Fifty Years of Comparative Education

This edited collection was produced to celebrate the 50th anniversary of the journal *Comparative Education*, one of the most established and prestigious journals in the field. Each chapter was written by a leading scholar of comparative and international education. The collection marks a creative and critical engagement with some of the most important topics in contemporary comparative education, including 'big data', pedagogy, adult education, scholarly mobility and gender. The theme of 'silences' connects the chapters: while comparative education covers the breadth and depth of educational concerns, it has its own obsessions, but which themes do not receive the attention they deserve?

This book will be of interest to anyone interested in the theory, method and practice of comparative education today or in its development over the past 50 years. It will be informative to all scholars and graduate students concerned with education in its global contexts. In addition, to those readers who situate themselves within the field of comparative and international education, it offers a unique perspective on this important area of inquiry and the activities, preoccupations, absences and communities within it.

This book was originally published as a special issue of *Comparative Education*.

Michele Schweisfurth is Professor of Comparative and International Education and Co-Director of the Robert Owen Centre for Educational Change at the University of Glasgow, UK. She was Editor of the journal *Comparative Education* from 2009 through 2014. Her research interests include tensions between global frameworks (such as children's rights, and notions of 'best practice' in teaching and learning) and local and cultural imperatives. She is the author of *Learner-Centred Education in International Perspective: Whose Pedagogy for Whose Development?* (2013) and *Comparative and International Education: An Introduction to Theory, Method and Practice* (2014, with David Phillips).

Fifty Years of Comparative Education

Edited by
Michele Schweisfurth

Routledge
Taylor & Francis Group
LONDON AND NEW YORK

First published 2015
by Routledge
2 Park Square, Milton Park, Abingdon, Oxon, OX14 4RN, UK

and by Routledge
711 Third Avenue, New York, NY 10017, USA

Routledge is an imprint of the Taylor & Francis Group, an informa business

© 2015 Taylor & Francis

All rights reserved. No part of this book may be reprinted or reproduced or utilised in any form or by any electronic, mechanical, or other means, now known or hereafter invented, including photocopying and recording, or in any information storage or retrieval system, without permission in writing from the publishers.

Trademark notice: Product or corporate names may be trademarks or registered trademarks, and are used only for identification and explanation without intent to infringe.

British Library Cataloguing in Publication Data
A catalogue record for this book is available from the British Library

ISBN 13: 978-1-138-85333-1

Typeset in Times New Roman
by RefineCatch Limited, Bungay, Suffolk

Publisher's Note
The publisher accepts responsibility for any inconsistencies that may have arisen during the conversion of this book from journal articles to book chapters, namely the possible inclusion of journal terminology.

Disclaimer
Every effort has been made to contact copyright holders for their permission to reprint material in this book. The publishers would be grateful to hear from any copyright holder who is not here acknowledged and will undertake to rectify any errors or omissions in future editions of this book.

Contents

Citation Information — vii
Notes on Contributors — ix

Introduction — 1
Michele Schweisfurth

1. Comparative education: stones, silences, and siren songs — 3
   Robert Cowen

2. Global league tables, big data and the international transfer of educational research modalities — 15
   Michael Crossley

3. Lessons from abroad: whatever happened to pedagogy? — 27
   Julian G. Elliott

4. From adult education to lifelong learning and beyond — 45
   Peter Jarvis

5. The intellect, mobility and epistemic positioning in doing comparisons and comparative education — 58
   Terri Kim

6. 'Comparatography', history and policy quotation: some reflections — 73
   David Phillips

7. Neither orthodoxy nor randomness: differing logics of conducting comparative and international studies in education — 84
   Jürgen Schriewer

8. Among the comparativists: ethnographic observations — 102
   Michele Schweisfurth

9. Thinking about gender in comparative education — 112
   Elaine Unterhalter

Index — 127

Citation Information

The chapters in this book were originally published in *Comparative Education*, volume 50, issue 1 (February 2014). When citing this material, please use the original page numbering for each article, as follows:

Introduction
Originally published as: *Editorial: The 50th anniversary special issue*
Michele Schweisfurth
Comparative Education, volume 50, issue 1 (February 2014) pp. 1–2

Chapter 1
Comparative education: stones, silences, and siren songs
Robert Cowen
Comparative Education, volume 50, issue 1 (February 2014) pp. 3–14

Chapter 2
Global league tables, big data and the international transfer of educational research modalities
Michael Crossley
Comparative Education, volume 50, issue 1 (February 2014) pp. 15–26

Chapter 3
Lessons from abroad: whatever happened to pedagogy?
Julian G. Elliott
Comparative Education, volume 50, issue 1 (February 2014) pp. 27–44

Chapter 4
From adult education to lifelong learning and beyond
Peter Jarvis
Comparative Education, volume 50, issue 1 (February 2014) pp. 45–57

Chapter 5
The intellect, mobility and epistemic positioning in doing comparisons and comparative education
Terri Kim
Comparative Education, volume 50, issue 1 (February 2014) pp. 58–72

CITATION INFORMATION

Chapter 6
'Comparatography', history and policy quotation: some reflections
David Phillips
Comparative Education, volume 50, issue 1 (February 2014) pp. 73–83

Chapter 7
Neither orthodoxy nor randomness: differing logics of conducting comparative and international studies in education
Jürgen Schriewer
Comparative Education, volume 50, issue 1 (February 2014) pp. 84–101

Chapter 8
Among the comparativists: ethnographic observations
Michele Schweisfurth
Comparative Education, volume 50, issue 1 (February 2014) pp. 102–111

Chapter 9
Thinking about gender in comparative education
Elaine Unterhalter
Comparative Education, volume 50, issue 1 (February 2014) pp. 112–126

Please direct any queries you may have about the citations to
clsuk.permissions@cengage.com

Notes on Contributors

Robert Cowen, Institute of Education, University of London, UK

Michael Crossley, Graduate School of Education, University of Bristol, UK

Julian G. Elliott, Principal of Collingwood College, School of Education, Durham University, UK

Peter Jarvis, School of Politics, University of Surrey, Guildford, UK

Terri Kim, Cass School of Education and Communities, University of East London, UK

David Phillips, St Edmund Hall, University of Oxford, UK

Jürgen Schriewer, Philosophische Fakultät IV, Humboldt University, Berlin, Germany

Michele Schweisfurth, Robert Owen Centre for Educational Change, University of Glasgow, UK

Elaine Unterhalter, Institute of Education, University of London, UK

INTRODUCTION

A.D.C. Peterson wrote in the editorial of the first issue of *Comparative Education* in 1964:

> We hope to serve the cause and attract the attention not only of comparative education and comparativists, but of education as a whole and its administrators and practitioners. (Peterson 1964, 3)

Fifty years later, these aims remain current and laudable, and the combination of theory, methodology, and policy and practical applications advocated in Peterson's inaugural editorial resonate with the concerns of the field and the journal in 2014. All of these aspirations continue to be reflected in our aims and scope, and in our review processes.

Comparative education and *Comparative Education* have been through significant developments in that half century. Editors past and present surveyed these developments a few years ago in a collection celebrating the journal (Crossley, Broadfoot, and Schweisfurth 2007). We identified four major categories of intellectual and professional shifts over time: paradigms and positioning; neo-liberal challenges: market forces, accountability and international transfer; changing contexts, globalisation and difference; and comparative research, identity and the Other. All of these reflect developments in the wider social sciences as well as the lived realities of education worldwide. Articles published since that 2007 collection point to the continuing salience of these categories and to an intensification of debate over some of them. We concluded the editorial piece of the collection by looking forward ' … to a new era of productive, critical and creative engagement within the field, in ways that maintain and enhance the original spirit of its founders' (Crossley, Broadfoot, and Schweisfurth 2007, 12).

This special issue celebrating our 50th anniversary is part of that creative and critical engagement, with a personal twist. Each article is written by a member of the current editorial board, and we have written on topics about which we individually feel passionate and which we feel reflect important concerns of the contemporary field. We gave ourselves permission to write from our personal perspectives, given the depth and range of expertise that board members possess, and the distinctive occasion. One of the themes that emerges across the articles is 'silences'. The research and scholarship underpinning the field have a number of well-documented concerns and obsessions: but about which topics are we silent? Which do not receive the attention they deserve or need, and why?

I hope we are allowed to crow a little on such a milestone birthday. *Comparative Education* is not only one of the longest-standing journals in the field, it is one of its leading and most well-respected publications. We are proud of our history and heritage as well as our contemporary contribution, and we look forward both to continuing the best of our traditions and to injecting fresh thinking into the study of education in comparative and global contexts. In a more humble vein, we welcome responses to our special issue and to the debates and silences which it has opened.

Michele Schweisfurth
Professor of Comparative and International Education Co-Director
Robert Owen Centre for Educational Change, University of Glasgow

References

Crossley, M., P. Broadfoot, and M. Schweisfurth, eds. 2007. *Changing Educational Contexts, Issues and Identities: 40 years of Comparative Education*. Abingdon: Routledge.

Peterson, A. D. C. 1964. "Editorial." *Comparative Education* 1 (1): 1–3.

Comparative education: stones, silences, and siren songs

Robert Cowen

Institute of Education, University of London, London, UK

> This article tries to look forward and backward simultaneously – the normal uncomfortable perspective used within articles written for anniversary issues. The theme of the paper is the need for some academic housekeeping. The main motif is that 'comparative education' does not have an essential identity but that earlier debates which struggled to assert one have left a number of blockages to rethinking comparative education. This academic rubble needs clearing away. The second much briefer motif emphasises our current 'siren songs' – the voices of attraction which beckon us forward academically – and how they can be harmonised. There is a last short anxiety fit and a brief discussion of 'visions'; but there is no conclusion. The article is supposed to clear things out and open things up; not close them down.

Introduction

In the last decade or so, 'comparative education' has changed. This is partly because the world has changed, and the political processes of that world and the words we use have become irritants and stimulants: information societies, post-colonial, neo-liberal, post-modern, globalised, post-socialist, knowledge economies, and so on. This has generated a flurry of new theorisation, not least because a new generation of scholars with their own fresh perspectives has reinterpreted the world that comparative education sees (Alexiadou 2007; Beech 2011; Carney 2010; Klerides 2012; Larsen 2011; Manzon 2011; Ninnes and Mehta 2004; Rappleye 2012; Silova 2009; Sobe 2009; Takayama 2011). The bonus which the fresh voices have given us – along with powerful creativities from Roger Dale, Erwin Epstein, Martin Lawn, António Nóvoa, Jenny Ozga, Susan Robertson, Gita Steiner-Khamsi and from my colleagues on the Board of this journal and from within the Comparative Education Society in Europe – is that it is even clearer that there are many more 'comparative educations' than I had anticipated when I first used that expression (Cowen 1990). All I was attempting to do, then, was to edge towards some simple distinctions between forms of comparative education and to develop some sense of what might be seen as the institutional infrastructures and superstructures of 'comparative education'.

Now, it is very clear that there are forms of 'comparative education' aimed at solutions to economic problems (the World Bank, OECD); forms of comparative education aimed at 'closing gaps' and developing the Third World; and forms of comparative education, in many countries, which are university-based and worry a lot about epistemology and modes of academic understanding. Emphasising that there are varieties of 'comparative education' permits sharper sensibilities about: (i) their orientations to action; (ii) their agendas of attention – their 'hot topics'; (iii) their agendas of approach – their social ontologies and 'methodologies'; and (iv) their 'agendas of agglutination' – who you are prepared to ally with while you do your work. All of the varieties of comparative education are constructed within and address a different politics of commitment, define 'the global' differently, and have agendas of agglutination that mutate differently.

New varieties of 'comparative education' embrace new names when what they study changes. Thus in the historical vocabulary of the Institute of Education in the University of London, the label 'education in tropical areas' was embedded in a different politics of naming from that which later linked 'the Third World' with a 'Department of Education in Developing Countries'. More contemporaneously (Lawn 2013), we will no doubt identify a branch of comparative education which someone sooner or later [probably within Gemma Moss's (ed.) (2014) Special Issue of *Comparative Education*: in preparation] will call 'big data' comparative education. We already have a form of 'comparative education' called 'PISA' (Cowen 2011a, 2011b) and TIMSS and AHELO…

In other words, 'comparative education' changes as the world changes because it is part of the international relations of political, economic and cultural power which it studies – in addition, of course, to being labelled in complex ways in a range of languages and having to live with ambiguities within any one of them. 'International education' in England can certainly include teaching about the world in English schools so that children begin to understand cultures and 'other countries' outside of England; but 'international education' is also part of the official title of the British academic and professional society (BAICE) which studies 'comparative education'. The same ambiguities exist, in English, for the words 'development education' (Ishii 2001).

Living with professional ambiguities is difficult. Perhaps for this reason (as well as for reasons of resource acquisition within the politics of universities) much of the literature in the specialist comparative education journals has been concerned to refuse ambiguities and, firmly, to define 'the subject'.

Many of these efforts to routinise what we know, to establish and confirm iconographies, I will call 'stones'. I accept that some stones are pebbles, some are boulders, and there is often a lot of shingle in between.

Stones

The anxiety to define 'the subject' was with us early in our history and, even after the Methods Wars of the 1960s, that work continued (Adams 1977; Altbach 1991; Arnove 2007; Bray 2007; Broadfoot 1999; Cowen 2000; Crossley 1999; Epstein 1983, 2008; Fletcher 1974; Halls 1990; Little 2000; Parkyn 1977; Price 1992; Rust 1991; Schriewer 2000; Trethewey 1976; Wilson 1994). Clearly this discussion across the decades hints at something important – efforts are being made to stabilise the field while it is changing over time. But change it does – under the press of a range of politics (international and domestic as well as the internal politics of universities and the games which academics play while they work in them) as well as through reinterpretations (Ninnes and Burnett 2003) of what are seen as 'saviour sciences' or theoreticians that would be able – coming in from outside – to rescue the 'comparative education' of the period from its trivialities.

This concern to stabilise 'the subject' is perhaps at its most neurotic when it is concerned to define 'the discipline'. Fretting on, at least in the English language for 40 years (Heath 1959; Higginson 2001), about comparative education as a 'discipline' is to echo the asociological perspective of Richard Peters who was concerned to define epistemic principles that distinguished his serious 'philosophy of education' from earlier traditions of studying 'the principles of education' embedded in the writings of great philosophers, so that teachers might benefit from such wisdom. His 'philosophy of education' was a discipline and most other forms of educational studies were not (Tibble 1966). The moment the terms of debate asserted by Richard Peters and Paul Hirst (1966) are accepted, it is instantly clear that 'comparative education' is not 'a discipline' (cf. Becher and Trowler 2001). Equally obviously: the 'comparative educations' are comprehensible – in their locations, construction and modes of application – as both Mode One and Mode Two knowledges (Gibbons et al. 1994). Only in its mad moments, when it was messianic about its intention to be 'a science', has university-based comparative education attempted an exclusionary 'disciplined' form.

However, the sad echo in the word 'discipline' does not end there. There is in the word 'discipline' an implicit hankering for security and permanence. I recently argued that this motif is offered to us by the academic name (at least in English) of the field of study itself. In the Foreword to Maria Manzon's book, *Comparative education: The construction of a field*, I suggested:

> ... gazing upon the two words 'comparative education' and insisting on their literal-and-conjoined interpretation creates an account of the field which emphasises its potentially stable and permanent nature. The implicit argument, in the juxtaposition of the words ('comparative' and 'education'), generates an epistemic position: there is an essential and permanent act of 'comparison' and an essential and permanent institutional entity 'education'. Those words, acted upon together in a certain way, will give us lists of similarities and differences in education-in-context; and, after much work, the identification of the causes of those similarities and differences will become known. Finally there will have been so many 'comparative' investigations done that a 'universal and useful science' of comparative education will have been created, firmly based on fact. (Manzon 2011, xv)

Clearly there are some smooth time-worn pebbles to be cleared away here: the mantra of similarities and difference; the routine assumption that 'comparative education' seeks out 'the causes of things' using principles of method defined in the nineteenth century by J. S. Mill; the search for a 'universal and useful science' of comparative education. However there is, in addition, a peculiarly irritating 'stone' (a stonefish[1]) to be cleared away.

This stone is almost invisible – until you actually step on it in anniversary issues. There you can often find fatuous systems for the classification and counting of 'comparative' articles. Articles are separated into those which, as measured by juxtapositions within the article, are 'comparative' and those which are not. In other words, if the article has the *surface form* of a comparison (say, apples versus oranges; Argentina versus Zanzibar) then it is 'comparative'. If it is an essay on the compression of social power into educational patterns on a 'global' scale at the intersection of changing international and domestic politics – such as the dominance of Latin as a *lingua franca* in some societies and in some forms of education for centuries – then it is not (unless a special classificatory *caveat* has been entered).

That specific issue is a small version of a broader problem: juxtapositions themselves.

I argued in the same Foreword (Cowen 2011a, 2011b, xv) that the broader '... academic problem is to refuse ... juxtaposed educational systems as the central unit of comparison; and juxtaposed social contexts ... as the definition of a permanent truth about our field of study'. According to at least one routine history of the field of study (Cowen and Kazamias 2009, 1–156), this difficulty – that most forms of 'comparative education' need to account for 'context' – comes from Sir Michael Sadler. Unfortunately, his theorisation of the concept of social context was in a literary vocabulary which mellifluously murmured about 'gardens' and 'battles long ago' and 'intangible forces' (Sadler 1900). He thus gave to comparative education a 'stone' which will simply not go away, despite the extremely valiant continuous and contemporary efforts of Michael Crossley (2009) to get the concept sorted out. The combination of the concept of 'context' with the Sadlerian assumption that our duty is to 'learn things of practical value' means we work in the shadow of a stone about the size of an Easter Island statue. This expectation (about practicality) has affected all comparative education*s*, even academic comparative education.[2]

However, even within the tradition of academic comparative education – a long trajectory which stretches from the work of C. A. Anderson, George Bereday, Nicholas Hans, Brian Holmes, Edmund King and Joseph Lauwerys in the 1960s and earlier, to recent serious 'academic comparative' work (Steiner-Khamsi and Waldow 2012), the repetition of the word 'policy' and our contribution to its formulation for the reform of educational systems (or parts thereof – teacher education or higher education or vocational technical education, and so on) constructs a big stone.

The argument so far (if I take a literary turn with Sir Michael Sadler) is that we have assembled a rockery and the stones in it have names: 'the subject'; discipline; similarities and differences; useful science; comparison as juxtaposition; context; learning from foreign systems of education; policy and reform. Therefore, right now, we have a lot of stones.

We need to decide – particularly in terms of 'academic comparative education' – whether we have stones that provide stability and shelter. Or do we have a pile of rubble which needs clearing away? Just how much of the traditional anguish – seeking similarities and differences; defining ourselves as a useful science; stressing comparison as juxtaposition; repeating the mantras of 'context', 'learning from foreign systems of education' and acting as loyal Sherpas to Ministers who wish to change educational policy (at home or overseas) – do we wish to retain?

The short answer is that if you guard what you think of as your intellectual capital too nervously and sternly, you find it very difficult to learn anything new: you know what you know, and you know what you know with certainty, and that leads to not-learning and to not-even-listening. Such commonsensical assertions may be true. Fortunately, an academic interpretation can also be offered, about how what I am calling rubble was once deliberately shaped to be an architectural masterpiece.

Silences

Contemporary academic comparative education is 'modernist'. I originally used this label in an analysis of the condition of academic comparative education in the *International handbook of comparative education* (Cowen and Kazamias 2009); not that I wish to claim a monopoly on the phrase. The phrase is used in a recent and extremely good book chapter by Dale and Robertson (2012) which is very much worth several re-readings. Similarly, my co-editor of the *International handbook* used the expression with his co-author Pella Kaloyannaki in their chapter 'The modernist beginnings of comparative education – the proto-scientific and the reformist/meliorist administrative motif'. They argued that

> The modernist beginnings of comparative education (CE) as a field of study are conventionally traced to the post-Enlightenment period in the early and mid-decades of the nineteenth century, specifically to the pioneering work of Marc-Antoine Jullien de Paris and to discourses of educational policy-makers/reformers and administrators in Europe and the United States, such as Horace Mann, Calvin Stowe and Henry Barnard in the United States, Victor Cousin in France and the poet–school inspector Matthew Arnold in England ...
>
> (Kaloyannaki and Kazamias 2009, 8)

I would not wish to disagree about the approximate timing of the birth, nor would I wish to quibble about the detailed relationships between the Scottish, Swedish and French Enlightenments and the new beginning. My interest is: what happened after the beginning?

My argument (I quote, although in the interests of space I have taken the liberty of removing bullet points) was that in modernist comparative education:

> The intellectual agenda of comparative education becomes limited in time (only studies of 'the educational system' count as comparative education); the classic form of comparative education becomes the juxtaposition of educational descriptions, perhaps with unsystematic comments about context. Anything educational can be compared – the number of hours spent on homework in two or more countries, attitudes to first-cycle schools by mothers; whether teachers are happy. However in general what is described in routine comparative work is some salient, contemporary aspect of educational policy. (Cowen 2009a, 2009b, 950)

It is this modernist trap, I argue here, which legitimates our nineteenth century positivist classification and methodological patterns including juxtaposition and notions of the gradualist improvement of societies through the power of social science; but which also imposes severe limitations on our intellectual imagination. My argument, then and now, is that after 1817 and the iconic writing of Jullien de Paris we move ourselves steadily into a trap which creates startling silences:

> (i) only certain space–time patterns are worth serious investigation; (ii) investigations outside such space–time patterns of contemporary history are proto-comparative education because they do not investigate 'the educational system'. Thus most of the educational experiences of the world are left undisturbed and unexplored; (iii) 'the educational system' and advice on salient policy problems becomes the point of comparative education – both its praxis and its intellectual work; (iv) among policy problems, the urgent and visible ones are the work agenda – this confirms comparative education as being accountable and relevant and useful; (v) and the anterior work for this needs to be informed by the specification of similarities and differences in educational provision and an understanding of the causes of these differences through 'the comparative method'. (Cowen 2009a, 2009b, 950)

In other words, within modernist comparative education, the range of our academic imagination narrows.

Despite claims that history has always been important to comparative education, despite Isaac Kandel's aphorism that 'comparative education is the continuation of the study of history into the present', and despite claims that history should really be 'the main method' of comparative education (Kazamias, *passim*), it is precisely history which we begin to cancel when we step into the discourse of modernist comparative education. We silence history – and peoples. There are multiple silences, some of which are huge in human terms, notably silences about revolution, war and Empires. Given we live in a period marked by the work of Theda Skocpol on revolutions, Tony Judt on the post-war period (after 1945) and excellent historical writing on Empire (such as Elkins on Kenya, Elliot and Thomas on the Spanish Empire, Hochschild on the Belgian Congo, Hoskin and Lieven on Russia, and Lawrence James on India) why has the comparative education literature has been relatively silent (Cowen 2013)?

Here my core point in the present analysis is that (in much of the English-language work) we committed ourselves to the creation of a gradualist, ameliorative, equilibrium-restoring policy-focussed 'modernist' comparative education – and then discussed method for a decade – before, in a soft-radical moment in the Cold War period, taking up a discussion of education as cultural imperialism and education and colonialism.

We did not take up the far more historically, sociologically, anthropologically and culturally complex issues involved in analysing and understanding education and Empires.

The point about Empires is significant. Nóvoa and Yariv-Mashal (2003) offer a brilliant argument which is counterpoint to the analysis being constructed here. First, in a few startling lines, they create a strategic case for the need to write a revisionist history of the field of study. Second, and here of very specific interest, their argument (2003, 424) – which emphasises that the legitimacy and popularity of the field of study clustered in the 1880s around 'knowing the other', in the 1920s around 'understanding the other', and in the 1960s around 'constructing the other' – does not acknowledge Empires. I interpret this as indicating that Empires (cf. 'India'; cf. 'Canada') were invisible within the perspectives of modernist comparative education. There was a silence.

Siren songs

And that means a major amount of creativity has to be generated now, when we are faced with a flurry of new empires in non-classical forms. We must again 'read the global' (Cowen 2000) – a concept which Nóvoa and Yariv-Mashal illuminate succinctly in their 'periodisation' (sketched above) and their subsequent discussion of time–space for the contemporary world.

Of course, contemporary 'readings of the global' tend to use the word 'globalisation', and globalisation (like Mrs Thatcher) was a boon to comparative education. Manifestly, an insistence on the significance of various forms of 'globalisation' was and is useful and necessary; and the work of melding the theme into the comparative field continues (Brock and Alexiadou 2013) while at the same time a very strong strand of studies which deals directly with globalisation and education flourishes. Fortunately, many of the best writers on education and globalisation (such as Dale and Robertson and Lingard and Rizvi) have chosen to publish in the comparative literature also.

Nevertheless, I think it is still worthwhile, in an anniversary issue of a comparative journal, to ask what are the siren songs? I accept that these could be on topics (such as shadow education or BRICS) but in the nicest possible way I regard those hot topics as pop songs. My question is which symphonies might our very own Mozartian prodigies go on to write, having heard siren songs of mysterious power?

I would, of course, pick time (Cowen 2002; Sweeting 2007) and space (Dale and Robertson 2009; Larsen and Beech forthcoming, 2014; Schriewer 2012; Symaco and Brock 2013) and space–time (Nóvoa and Yariv-Mashal 2003). I would, balanced not too nervously between accusations of methodological nationalism and methodological individualism, remain fascinated by the State (which I think we have under-estimated in all its forms, expect perhaps as state-socialist, developmentalist and fascist). It is not merely that 'governance' is a powerful siren song currently – we probably also need to address theories (such as those of W. I. Robinson) about the emergence of the transnational State.

I would remain alert to several of the old siren songs – the classic factors of Nicholas Hans – which include religion and language and political philosophies and the identities which follow from those mixtures as they work themselves out – for example now, in societies such as Iraq and Libya and Syria with redefinitions of both 'the nation' and the educational system still to emerge. I would give increasing attention to the literature of intercultural education. Much of that literature merely adds dull fact to dull writing – though some adds hot gospelling to hot topics; but its theoretical forms can be impressive (Dietz and Mateos Cortés 2012). On social conflict and visions of societies, I would be keen to listen to a siren song which made a distinction between knowledge economies and knowledge societies with a long discussion about knowledge (Popkewitz 2000). Within such a treasure trove of song, I might even be prepared to have a new and critical look at 'policy' with the help of Tröhler (2011) and 'context' with the help of Sobe and Kowalczyk (2012).

However – overall – the siren songs I have noted are those which invite attention to what I termed, in the vocabulary which Robert Nisbet used to analyse sociology, the 'unit ideas' of comparative education (Cowen 2009a, 2009b). The fulcrum of those ideas is the unit idea of 'transfer'. It is that unit idea which focuses the significance of, say, the State or 'identity' in a specific analysis of educational shape-shifting in the multiple processes of transfer, translation and transformation. This challenge is, for me, a siren song – but invitational; hardly a demand that we mobilise around my 'unit ideas': in a very loose version of the Chinese joke at the time of Mao's revolutionary operas – 800 academics to work on only eight songs.

There is a marvellous moment in the history of comparative education wonderfully pinned by Silova and Brehm (2010, 461), when the field was to be saved from the inside:

> Noah threw the gauntlet down to the old cast of comparativists who emphasized humanistic and philosophical foundations, demanding their acceptance of his new genre:
>
> Systematic, controlled, empirical, and (wherever possible) quantitative investigation of explicitly stated hypotheses is the modus operandi of best practice in the contemporary social sciences; we must hope that it will soon become the hallmark of those who would call themselves comparative educators, too. (Noah 1969, 251)
>
> Scholars who did not heed the warning would be left behind, with blame placed squarely on the shoulders of the individual, not the new scientific method in the field.

It is nice to be that confident occasionally; perhaps unwise to be so continuously. Not everyone (and that used to include John Maynard Keynes) judges that the best way to understand the world is to think like economists, whether before 1929 or before 2009.

Nightmares and visions

That said, in a situation in which the collection of big data is likely to become (to adapt the phrasing of a BBC website about PISA) 'the most important exam in the world' and given probable EU research contracts to specify *new triple-helix triangulations which define a variable but reliable geometry of insertion that guarantees the delivery of a world class university to appropriate socio-locales within the European Union*,[3] it is of some importance to be confident enough to spend energy on ensuring the institutional survival of academic comparative education. In my view there is little point in the conferences of the academic professional societies getting larger and larger while the university base for academic work which does not have immediate economic impact gets smaller and smaller.

At least the British Academy is starting to raise such questions at the European level. In the interim, like comparative literature or the comparative study of religions or comparative history, academic comparative education has no instant utility. Therefore its institutional infrastructure, and thus much of its survival, is heavily dependent on the diminishing number of universities able to resist the ideology that universities should live (or die) by their immediate relevance to the world politicians think of as real (Cowen 2012).

In those circumstances, it is perhaps of importance to continue to understand what we are trying to save. What is the vision which we, in comparative education, hold of *education* itself? We can ask questions about relativism, banality, osmosis, praxis, and so on (Cowen 2009a, 2009b). We can ask about applied forms of comparative education (Cowen 2006). A disorienting question – for me at least given I grew up amid a lot of post-war rubble – is: are we still aiming at creating a science of policy transfer or are we emphasising what my colleague, Elaine Unterhalter, drawing in part on capability theory, calls 'ethical globalisation'?

The answers to such questions remain as elusive (to me) as they were in 1973 when, newly arrived in the USA, I wrote about them for a Canadian journal. I do not find that a nightmare; but I do find the vision elusive. And I find the vision elusive precisely because – in my view – 'the rubble' we need to clear away includes overconfident notions about the applicability of the social sciences in their present theoretical condition.

For the moment, I personally will stay captivated by the conviction that a serious education in comparative education releases the imagination in the way George Steiner does in his treatments of comparative literature; that an immersion in a serious comparative education creates a sense of awe about the human condition that can come for reading Durkheim on elementary forms of religious life; or Levi-Strauss' writings on 'the tropics'; or the shock that comes with Edmund de Waal's *The hare with amber eyes*.

And for day-to-day work? I will stay with the vision of C. Wright Mills: to try and think about the world in a way which permits a simultaneous understanding of historical forces, social structures and individual biography, and I will to write out a coherent version of the political and cultural 'codings' of educational processes; within a theoretically coherent 'academic comparative education' of course.

On that task, given our fixation with policy and other 'stones', we have – collectively – barely had time to begin.

Notes

1. Stonefish, associated with some of the beaches of the Indo-Pacific including Australian beaches where I first learned to fear them, can lie motionless in beach sand. They have

poisonous dorsal fins. Swimmers stepping on them suffer great pain and even death, though antidotes exist.
2. In this article so far the expression 'comparative education' has been used as a signifier of all comparative education*s*. At this point I wish to mark off 'academic comparative education' as a specific sub-form. I intend the expression 'academic comparative education' to mean a field of study, based in universities, which works to understand theoretically and intellectually the shape-shifting of 'education' as it moves transnationally amid the interplay of international political, cultural and economic, hierarchies and domestic politics and forms of social power. One of the minor advantages of this definition is that it abolishes the vocabulary of 'international education' as a synonym for studying education and the Third World and 'comparative education' as a synonym for studying what George Bereday called 'the northern crescent' – crudely speaking, Europe, Russia and China, North Asia and North America. Academic comparative education, as the study of transfer and educational shape-shifting, is my central intellectual concern.
3. In fairness to the EU and to Ministers of Education everywhere: as far as I know the draft specification of such a research contract has not been written out, by any public official, yet.

References

Adams, D. 1977. "Development Education." *Comparative Education Review* 21 (2–3): 296–310.
Alexiadou, N. 2007. "The Europeanisation of Education Policy: Researching Changing Governance and 'New' Modes of Coordination." *Research in Comparative and International Education* 2 (2): 102–116.
Altbach, P. 1991. "Trends in Comparative Education." *Comparative Education Review* 35 (3): 491–507.
Becher, T., and P. Trowler. 2001. *Academic Tribes and Territories: Intellectual Enquiry and the Culture of Disciplines*. Buckingham: Society for Research into Higher Education & Open University Press.
Beech, J. 2011. *Global Panaceas, Local Realities: International Agencies and the Future of Education*. Frankfurt-am-Main: Peter Lang.
Bray, M. 2007. "Actors and Purposes in Comparative Education." In *Comparative Education Research: Approaches and Methods*, edited by M. Bray, B. Adamson, and M. Mason, 15–38. Hong Kong: Comparative Education Research Centre, The University of Hong Kong, and Dordrecht: Springer.
Broadfoot, P. 1999. "Not So Much a Context, More a Way of Life? Comparative Education in the 1990s." In *Learning from Comparing: New Directions in Comparative Educational Research*, Vol. 1, edited by R. Alexander, P. Broadfoot, and D. Phillips, 21–31, Oxford: Symposium Books.
Broadfoot, P. 2009. "Time for a Scientific Revolution? From Comparative Education to Comparative Learnology." In *International Handbook of Comparative Education*, edited by R. Cowen and A. M. Kazamias, 1249–1266. London: Springer.
Brock, C., and N. Alexiadou. 2013. *Education Around the World: A Comparative Introduction*. London and New York: Bloomsbury.
Carney, S. 2010. "Reading the Global: Comparative Education at the End of an Era." In *New Thinking in Comparative Education: Honouring the Work of Robert Cowen*, edited by Marianne Larsen, 125–142. Rotterdam: Sense Publishers.
Cowen, R. 1990. "The National and International Impact of Comparative Education Infrastructures." In *Comparative Education: Contemporary Issues and Trends*, edited by W. D. Halls, 321–352. London and Paris: Jessica Kingsley Publisher/UNESCO.
Cowen, R. 2000. "Comparing Futures or Comparing Pasts?" *Comparative Education* 36 (3): 333–342.

Cowen, R. 2002. "Moments of Time: A Comparative Note." *History of Education* 31 (5): 413–424.
Cowen, R. 2006. "Acting Comparatively upon the Educational World: Puzzles and Possibilities." *Oxford Review of Education* 32 (5): 561–573.
Cowen, R. 2009a. "New Thinking." In *International Handbook of Comparative Education*, edited by R. Cowen and A. M. Kazamias, 947–950. Dordrecht: Springer.
Cowen, R. 2009b. "Then and Now: Unit Ideas and Comparative Education." In *International Handbook of Comparative Education*, edited by R. Cowen and A. M. Kazamias, 1277–1294. Dordrecht: Springer.
Cowen, R. 2011a. "Foreword." In *Comparative Education: The Construction of a Field*, edited by M. Manzon, xiii–xvi. Hong Kong: Comparative Education Research Centre, The University of Hong Kong, and Dordrecht: Springer.
Cowen, R. 2011b. "CODA." In *PISA Under Examination: Changing Knowledge, Changing Tests, and Changing Schools*, edited by M. A. Pereyra, H. G. Kotthoff, and R. Cowen, 259–264. Netherlands: Sense Publishers.
Cowen, R. 2012. "Robustly Researching the Relevant: A Note on Creation Myths in Comparative Education." In *Enlightenment, Creativity and Education: Polities, Politics, Performances*, edited by L. Wikander, C. Gustaffson, and U. Riis, 3–26. Rotterdam: Sense Publishers & CESE.
Cowen, R. 2013. "Generations and Degenerations: an Initial Note on Silences in Comparative Education." In *Conversaciones con un maestro (Liber Amicorum). Estudio interdisciplinar de discípulos y colegas en homenaje al profesor DR. D. José Luis García Garrido, Catedrático Emérito de Universidad*, edited by AA. VV, 139–152. Madrid: Ediciones Académicas-UNED.
Cowen, R., and A. M. Kazamias, eds. 2009. *International Handbook of Comparative Education*. Dordrecht: Springer.
Crossley, M. 1999. "Reconceptualising Comparative and International Education." *Compare: A Journal of Comparative Education* 29 (3): 249–267.
Crosslcy, M. 2009. "Rethinking Context in Comparative Education." In *International Handbook of Comparative Education*, edited by R. Cowen and A. M. Kazamias, 1173–1187. Dordrecht: Springer.
Dale, R., and S. Robertson. 2009. "Beyond Methodological 'Isms' in Comparative Education in an Era of Globalisation." In *International Handbook of Comparative Education*, edited by R. Cowen and A. M. Kazamias, 1113–1127. Dordrecht: Springer.
Dale, R., and S. Robertson. 2012. "Towards a Critical Grammar of Policy Movements." In *World Yearbook of Education 2012: Policy Borrowing and Lending in Education*, edited by G. Steiner-Khamsi and F. Waldow, 21–40. London and New York: Routledge, Taylor and Francis.
Dietz, G., and L. S. Mateos Cortés. 2012. "The Need for Comparison in Intercultural Education." *Intercultural Education: Special Issue: Intercultural and Comparative Education: Possibilities and Problems* 23 (5): 411–414.
Epstein, E. H. 1983. "Currents Left and Right: Ideology in Comparative Education." *Comparative Education Review* 27 (1): 3–28.
Epstein, E. H. 2008. "Setting the Normative Boundaries: Crucial Epistemological Benchmarks in Comparative Education." *Comparative Education* 44 (4): 373–386.
Fletcher, L. 1974. "Comparative Education: A Question of Identity." *Comparative Education Review* 18 (3): 348–353.
Gibbons, M., C. Limoges, H. Nowotny, S. Schwartzman, P. Scott, and M. Trow. 1994. *The New Production of Knowledge: The Dynamics of Science and Research in Contemporary Societies*. London: Sage.
Halls, W. D. 1990. "Trends and Issues in Comparative Education." In *Comparative Education: Contemporary Issues and Trends*, edited by W. D. Halls, 21–65. Paris: UNESCO & London: Jessica Kingsley.
Heath, K. G. 1959. "Is Comparative Education a Discipline?." *Comparative Education Review* 2 (2): 31–32.
Higginson, J. H. 2001. "The Development of a Discipline: Some Reflections on the Development of Comparative Education as seen through the Pages of the Journal Compare." In *Doing Comparative Education Research: Issues and Problems*, edited by K. Watson, 373–388. Oxford: Symposium Books.

Hirst, P. H. 1966. "Educational Theory." In *The Study of Education*, edited by J. W. Tibble, 29–58. London: Routledge & Kegan Paul.

Ishii, Y. 2001. "Teaching about International Responsibilities: A Comparative Analysis of the Political Construction of Development Education in Schools." *Comparative Education* 37 (3): 329–344.

Kaloyannaki, P., and A. Kazamias. 2009. "The Modernist Beginnings of Comparative Education: The Proto-Scientific and the Reformist-Meliorist Administrative Motif." In *International Handbook of Comparative Education*, edited by R. Cowen and A. M. Kazamias, 11–36. London: Springer.

Kazamias, A. M. 2009. "Reclaiming a Lost Legacy: The Historical Humanist Vision in Comparative Education." In *International Handbook of Comparative Education*, edited by R. Cowen and A. Kazamias, 1267–1276. London: Springer.

Klerides, E. 2012. "Comparing Identities in Dissimilar Spaces and Times: Hybridity, Border Crossing, Indeterminacies, Pluralism." In *Enlightenment, Creativity and Education: Polities, Politics, Performances*, edited by L. Wikander, C. Gustaffson, and U. Riis, 193–208. Rotterdam: Sense Publishers & CESE.

Larsen, M. 2011. *The Making and Shaping of the Victorian Teacher: A Comparative New Cultural History*. London/New York: Palgrave McMillan.

Larsen, M., and J. Beech. forthcoming, 2014. Spatial theorizing in comparative and international education research.

Lawn, M. 2013. "The Internationalization of Education Data: Exhibitions, Tests, Standards and Associations." In *The Rise of Data in Education Systems: Collection, Visualisation and Uses*, edited by M. Lawn, 11–25. Oxford: Symposium Books.

Little, A. 2000. "Development Studies and Comparative Education: Context, Content, Comparison and Contributors." *Comparative Education* 36 (3): 279–296.

Manzon, M. 2011. *Comparative Education: The Construction of a Field*. Hong Kong: Comparative Education Research Centre, The University of Hong Kong & Springer.

Ninnes, P., and G. Burnett. 2003. "Comparative Education Research: Poststructuralist Possibilities." *Comparative Education* 39 (3): 279–297.

Ninnes, P., and S. Mehta, eds. 2004. *Re-imagining Comparative Education: Postfoundational Ideas and Applications for Critical Times*. New York: Routledge.

Nóvoa, N., and T. Yariv-Mashal. 2003. "Comparative Research in Education: A Mode of Governance or a Historical Journey?." *Comparative Education* 39 (4): 423–438.

Parkyn, G. W. 1977. "Comparative Education Research and Development Education." *Comparative Education* 13 (2): 87–93.

Popkewitz, T. S. 2000. "Globalization/Regionalization, Knowledge, and the Educational Practices." In *Educational Knowledge: Changing Relationships Between the State, Civil Society, and the Educational Community*, edited by T. S. Popkewitz. Albany: State University of New York Press.

Price, R. F. 1992. "Comparative Education Redefined?." In *Contemporary Perspectives in Comparative Education*, edited by R. J. Burns and A. R. Welch, 69–87. New York: Garland Publications.

Rappleye, J. 2012. *Educational Transfer in an Era of Globalization: Theory, History, Comparison*. Berlin: Peter Lang.

Rust, V. 1991. "Postmodernism and its Comparative Education Implications." *Comparative Education Review* 35 (4): 610–626.

Sadler, M. 1900 [reprinted 1964]. "How Far Can We Learn Anything of Practical Value from the Study of Foreign Systems of Education?." *Comparative Education Review* 7 (3): 307–314.

Schriewer, J. 2000. "Comparative Education Methodology in Transition: Towards a Science of Complexity?" *Discourse Formation in Comparative Education*, edited by J. Schriewer, 3–52. Frankfurt am Main: P. Lang.

Schriewer, J. S., ed. 2012. *Comparative Education: Special Issue 45: Reconceptuyalising the Global/Local Nexus: Meaning Constellations in the World Society*. 48 (4).

Seddon, T. 2002. "Coda: Europe, Social Space and the Politics of Knowledge." In *Fabricating Europe: The Formation of an Education Space*, edited by A. Nóvoa and M. Lawn, 157–161. Dordrecht: Kluwer.

Silova, I. 2009. "The Changing Frontiers of Comparative Education: A Forty-year Retrospective on European Education." *European Education* 41 (1): 17–31.

Silova, I. ed. 2010. *Post-socialism is not Dead: (re)reading the Global in Comparative Education*. UK: Emerald Group Publishing Limited.

Silova, I., and W. C. Brehm. 2010. "An American Construction of European Education Space." *European Educational Research Journal* 9 (4): 457–469.

Sobe, N. ed. 2009. *American Post-Conflict Educational Reform: From the Spanish-American War to Iraq*. New York: Palgrave Macmillan.

Sobe, N. W., and J. Kowalczyk. 2012. "The Problem of Context in Comparative Education Research." *ECPS Journal* 55–73. Accessed December 31, 2012. http://www.ledonline.it/ECPS-Journal/

Steiner-Khamsi, G., and F. Waldow, eds. 2012. *World Yearbook of Education 2012: Policy Borrowing and Lending in Education*. London and New York: Routledge, Taylor and Francis.

Sweeting, A. 2007. "Comparing Times." In *Comparative Education Research: Approaches and Methods*, edited by M. Bray, B. Adamson, and M. Mason, 145–163. Hong Kong: CERC.

Symaco, L. P., and C. Brock, eds. 2013. "Comparative Education." *Special Issue (47): The Significance of Space, Place, and Scale in the study of education* 49 (3).

Tibble, J. W., ed. 1966. *The Study of Education*. London: Routledge & Kegan Paul.

Trethewey, A. R. 1976. *Introducing Comparative Education*. Rushcutters Bay, Australia: Pergamon Press.

Tröhler, D. 2011. "The Global Language on Education Policy and Prospects of Education Research." In *The Future of Education Research: Education Systems in Historical, Cultural, and Sociological Perspectives*, edited by D. Tröhler and R. Barbu, 55–73. Rotterdam, Netherlands: Sense Publishers.

Wilson, D. 1994. "Comparative and International Education: Fraternal or Siamese Twins? A Preliminary Genealogy of Our Twin Fields." *Comparative Education Review* 38 (4): 449–486.

Global league tables, big data and the international transfer of educational research modalities

Michael Crossley

Graduate School of Education, University of Bristol, UK

> The international transfer of educational policy and practice has long been a key theme in comparative research and scholarship. Recent years have seen renewed attention to the processes of international policy transfer, with new understandings emerging from innovative theorising and analysis. This article examines the nature and implications of such work, explores the potential for further theoretical and methodological advances, and considers why and how future comparative research might engage in: critical analyses of the use of findings derived from international comparisons of performance and achievement; socio-cultural contributions to the emerging 'big data' debate; and empirically grounded studies of the international transfer of educational research and evaluation modalities.

Introduction

In the twenty-first century comparative education is a very different field, and one that has experienced fundamental transformations since it flourished within university programmes in the UK, USA, Europe and beyond during the 1960s and 1970s (Crossley and Watson 2009). Much has also changed since the last time that the Editorial Board for this journal reflected upon the 'state of the art' in two linked Millennium Special Issues (Crossley and Jarvis 2000, 2001). This contribution to the 50th Anniversary of *Comparative Education* reflects upon three key issues and challenges that have emerged since the turn of the century, and that demand urgent and critical attention within and beyond the field in coming years. Running throughout the article is an overarching theme that has long characterised both comparative studies and my own research – concern with uncritical international policy transfer in education.

The first set of issues and related challenges stem from familiar territory for comparativists – the increasing influence and public visibility of international comparative studies of performance, be it by pupils, schools, universities or others, and the public and policy impact of related league tables. Since the year 2000 the OECD's Programme for International Student Assessment (PISA) studies have commanded perhaps the greatest level of global attention, and generated some of the most pertinent and insightful analyses and critiques (see Mayer and Benavot 2013). Significant attention has also been given in the comparative literature to the longer running International Association for the Evaluation of Educational Achievement (IEA) studies of student achievement (Postlethwaite 1999). Such studies and associated league tables are now being recognised for their increasingly powerful influence upon policy formulation across all sectors of education and wider society (Grek et al. 2009; Ozga 2012).

The second set of issues relates to the theoretical and epistemological assumptions that increasingly legitimise metrics and 'big science' approaches to research across the social sciences. More recently this has been combined with the emergence of what has become known as the big data movement (Uprichard 2013). The implications of this constellation of related developments for educational research, and for comparative education in particular, are only just beginning to be explored in any significant depth but, it is argued here, that they now deserve concerted and critical interrogation.

The third and final challenge, a challenge that is seen to connect very closely to those identified above, engages with the political economy of educational research; the growing privileging and prioritisation of expensive, large-scale quantitative research initiatives, designed primarily to meet the expectations of policy makers and influential research funders; and tendencies towards the hegemony and uncritical international transfer of such research modalities from the Western contexts in which they are currently being developed to a diversity of educational contexts, systems and cultures – rich and poor, large and small – worldwide.

The evolution of large-scale international comparative surveys and related league tables

The potential of large, cross-national surveys of education was recognised when the field of comparative education was first formally defined and systematised in the work of the French scholar Marc-Antoine Jullien (1817). Jullien's Plan (see Fraser 1964, 20) envisaged the collation, comparison and analysis of statistical information on, for example, student enrolments, pedagogy, numbers of teachers and finance, 'to deduce true principles and determined routes so that education would be transformed into an almost positive science' (Jullien 1817, cited in Fraser 1964, 20). This reflected the scientific preoccupations of this period in Western European history, and it remains deeply embedded within much contemporary survey research carried out by multilateral organisations and research and development agencies, including work by the OECD, UNESCO, the IEA and the World Bank.

In Jullien's day, much as it is today, the primary motivation for such comparisons came from economic competition between nation-states – with France looking to strengthen its position through the strategic use of high quality education. Also reflecting, but pre-dating the modern rationale, Jullien's research aimed to generate a robust evidence base for the direction of educational development and reform; the search was on to find out 'what works'; and, without using these exact words, it was assumed that 'best practice' could be identified and successfully adopted and transferred elsewhere.

While the twin fields of comparative and international education evolved in a diversity of ways in subsequent years, many of the epistemological assumptions and values that characterised Jullien's Plan can be seen to underpin the rapid growth of contemporary interest in cross-national studies such as the PISA series (OECD 2001, 2004, 2007, 2010). This includes the associated international league tables that both inspire and inform new and intensified forms of educational policy borrowing – and the flight of educational policy makers to observe and learn from top performing systems such as Finland in Europe and Singapore and Hong Kong in South-East Asia.

The impact of these large-scale comparative studies on education policy worldwide can be seen in national policy documents, in specific reform initiatives and in the nature and shape of much public debate. The 2010 Schools White Paper for England titled *The importance of teaching*, for example, draws significantly upon reports produced by McKinsey consultants (Barber and Mourshed 2007), related interpretations of OECD/PISA data, and the experience of 'high performing systems' in justifying its own policy trajectories and proposals (Department for Education 2010). The UK Secretary of State for Education thus told the Parliamentary Select Committee on Education that 'I have been to Singapore and Hong Kong, and what is striking is that many of the lessons that apply there are lessons that we can apply here' (Gove 2010). Indeed, in a speech to the World Education Forum in January 2011 he argued that:

> No nation that is serious about ensuring its children enjoy an education can afford to ignore the PISA and McKinsey studies. Doing so would be as foolish as dismissing what control trials tell us in medicine. It means flying in the face of the best evidence we have of what works ... our recently published Schools White Paper was deliberately designed to bring together – indeed, to shamelessly plunder from – policies that have worked in other high-performing nations. (Gove 2011)

In the light of such developments, it is not surprising that critical analysts such as Nóvoa and Yariv-Marshal (2003) have argued that comparative studies are being used as political tools to legitimate educational policy positioning. To cite their own text:

> ... we are witnessing a growing interest in comparative approaches ... politicians are seeking 'international education indicators', in order to build educational plans that are legitimised by a kind of 'comparative global enterprise'. (Nóvoa and Yariv-Marshal 2003, 425)

For Nóvoa and Yariv-Marshal the influence of such trends also represented a challenge to the field of comparative education in itself – for fostering the forms of research that underpin and reinforce the positivistic values and aspirations of the emergent large-scale cross-national comparisons industry. Here, however, it is argued that, while Nóvoa and Yariv-Marshal advance a powerful and timely critique, this dimension of their analysis underplays the fact that many stakeholders involved in, for example, the PISA studies, are statisticians and data analysts with little first-hand involvement in education, rather than disciplined comparativists. At the same time, it can also be argued that substantial challenges to the uncritical international transfer of contemporary best practice continue to be strong within the field (see details in Crossley and Watson 2003).

More specifically, comparative perspectives are now increasingly, if belatedly, being applied in challenging both the nature and application of international comparisons of student achievement. Grek et al. (2009, 5), for example, adopt a critical stance highlighting the:

> ... rise of Quality Assurance and Evaluation mechanisms and processes as providing the overarching rationale for data demands, both for accountability and performance improvement purposes.

More recently, Ozga (2012, 19) has argued that comparative research has the potential to reveal how PISA can be seen as:

> ... a very powerful policy instrument that is able to penetrate different kinds of policy-making regimes and very diverse political circumstances, because of its high level of credibility and trustworthiness as the 'gold standard' of performance assessment, and because of its apparent adaptability to many disparate political ends.

She goes on to suggest that PISA data:

> ... encourage the production and circulation of technical 'objective' knowledge, and privilege the production of knowledge that is simplified, comparative, normative and transportable ... [strengthening] the influence of the non-governmental actors who construct it and claim to understand it: the external experts, commercial agencies and consultancies that service PISA and generate income from it. (Ozga 2012, 19)

Auld and Morris (2013) further demonstrate how, in these rapidly globalising times, policy makers frequently turn to this 'new paradigm of comparative education' and its 'influential intermediary network' of consultants, seeking what they see as authoritative, applied and accessible guidance. This 'what works' paradigm (see, for example, International Initiative for Impact Evaluation 2013) is persuasive – partly because it is backed up by the sort of large-scale quantitative evidence that is increasingly favoured by decision makers and research funders alike. This contemporary approach to evidence-based educational policy is supported by the transfer of epistemological assumptions from research in the natural sciences and the model of randomised controlled trials (RCTs) in the field of medicine. Given the connections between these developments and the contemporary resurgence in prestige given to large-scale, quantitative social science research, these and related issues are returned to again in the following sections dealing with the emergence of 'big data', and its implications for education and for comparative research in particular.

In the context of this journal, however, it is first pertinent to remember how the distinctive socio-cultural tradition of research in comparative education has long challenged the forms of simplistic policy borrowing – or uncritical international policy transfer – that large-scale cross-national surveys and related global league tables too often generate. While this tradition dates back to the pioneering work of writers such as Sir Michael Sadler at the outset of the twentieth century (Sadler 1900), the contemporary league tables debate has stimulated a resurgence of interest in educational policy transfer processes, and, in turn, this has generated a diversity of new contributions to the policy transfer literature. This includes theoretical formulations that pay close attention to the politics of change and to ways in which policy prescriptions are mediated and reshaped by local agency during the transfer process (Cowen 2009; Schriewer 2006). Others have made concerted efforts to develop analytic models (Phillips and Ochs 2004), to extend earlier thinking, and to develop innovative theoretical and applied applications (Beech 2006; Rappleye 2012). Testifying to the scope and reach of this resurgence of interest, the World Yearbook of Education for 2012 adopted the title theme of *Policy borrowing and lending in education* (Steiner-Khamsi and Waldow 2012).

Collectively, such research helps greatly in understanding contemporary preoccupations with cross-national studies of achievement and global league tables that purport to represent differences in the quality of education between nations – and to evaluate the strengths and limitations of such studies in different contexts. Thus, with regard to her European research, Ozga (2012, 19) reports that:

> ... we explored the degree of penetration of the PISA regulation tool into the policy and scientific community in each national context in the study. This varied according to the strength of the scientific community.

With this in mind, and returning to the 2010 White Paper for English schools, Morris (2012) demonstrates the potential of disciplined comparative analysis by interrogating the 'pick and mix' approach to policy borrowing that he argues is applied selectively in the White Paper to support the greater marketisation and privatisation that its architects aspire to. In doing so Morris's analysis points to an ideologically inspired shift in teacher education policy that is consistent with government efforts to move away from university sector provision towards school-based teacher training in the form of the Teach First and related initiatives. Revealingly, it is also interesting to see how UK policy makers have increasingly looked East (Sellar and Lingard 2013) for such policy justification – as opposed to the successful European case of Finland where policy and practice is less in tune with UK governmental values and priorities. Here the politics of policy transfer are revealed, and strong national agency can be seen to actively select the forms of comparative evidence that best support its own preferred policy orientation.

In contrast, in the arena of international development cooperation, additional issues arise relating to the powerful influence of development agencies and organisations such as the World Bank, the UK Department for International Development (DFID) and UNESCO. Where, what Ozga labels as 'the strength of the scientific community' is limited, as in many poor or small countries, the potential for the control or mediation of internationally inspired policy interventions is often significantly reduced. This can lead to more direct forms of policy transfer, importation or imposition – and to the limited degrees of success that have repeatedly been well-documented at the level of implementation (see, for example, Crossley 1984; Samoff 1999; Tikly 2004). It is in the light of these dilemmas that, if more successful change is to be achieved, my own work has consistently maintained that 'context matters' more than many policy makers and international agencies realise (Crossley, 2010).

For the above reasons, it is argued here that research on the nature and implications of large-scale, cross-national comparisons of educational achievement, and the impact of related league tables, warrants further critical, theoretical and applied analysis. This is a core priority for attention and one that is closely connected to the second of the key issues considered here – the emergence of big data and its implications for the future of comparative and international research in education.

Implications of the big data debate for comparative and international research in education

In the previous section attention was given to the impact of large-scale, cross-national studies of educational achievement on the governance of educational policy worldwide. Underpinning this is the legitimating influence of large-scale data sets that 'speak the language of power'. While the increasing significance of such work can certainly be seen throughout the previous discussion, it is also visible in a wider range of global initiatives that include: the production and use of the Annual Global Monitoring Reports (GMRs) that assess progress toward Education for All Goals and targets (EFA) (UNESCO 2012, 2013); investment in educational data bases such as those produced by the UNESCO Institute for Statistics (UNESCO 2011); the annual compilation of World Development Indicators published by the World Bank (World Bank 2013); the current work of the Brookings Institution and the Learning Metrics Task Force (Brookings Institution 2013); global planning processes for the post-2015 Development Agenda (Mohammed 2013); and the increasing prioritisation of quantitative research and associated quantitative research skills and training by leading research funders across the social sciences.

It is in this broader intellectual and professional context that the emergence of the big data movement can be seen to offer both further advances and significant challenges for the educational research community and for the social sciences in general. At present, the advocates of a proposed 'big data revolution' are many, with writers such as Victor Mayer-Schönberger and Kenneth Cukier (2013) arguing that recent developments in technical and computational power mean that specialists can now process vast amounts of statistical material, so thoroughly and so quickly, that this has the potential to solve many contemporary social and economic problems. Thus, according to Uprichard (2013):

> The world of data has gone from being analogue and digital, qualitative and quantitative, transactional and by-product to, simply, BIG. It is as if we couldn't quite deal with its omnipotence and just ran out of adjectives. BIG.

Looking to the future she goes on to argue that:

> ... organisations, public and private firms and governments [are] preparing for all that it will bring. Some say that big data is already here and always has been, since we have always had more data than we know what to do with. Others say it is unlike anything that has been before because its v-dimensionality makes it different, new and powerful. The four big Vs are: Velocity, because it's 'live' and coming in all the time, e.g. Twitter, Flickr; Variety, because there's so many different kinds, from images (YouTube), to text (blogs), to numbers (transactions, automated logs); Veracity, because it's uncertain or imprecise and we don't always know what's there; and Volume, because there's so much of it, it's big.

Much of the related discussion draws further legitimacy from the predominance of economic discourse in contemporary society, from a quest to measure and evaluate performance in all walks of life, and from what some see as a search for 'certainty' in times when this is hard to find.

While much can be gained from these developments the potential hegemony of statistical evidence in educational research and the social sciences – and in comparative and international education in particular – deserves ongoing critical attention. As Lawn (2013, 8) points out the 'rise of data in education systems' has a long history, but by the late twentieth century 'quantitative data had gained enormous influence in education systems through the work of the OECD, the European Commission and national system agencies'. The limitations of such forms of evidence, the place of judgement and interpretation in their use, and the challenges faced by all users and stakeholders in being able to realistically evaluate and question the significance of decisions made on the basis of big data will become increasingly important. In reflecting upon the influence of PISA on educational governance, for example, Meyer and Benavot (2013, 9) propose that:

> PISA's dominance in the global educational discourse runs the risk of engendering an unprecedented process of worldwide educational standardisation for the sake of hitching

schools more tightly to the bandwagon of economic efficiency, while sacrificing their role of preparing students for independent thinking and civic participation.

In the light of such challenges, it is important for the comparative field, and the wider academy, to actively engage in this debate, as demonstrated by CESE's (Comparative Education Society in Europe) focus upon the theme of 'Governing Educational Spaces: Knowledge, Teaching and Learning in Transition' for its XXVI Conference in 2014. Similarly, in 2012 the British Academy hosted 'The Big Data Debate' as part of the UK's ESRC (Economic and Social Research Council) Festival of Social Science. This explored the opportunities offered by big data, along with the challenges to be faced and the skills, training and resources needed.

Training in the advanced statistical skills needed to both work with and evaluate big data is certainly important (MacInnes, 2013). But so too is the need to ensure that preoccupations with big science and big data do not 'take ever-larger bites from a modest and diminishing funding pot' (Amos 2013, 29) and so starve and marginalise other forms of research and scholarship in the wider educational and social science research community. Working from within the quantitative tradition, Goldstein (1996, 2013) has long cautioned against the uncritical application of international educational league tables, and has more recently challenged the transfer of the RTC model into the educational research landscape – arguing that this could 'undermine a great deal of good educational research, including that done in collaboration with teachers' (Goldstein, email correspondence). Torrance (2013, 28) develops such arguments further, in defending a wide range of approaches to educational research in the face of what he portrays as a 'disciplinary land grab for resources'. This leads to the third related challenge raised here, in the form of the uncritical international transfer of dominant educational research modalities.

The international transfer of educational research modalities

This section of the article develops the arguments raised above, and draws upon the text for a presentation made at the Centre for Research in International and Comparative Education (CRICE) at the University of Malaya in 2012 (Crossley 2012). In doing so, it extends the literature on international policy transfer to the critical analysis of research processes, collaborative capacity building and international partnerships.

To understand the magnitude of these issues, it is revealing to examine the global political economy of educational research in a little more detail. St Clair and Belzer (2007), for example, challenge the increasing dominance of powerful discourses that have come to dominate the shape of contemporary educational research cultures in the UK and the USA. In brief they argue that rather than improving the quality of educational research many of the 'structural transformations' that have been introduced over recent decades, 'can be seen as an attempt to promote market managerialism in educational research for political ends' (St Clair and Belzer 2007, 471). For these authors the continued globalisation of related research modalities warrants critical, comparative interrogation at home and abroad. Providing what is, perhaps, a clearer glimpse of these dangers, Vulliamy addressed an audience of comparativists directly by arguing that:

> A concern for sensitivity to cultural context has been a key part of the field of comparative education in England – all the way from its pioneers ... to current exponents ... Such

concern for cultural context also pervades sociological traditions underpinning the development of qualitative research ... The challenge for future comparative and international researchers in education is to harness the symbiosis of these two traditions to resist the increasing hegemony of a positivist global discourse of educational research and policy-making. (2004, 277)

Building upon Vulliamy, it is argued here that while research capacity building is important within the field of international development, and within the comparative education constituency itself, the international transfer of currently dominant Western research models and modalities is a further issue that deserves urgent and critical attention. In doing so, comparativists should ask whose capacity will be strengthened by new initiatives, whose values and approaches to research will be prioritised, whose modalities will be applied – and do these meet local needs, priorities and agendas? Do, for example, the expensive big science approaches to social research that are increasingly favoured in the UK have the best potential to foster the strengthening of research capacity within low-income countries? What are the implications of the big data debate for the nature and future of international research collaboration? And are the large-scale quantitative surveys increasingly promoted by international development agencies, and the currently fashionable international studies of student achievement, generating data that are context-sensitive enough to assist in the improvement of the quality of education in low-income countries with diverse cultural heritages and traditions?

With references to my own work in Kenya and Tanzania there is much evidence to suggest that locally-grounded, mixed methods research, carried out by African researchers, perhaps in partnership with international colleagues, has much to offer, if a greater proportion of educational reform initiatives are to be translated into successful practice. Studies of the implementation of the Primary School Management Project (PRISM) in Kenya (Crossley et al. 2005), for example, demonstrate how in-depth, qualitative field research played a central role in the shaping of this successful national in-service training programme for primary school head-teachers; and how research partnerships between specialist researchers and practitioners, insiders and outsiders, and local and international personnel were essential for generating crucial insights into grass-roots perspectives, problems and realities.

More recent work in Tanzania also demonstrates how research capacity building was supported by the development of long-standing international collaborative research partnerships. This work also highlighted the importance of such partnerships avoiding research modalities that perpetuate the hegemony of the North (Barrett, Crossley, and Dachi 2011; Barrett, Crossley, and Fon 2014). In recognising these issues and dilemmas, work like this is beginning to address the implications of uncritical international transfer in the research arena, but more needs to be done – including empirically grounded reflexive studies relating to the conceptual and ethical implications of international research collaboration. International research partnerships, for example, are increasingly encouraged by development agencies as a way of strengthening local engagement (Rizvi 2012; Stephens 2009). However, if such partnerships perpetuate imbalances in collaboration that prioritise Northern expertise, leadership and control, the simplistic transfer of fashionable or currently dominant approaches and modalities from the North to the South could help to reinforce dependency and what Tikly characterises as the 'New Imperialism' (Tikly 2004). Moreover, this draws attention to the dangers of some forms of educational research marginalising the role of the independent academic voice, undermining the place of the public intellectual, and becoming too closely associated with policy-making processes and the role of the state. More also needs to be done to support research from diverse cultural perspectives, as demonstrated by a recent special issue of *Comparative Education* on the theme of 'Educational Research in Confucian Heritage Cultures' (Evers, Katyal, and King 2011).

We should, in sum, be careful not to let one conception of research, and research capacity building, to overly dominate our thinking, especially where assumptions about the relative merits of different philosophical and epistemological paradigms, cultures, management structures and evaluation systems are embedded within. Without this, it is argued, educational research capacity, within a diversity of international contexts, may come to be shaped and 'built' in ways that do more to maintain dependency and hegemony than they will to strengthen stakeholder ownership and voice, and to genuinely meet local needs.

Conclusions

For the 50th Anniversary of the journal *Comparative Education* this article identifies three, closely related, key issues and associated challenges that demand critical attention from the comparative and international research community. Together these highlight the implications of global league tables, big data and the international transfer of educational research modalities. It is argued that powerful global trends and agendas are increasingly prioritising, and internationalising, broad modalities of educational and social research that are underpinned by positivistic assumptions and orientations. Within the field of comparative and international education this is both a familiar and a revealing story. The impact of large-scale international surveys of student achievement on the governance of education worldwide helps to legitimise such developments – as does the emergence of the big data movement itself. While there are advances to be gained from such developments, these are well-documented elsewhere. This analysis, therefore, draws attention to the challenges that they generate, and for the need for comparativists to pay close attention to the implications of this for the future of our own distinctive, cross-cultural and multi-disciplinary field.

Acknowledgements

Thanks are extended to Terra Sprague and Anne Crossley who provided helpful feedback and support in the production of this article.

References

Amos, B. 2013. "A Discipline Withers in Big Science's Shadow." *Times Higher* 27 June: 28–29.

Auld, E., and Morris, P. 2013. "Comparative Education, the 'New (What Works) Paradigm' and Policy Borrowing." *Comparative Education* Doi: 10.1080/03050068.2013.826497

Barber, M., and M. Mourshed. 2007. *How the World's Best Performing School Systems Came out on Top*. London: McKinsey and Company.

Barrett, A. M., M. Crossley, and H. A. Dachi. 2011. "International Collaboration and Research Capacity Building: Learning from the EdQual Experience." *Comparative Education* 47 (1): 25–43.

Barrett, A. M., M. Crossley, and T. P. Fon. 2014. "North-South Research Partnerships in Higher Education: Perspectives from South and North." In *Internationalization of Higher Education and Global Mobility. Oxford Studies in Education*, edited by B. Streitwieser. Oxford: Symposium Books.

Beech, J. 2006. "The Theme of Educational Transfer in Comparative Education: a View over Time." *Research in Comparative and International Education* 1 (1): 2–13.

Brookings Institution. 2013. *Toward Universal Learning: Recommendations from the Learning Metrics Task Force*. Washigton, DC: Brookings Institution.

Cowen, R. 2009. "The Transfer, Translation and Transformation of Educational Processes: And their Shape-Shifting?" *Comparative Education* 45 (3): 315–327.

Crossley, M. 1984. "Strategies for Curriculum Change and the Question of International Transfer." *Journal of Curriculum Studies* 16 (1): 75–88.

Crossley, M. 2010. "Context Matters in Educational Research and International Development: Learning from the Small States Experience." *Prospects* 40 (4): 421–429. doi:10.1007/s11125-010-9172-4.

Crossley, M. 2012. "Comparative Education and Research Capacity Building: Reflections on International Transfer and the Significance of Context." *Journal of International and Comparative Education* 1 (1): 4–12.

Crossley, M., A. Herriot, J. Waudo, M. Mwirotsi, K. Holmes, and M. Juma. 2005. *Research and Evaluation for Educational Development. Learning from the PRISM Experience in Kenya*. Oxford: Symposium Books.

Crossley, M., and P. Jarvis, eds. 2000. "Comparative Education for the 21st Century." *Special Issue of Comparative Education* 3 (36).

Crossley, M., and P. Jarvis, eds. 2001. "Comparative Education for the Twenty-First Century: An International Response." *Special Issue of Comparative Education* 37 (4).

Crossley, M., and K. Watson. 2003. *Comparative and International Research in Education: Globalisation, Context and Difference*. London: RoutledgeFalmer.

Crossley, M., and K. Watson. 2009. "Comparative and International Education: Policy Transfer, Context Sensitivity and Professional Development." *Oxford Review of Education* 35 (5): 633–649.

Department for Education. 2010. *The Importance of Teaching – the Schools White Paper*. London: Crown Copyright.

Evers, Colin W., Kokila Roy Katyal and Mark King, ed. 2011. "Special Issue: Educational Research in Confucian Heritage Cultures." *Comparative Education* 47 (3).

Fraser, S. E. 1964. *Jullien's Plan for Comparative Education 1816–1817*. New York: Bureau of Publications, Teachers' College, Columbia University.

Goldstein, H. 1996. "Introduction." *Assessment in Education: Principles, Policy & Practice* 3 (2): 125–128.

Goldstein, H. 2013. *School League Tables. A Short Guide For Head-Teachers and Governors*. London: British Academy.

Gove, M. 2010. "Oral evidence on the Schools White Paper." The Schools White Paper 2010, 14th December 2010. Accessed May 19, 2012. www.parliament.co.uk

Gove, M. 2011. "Michael Gove to the Education World Forum." *Department for Education: Speeches*. January 11. http://www.education.gov.uk/inthenews/spccches/a0072274/michael-gove-to-the-education-world-forum

Grek, S., M. Lawn, B. Lingard, J. Ozga, R. Rinne, C. Segerholm, and H. Simola. 2009. "National Policy Brokering and the Construction of the European Education Space in England, Sweden, Finland and Scotland." *Comparative Education* 45 (1): 5–21.

International Initiative for Impact Evaluation. 2013. Quality Education for all Children? What Works in Education in Developing Countries. www.3ieimpact.org/en/evaluation/working-paper-20

Jullien, M. 1817. *Esquisse d'un Ouvrage sur L'Éducation Comparée*. Paris: De Fain. Reprinted by the Bureau International d'Éducation, Genéve, 1962.

Lawn, M., ed. 2013. *The Rise of Data in Education Systems. Collection, Visualisation and Use*. Oxford: Symposium Books.

Mayer, H. D., and A. Benavot, eds. 2013. *PISA, Power and Policy. The Emergence of Global Educational Governance*. Oxford: Symposium Books.

Mayer-Schönberger, V. and Cukier, K. 2013. *Big Data: A Revolution that will Transform how we Live, Work and Think*. London: John Murray Publishers.

MacInnes, J. 2013. "Sexy Statistics?" *Society Now. ESRC Research Making an Impact* 17: 16–17.

Morris, P. 2012. "Pick'n'Mix, Select and Project; Policy Borrowing and the Quest for 'World Class' Schooling. An Analysis of the 2010 Schools White Paper." *Journal of Education Policy* 27 (1): 89–107.

Mohammed, A. J. 2013. "Education in the Post-2015 Development Agenda: Translating Knowledge into Development." Keynote Address presented at the 12th UKFIET International Conference on Education and Development, September 10, Oxford, UK.

Nóvoa, A., and T. Yariv-Marshal. 2003. "Comparative Research in Education: A Mode of Governance or a Historical Journey?" *Comparative Education* 39 (4): 423–438.

OECD. 2001. *Knowledge and Skills for Life. First Results from PISA*. Paris: OECD Publishing.

OECD. 2004. *Learning for Tomorrow's Wold: First Results from PISA 2003*. Paris: OECD Publishing.

OECD. 2007. *PISA 2006: Science Competencies for Tomorrow's World*. Paris: OECD Publishing.

OECD. 2010. *PISA 2009 Results: Overcoming Social Background: Equity in Learning, Opportunities and Outcomes (Volume II)*. Paris: OECD Publishing.

Ozga, J. 2012. "Comparison as a Governing Technology: The Case of PISA." *Research Intelligence* 1 (19): 18–19.

Phillips, D., and K. Ochs. 2004. "Researching Policy Borrowing: Some Methodological Challenges in Comparative Education." *British Educational Research Journal* 30 (6): 773–784. doi:10.1080/0141192042000279495.

Postlethwaite, T. N. 1999. *International Studies of Educational Achievement: Methodological Issues*. Hong Kong: The University of Hong Kong, Comparative Education Research Centre.

Rappleye, J. 2012. *Educational Policy Transfer in an Era of Globalization: Theory - History - Comparison*. Oxford and New York: Peter Lang.

Rizvi, S., ed. 2012. *Multidisciplinary Approaches to Educational Research*. New York and Oxon: Routledge.

Sadler, M. 1990. "How Far Can We Learn Anything of Practical Value from the Study of Foreign Systems of Education?" In *Selections from Michael Sadler*, edited by J. H. Higginson, published 1979. Liverpool: Dejall & Meyorre.

Samoff, J. 1999. "Institutionalising International Influence." In *Comparative Education: The Dialectic of the Global the Local*, edited by R. F. Arnove and C. A. Torres, 51–89. Lanham: Roman and Littlefield.

Schriewer, J. 2006. "Comparative Social Science: Characteristic Problems and Changing Problem Solutions." *Comparative Education* 42 (3): 299–336.

Sellar, S., and B. Lingard. 2013. "Looking East: Shanghai, PISA 2009 and the Reconstitution of Reference Societies in the Global Education Policy Field." *Comparative Education* 49 (4): 464–485.

St Clair, R., and A. Belzer. 2007. "In the Market for Ideas: How Reforms in the Political Economy of Educational Research in the US and UK Promote Market Managerialism." *Comparative Education* 33 (4): 471–488.

Steiner-Khamsi, G., and F. Waldow, eds. 2012. *World Yearbook of Education 2012: Policy Borrowing and Lending in Education*. City: Routledge.

Stephens, D. ed. 2009. *Higher Education and International Capacity Building. Twenty-five Years of Higher Education Links*. Bristol Papers in Education: Comparative and International Studies. Oxford: Symposium Books.

Tikly, L. 2004. "Education and the New Imperialism." *Comparative Education* 40 (2): 173–198.

Torrance, H. 2013. "Building Evidence into Education: Why Not Look at the Evidence?" *Research Intelligence* 121: 28–29.
UNESCO. 2011. *UNESCO and Education*. Paris: UNESCO.
UNESCO. 2013. *EFA Global Monitoring Report 2012: Youth and Skills, Putting Education to Work*. Paris: UNESCO.
Uprichard, E. 2013. "Focus: Big Data, Little Questions?" Accessed October 1st, 2013. http://www.discoversociety.org/focus-big-data-little-questions
Vulliamy, Graham. 2004. "The Impact of Globalisation on Qualitative Research in Comparative and International Education." *Compare* 34 (3): 261–284.
World Bank. 2013. *World Development Indicators 2013*. Washington, DC: The World Bank.

Lessons from abroad: whatever happened to pedagogy?

Julian G. Elliott

Principal of Collingwood College, School of Education, Durham University, Durham, United Kingdom

> This paper considers attempts to import pedagogic practices from other educational systems. In so doing, it focuses upon policymakers' attempts to: (a) import interactive whole class teaching approaches to the UK (and, to a lesser extent, the US); and (b) export learner-centred pedagogies, largely derived from Anglo-American theorising and practice, to industrialised and developing countries that often vary greatly in educational performance. The paper explains why such initiatives have largely proven ineffective, yet notes that while UK policymakers have largely moved away from pedagogic concerns to issues of teacher quality and expectation, learner-centred approaches continue to be proffered as a solution to the educational problems of many traditional societies. Finally, the paper concludes by emphasising student academic motivation and engagement, rather than specific pedagogic practices, as key to the differential performance of industrialised countries in international comparisons.

Introduction

In the second half of 2013, the Organisation for Economic Co-operation and Development (OECD) reported comparative findings of the educational performance of 16–24 year olds in 24 nations. Young adults in England were found to rank 22nd in literacy and 21st for numeracy. The highest performing countries for numeracy were the Netherlands, Finland and Japan, and for literacy, Finland, Japan and South Korea. Despite frequent criticisms of the methods and procedures employed in large-scale assessments of this kind (Gaber et al. 2012; Goldstein 2004; Prais 2003, 2007; Roth et al. 2006), and the problems of reducing complex datasets to simplistic aggregated rankings (Wrigley 2004) the OECD findings confirmed the long-standing superiority of Finland and South East Asian countries across multiple international comparative studies of literacy and numeracy.

As has typically been the case for such analyses, the findings were met with no little anguish [the so-called PISA 'shock' phenomenon (Wiseman 2013)] by policymakers in those countries where modest standings in the league table were held to be unacceptable. Once again, commentators looked to countries at the top of the league tables to provide clues as to where problems in their own countries lay and to indicate what could be done to improve performance. Although, in the UK, poor classroom practice was once again held up as the primary culprit, there was now little suggestion that this related to particular forms of pedagogy. No longer was the main solution to inferior UK performance seen to be the importation of whole class teaching as practised in high-achieving countries [the supposed 'miracle' cure of the 1990s (Alexander

2012a)]. Instead, the focus shifted away from pedagogy towards other educational policy-related features of high-performing countries such as Finland, Taiwan, Singapore, Japan, China (Shanghai) and South Korea.

It is perhaps something of an irony that while the US and UK have looked to Asian societies for pedagogic inspiration, the learner-centred forms of pedagogy, criticised as one reason for poor Western performance, have continued to be admired by many reformers in high-performing countries, and attempts to export such practices to cultures in the developing world (Vavrus, Thomas, and Bartlett 2011) have persisted, despite consistently disappointing results (Schweisfurth 2013).

Learning from others

There is a long tradition of educationalists looking overseas to 'reference societies' in order to learn and borrow effective practices (Alexander 2000; Phillips and Och 2004) and justify and legitimate the desire for reform (Waldow 2012). At the end of the nineteenth century the major European nations, concerned about their military and industrial competitiveness, cast anxious eyes at one another's education systems. During the Cold War, the launch of Sputnik in 1957 resulted in apprehensive examination as to whether the Soviet system of education was superior, with a seminal text by Bronfenbrenner (1970) extending Western angst to issues of wider childhood socialisation practices. Concern by American policymakers that educational standards were lagging behind those of other nations, and that the performance of current American students was, for the first time, inferior to that of previous generations, later found expression in *A nation at risk* (National Commission on Excellence in Education 1983). This report stated that the educational foundations of the United States were being

> ... eroded by a rising tide of mediocrity that threatens our future as a Nation and a people .... If an unfriendly foreign power had attempted to impose on America the mediocre educational performance that exists today, we might well have viewed it as an act of war. (5)

Shortly after its publication, a US Presidential visit to Japan, at a time when the Japanese economy was buoyant, resulted in political fascination with its education and what could lessons be learned (Rappleye 2012).

Anxiety in the US about poor national performance was fuelled by a series of studies consistently showing significantly higher academic achievement in a number of Asian countries (Song and Ginsburg 1987; Stevenson and Lee 1990; Stevenson and Stigler 1992; Stigler, Lee, and Stevenson 1990). Similar concerns were being voiced in England, fuelled by the results of a series of international comparisons undertaken by the International Association for the Study of Educational Achievement (IEA) and a rival group, Educational Testing Services' International Assessment of Educational Progress (IAEP). Particularly influential at this time were the Second International Assessments of Mathematics (IAEPM2) and Science (IAEPS2) (Foxman 1992). The performance of children aged nine and 13 was compared across 20 countries. As for other studies, children from China, Korea and Taiwan were the highest achievers, significantly ahead of children from England and the United States.

Despite deserved criticism of the methodological flaws of these studies this mounting body of findings was also gaining the attention of UK policymakers. Calling for change, Barber (1996), the Head of the Department for Education and Employment's Standards and Effectiveness Unit, stated that, irrespective of the methodological weaknesses of individual studies, the results were so consistent that we, ' … would be living in a fool's paradise if we chose to ignore the results' (24). In 1996, the Office for Standards in Education commissioned a *Review of international surveys involving England between 1964 and 1990* (Reynolds and Farrell 1996). The ensuing report examined the IEA and IEAP studies, together with other smaller-scale comparisons and concluded that the performance of English children in mathematics and science was poor and had deteriorated relative to other nations. As was the case for Japan in the 1980s, these findings became associated with the perceived threat of competing economic powers.

In attempting to explain why these countries were seemingly outperforming children in England, Reynolds and Farrell (1996) clustered reasons under four headings: cultural, systemic, school and classroom factors. Key cultural factors were the high status of the teacher, the emphasis on working hard, high parental aspirations, the academic quality of teachers, and high levels of student commitment. Important systemic factors were greater time in school, with more and longer school days, a prevalent belief that all children are able to succeed, and concentration on a small number of attainment goals, most of which were academic in content. For factors relating to the school, the report's authors highlighted the strong emphasis upon whole class collaborative and supportive group processes, the use of specialist teachers, free time for lesson planning and teacher collaboration, and close monitoring by regular testing and scrutiny from the school Principal. At the level of the classroom, the key factor identified was the use of whole class interactive teaching whereby the teacher's and students' joint task was to ensure that all members of the class kept up with the material together and that the range of achievement was minimised. Tight lesson timings ensured that attention was maximally focused. Widespread use of textbooks was held to be a valuable means to minimise the need for teachers to construct their own materials.

Shortly after the publication of Reynolds and Farrell's report, the first results of the Third International Maths and Science Study (TIMSS), involving 500,000 students in 41 countries, reached the front pages of the world's newspapers. English children scored significantly poorer in mathematics than their counterparts in several Pacific Rim and Eastern European countries. Indeed, while their performance was similar to that of children in Germany and Denmark, it was significantly lower than those in Austria, Belgium, Sweden, France, Switzerland and the Netherlands. While performance of English children in science was equal or better to most of Western Europe, it was still inferior to Pacific Rim and some East European countries. In the US, it was noted that the relative performance of American students declined as they progressed through the school years. By the end of their time in high school (12th grade), US students were among the lowest from 21 participating nations in both mathematics and science with only Cyprus and South Africa scoring significantly worse. Examination of the most able 10–20% of students in mathematics and physics (16 participating nations) proved particularly unsettling as, in both subjects, the US students were outperformed by every other country.

The political and educational fall-out from the TIMSS findings dovetailed with Reynolds and Farrell's (1996) call for changed patterns of teaching. High-profile attacks were made upon child-centred approaches with particular complaint that the emphasis upon individualisation and differentiation was leading to underachievement. Critics suggested that providing each child with material designed to their own particular needs, and operating at a pace that varied according to their own level, only served to increase differences between children and this inevitably resulted in a large tail of underachievers. In contrast, high-performing countries, such as the heavily cited Taiwan, encouraged practices that ensured that the range of achievement was kept to a minimum. Here, a strong emphasis upon group cohesion and cooperation appeared to be important, as was the general willingness of students to engage in additional work outside of the classroom.

Drawing upon observations in highly successful Pacific Rim countries, and studies of practice in Switzerland (Bierhoff 1996; Bierhoff and Prais 1995), Reynolds and Farrell (1996) argued for an increase in whole class teaching:

> ... not simply of the 'lecture to the class' variety, but high quality *interactive* teaching in which the teacher starts with a problem and develops solutions and concepts through a series of graded questions addressed to the whole class. (56, emphasis as in original)

Such an approach was held to be different from traditional whole class teaching which had:

> ... become associated with too much teacher talk and too many passive, tuned-out students ... whole-class instruction in Japanese and Chinese classrooms is a very lively, engaging enterprise. Asian teachers do not spend large amounts of time lecturing. They present interesting problems; they pose provocative questions; they probe and guide. The students work hard, generating multiple approaches to a solution, explaining the rationale behind their methods, and making good use of wrong answers. (Stevenson and Stigler 1992, 146–147)

The call for the introduction of successful practices from abroad was taken up enthusiastically by the then Chief Inspector of Schools in England and Wales (Woodhead 1996) who argued that 50% of primary school lesson time (60% in the case of mathematics) should take the form of whole class teaching. In a highly publicised initiative, the London Borough of Barking and Dagenham, sought to model its primary school mathematics teaching on practices observed in Switzerland and Germany (Luxton and Last 1997). This involved far greater emphasis upon whole class instruction in which the use of overhead projectors and oral discussion featured prominently.

Similar procedures were advocated in secondary schools. Drawing upon the Hungarian model of mathematics teaching, Burghes (1996) established a widely publicised intervention that was taken up in a variety of UK schools. The approach emphasised the need for greater clarity, precision and focus in teaching mathematical concepts, the value of examining student errors as illustrations for class learning, the use of homework as a central component of learning, and greater emphasis upon whole class, interactive teaching. Mathematics teaching was also under the spotlight in the US and, in a widely publicised initiative, Stigler and Herbert (1999) compared mathematics teaching approaches in the US, Japan and Germany and argued for the adoption of Japanese teaching practices. However, as Heyneman and Lee (2014) point out, a key factor, not brought into their analysis, was the widespread attendance of Japanese children at private tutoring schools (*juku*) where much of the preparatory work for university entrance examination was covered. As a result, Japanese teachers in state schools may be freed from the more pedestrian activities that encumber their peers in countries such as the US.

Beyond pedagogy: factors associated with high-achieving countries

It is notable that while classroom pedagogy in successful Asian countries has been a dominant concern of UK policymakers, local commentators in these countries have tended to focus upon other factors to account for their achievements. Thus, in accounting for the high performance of Singapore in international assessments, Ng (2013) lists five key factors: the existence of a government-led common goal for education with close monitoring of standards; financial investment geared to educational improvement; high status for the teaching profession offering prestige and attractive salaries; strong home support resulting in high levels of study out of school hours; and a sense of safety in the school environment. For South Korea, Shin (2013) identifies the importance of high levels of achievement motivation, fuelled both by the Confucian value placed upon scholarship and more instrumental career concerns, the proportion of time spent studying each week, and parental expectations and involvement. This latter factor has been emphasised as contributing towards a high degree of 'educational zeal' (Sorensen 1994, 21) with parents spending considerable time selecting and monitoring private tutoring for their children (Bray 2010; Park, Byun, and Kim 2011). As Sorenson points out, the academic success of South Korean students is less a matter of curriculum, pedagogy or structural factors such as class size than the result of how education is embedded within the fabric of Korean society. Interestingly, one important pedagogic element, the general absence of differentiated instruction in South Korea (Sung 2006), an approach that was perceived by Reynolds and Farrell (1996) to be a weakness in England, is held by Shin (2013) to be a reason for Korean underperformance.

A similar picture to Korea is provided for Taiwan (Liu 2013). Here, the key factors are seen to be the value placed upon education success that finds expression through the use of supplementary education – after class guidance, additional tutoring and private 'cram schools' (Liu 2009, 2011). Out of school tuition not only helps to drive up overall standards, it also enables struggling learners to catch up with their peers – thus reducing achievement gaps within class groups (Ma, Jong, and Yuan 2013). In a telling echo of Stigler and Herbert's US/Japanese comparison (1999), the key role of out of school activity was also downplayed in Reynolds' much publicised *Panorama* BBC television documentary (BBC 1996) where the high levels of Taiwanese performance in mathematics were attributed to whole class teaching and the concomitant lack of individualised teaching through differentiation (Reynolds 2010).

Shanghai, a top performer in PISA 2009, has recently gained much attention as a new reference society for educational policy (Sellar and Lingard 2013). Once again, cultural factors leading to high academic achievement have been identified as key – a powerful work ethic underpinned by Confucian principles, parental pressure (that also operates within low socio-economic status families) and a fiercely competitive examination system (Tan 2013). Others, however, have also highlighted policy initiatives that have sought to improve the quality of teaching and learning and address the problem of low performing schools (Cheng 2011).

During the past decade, the attention of policymakers has embraced a country with greater cultural similarity to other Western nations, and one that has achieved a premier position in the PISA surveys of 2000, 2003, 2006 and 2009. While the performance of Finnish children in earlier assessments by the International Association for the Evaluation of Educational Achievement (IEA) was unremarkable (Sahlberg 2007), it was the rather different nature of the PISA assessments, emphasising the application of knowledge and skills to real-life situations, that appears to have led to Finland's elevated position in international league tables for reading, science and mathematics.

This performance has resulted in policymakers and practitioners flocking to Finland from around the world in search of the key to success. Many factors have been suggested – a high level of preschool education, sound support for children with special educational needs, high levels of educational and welfare expenditure, a small immigrant population, and relatively low influence of socio-economic status on student performance. Another factor, echoing the Asian picture, is the high regard for education that permeates Finnish society. As a result, the profession is able to recruit high-quality student teachers who receive a lengthy and academically rigorous training (Chung and Crossley 2013).

In many ways, Finland has bucked the trend of most industrialised countries by resisting the emphasis upon formally measured national standards and teacher and school accountability (Sahlberg 2007). In line with the value accorded to the teaching profession in this country, commentaries upon Finnish teaching quality tend to emphasise the important role of teacher expertise in making decisions about practice. Professional understandings are underpinned by a strong focus upon research-based thinking and practice (Silander and Välijärvi 2013).

According to Chung and Crossley (2013) a particular strength of the Finnish system is its individualised provision for children with special educational needs. Such a strength appears to run counter to Reynolds and Farrell's (1996) recommendations for more whole class teaching and their claims that individualised approaches are, in part, to blame for the comparatively poor academic performance of children in England.

Why did imported pedagogies not take root?

There are two key reasons why in the UK and US, the preoccupation with imported pedagogy declined. Firstly, the warnings of Sadler, voiced in 1900, of the folly of cross-cultural educational cherry-picking have become more widely understood. Secondly, the principal reason why Asian countries are at the top of international league tables is that children in these countries typically work harder in and out of school.

Pedagogic practice and the culture of schooling

For some, identifying effective practices that will operate in any school system is a relatively simple empirical task; for others, such a belief is unrealistic. In discussing these opposing schools of thought, Fuller and Clarke (1994) identified camps with very different understandings about how schools work. One group, the 'policy mechanics', is associated with a neo-positive perspective in which controlled studies are advocated as a means to derive generalisable claims about reality. In respect of educational practices, their goal is to empirically isolate discrete teaching and wider school practices that are found to be universally associated with student achievement. Such information is of great interest both to national governments and to supra-national organisations who wish to identify elements of school and classroom effectiveness. This approach has thrived within a broader policy climate in which evidence-based approaches indicating 'What works' became de rigeur for politicians and policymakers across education, health and social services (Oakley 2002; Wiseman 2010). It is unsurprising, therefore, that education researchers in this tradition became the gurus of policymakers, ' … the academic community's jet-setting, high-tec, intellectual sharp dressers' (Alexander 1996, 6).

In contrast, the 'classroom culturalists', situated within a contextualist paradigm, reject any notion that educational practices can be considered independently of the culture in which they are situated. Rather, they emphasise a focus on the ' … implicitly modelled norms exercised in the classroom and how children are socialised to accept particular rules of participation and authority, linguistic norms, orientations towards achievement, and conceptions of merit and status' (Fuller and Clarke 1994, 119). For those who hold such a position, attempts to derive culture-free conceptions of educational inputs (class size, level of teacher education, pedagogic practice) considered to have consistent, universal effects upon achievement are naïve and unlikely to generate meaningful understandings.

One powerful contextualist theory is that developed by Urie Bronfenbrenner (1979, 2005) although it is important to note that context is just but one element of his process–person–context–time model. Particularly important in the theory are proximal processes – consistent and enduring forms of interaction between developing individuals and the people, objects and symbols that feature in their experience. Proximal processes are influenced by personal characteristics and the multiple spatial and temporal contexts in which these interactions occur. Contextual levels include the macrosystem, which may refer to a given society or region, microsystems, such as school or home (which are influenced by the macrosystem), and the chronosystem which concerns the impact of historical time on entire societies (and also the microsystems that operate within them) as major political, economic and social changes confront traditional values, beliefs and practices.

The policy mechanics can be criticised for ignoring many of these components. Proximal processes of interaction in many Asian settings are underpinned by deep respect for the importance of the educational process, for the knowledge and authority of teachers, for the demonstration of personal qualities of persistence and diligence, and for the priority placed upon the needs of the group over those of the individual. Such elements are likely to be important for the operation of interactive whole class teaching, an approach that will require a child to participate even at those times when the group activity is overly or insufficiently demanding for them. As collaborating participants in the learning process, class members need to respond to halting performance from struggling peers in ways that do not humiliate, alienate or deter. Such demands require a capacity to attend and concentrate for lengthy periods of time, a strong commitment to the group, and high standards of behaviour and self-discipline. Contrast this with Anglo-American classrooms, particularly those marked by socio-economic disadvantage or where there are high levels of variability in pupil attainment (Prais 1997). Here, the self-discipline necessary for coping with the lengthy passage of whole group interaction may routinely be lacking, and there will often be little desire to support the learning of peers who can be perceived as a competitors, stressors or harassers (Li 2012). Novice teachers, particularly in schools serving less affluent districts, may learn that it is often unproductive to try to draw out extended classroom discussion and rumination as this can too readily lead to restlessness, unruliness and disengagement. As Alexander (2012b) notes, one of the greatest hurdles to introducing a greater proportion of high-level dialogue to classrooms is the fear of teachers that this will make them more likely to lose control. Where student behaviour is a challenge, teachers will tend to favour forms of pedagogy that help them maximise task engagement and restrict student rowdiness. Oftentimes, this will involve a succession of short activities in which written, individual work forms a significant component.

The influence of the peer group is key to the operation of certain forms of pedagogy and here significant macrosystem and microsystem influences impact upon proximal processes. In examining patterns of interaction in classrooms, Elliott et al. (1999, 2001, 2005), for example, compared the role of peers in Russia with those in

England and the US. Since the pioneering work of Makarenko in the 1920s, socialisation practices in the Soviet Union have built upon the important role of the collective. From the age of three, most children were involved in group activities in which they were taught to recognise and respect the interests and needs of the group and defer to the authority of the adult (Markowitz 2000; Tudge 1991). This continued through the primary school years where children were taught to directly influence one another in ways that reflected the goals of the society. As Bronfenbrenner (1970) noted, the peer group championed 'desirable' behaviour within a culture in which students were encouraged to take personal initiative and responsibility for encouraging appropriate behaviour from their peers.

Elliott et al. (1999, 2001, 2005) noted that these traditions had persevered after the end of the Soviet period and Russian students were continuing to influence their classmates in ways that aided engagement and discipline in lessons. Academic enthusiasm and achievement were openly admired by peers as long as these were unencumbered by any signs of arrogance and able students were prepared to help those who were less accomplished. In contrast, peer influences in England and the US often militate against the outward show of enthusiasm for academic study to the extent that some students deliberately seek to underperform or, at least, conceal high grades from their peers [see also, Li (2012, 187), for a discussion of differing peer influences upon educational striving in Western and East Asian cultures]. However, without a strong climate of peer support, respect for teachers and the presence of strong student self-discipline, any attempt to establish significant levels of whole class interactive teaching is doomed.

Educational borrowing has not travelled in solely one direction, however. Policymakers, researchers and education reformers operating in traditional (both industrialised and developing) societies have also sought to import pedagogic practices from the UK and US. Such initiatives have been largely influenced by the primacy of Western (particularly American) educational and psychological theorising (American Psychological Association 1997) that emphasises the importance of individual wellbeing [for example, self-determination theory (Ryan and Deci 2000)] and a variety of democratic/emancipatory (Tabulawa 2003) agendas rather than the results of international comparative testing programmes. These practices can be described as component elements of learner-centred education, a somewhat generic term that is not easily encapsulated in a simple set of descriptors (Schweisfurth 2013) but which emphasises a view of knowledge as fluid rather than fixed, a diminution of teacher didacticism and authority in favour of democratic, student-led (often collaborative) learning, and a focus upon individual student interests and needs. According to academic work from the field of educational psychology, approaches based on such principles should result in greater levels of motivation and personal agency, higher quality learning and retention, greater capacity for critical thought, and an ability to apply knowledge meaningfully and imaginatively (Schweisfurth 2013).

Despite the modest league table standing of countries that are historically associated with learner-centred approaches, several high-achieving Confucian countries consider these to be a means of improving their students' creative, problem-solving and entrepreneurial performance (Ng 2008). Initiatives have not met with universal approval in these societies, however. Zhao (2005), for example, criticises the obsession of East Asian reformers with perceived American strengths – the production of happy, creative and socially responsible students – and the concomitant belief that Western approaches will help their own societies. Li (2012) notes that while learning from the *content* of Western education has proven helpful to China, accepting the associated learner-centred modes of teaching and learning has proven far more difficult. She cautions that unless managed carefully, the introduction of such approaches may have a deleterious effect upon relationships between children and their parents, teachers and peers and, in the light of this, questions:

> Why keep trying to change something that has failed to change for 150 years? Or perhaps the question ought to be posed in a different way: Is it worth the effort? And to what end? … I think it is time for them to stop and ponder. (Li 2012, 341)

However, according to Bronfenbrenner's theory, one would anticipate change not only at the level of the macrosystem (as a result of modernising influences) but also on the part of the developing individuals (the students) who are not mere passive recipients of social forces but also instigators. Changes in everyday practices do not occur solely because of changes at the level of culture or society but, in part, because of the experiences and personal characteristics of new generations. Despite the slow pace of change over those past 150 years it is conceivable, therefore, that longstanding proximal processes at home and at school will prove difficult to maintain indefinitely.

In this respect, Elliott and Tudge (2007) have described how globalising influences emphasising the importance of individual freedoms and autonomy led to calls for the importation of a range of Western approaches into hitherto academically successful Russian classrooms. Here, rather more than has been the case in East Asian societies, traditional teacher-dominated approaches, associated with the nation's Soviet past, were vilified by reformers as outdated and inefficient for modern industrialised societies (Polyzoi and Dneprov 2003). However, and as is noted above, far-reaching changes at the macrosystemic level are unlikely to be speedily translated into changes in proximal processes (e.g. classroom practices), especially where these have developed over many years. Thus, despite the initial attraction of Western approaches to teaching and learning to many Russian teachers, the power of longstanding proximal processes was such that early enthusiasms soon faltered and many teachers rapidly reverted to their former practices (Froumin 2005), much to the chagrin of many of their students who, in the long term, will surely exert a degree of influence upon future practices (Elliott 2013; Elliott and Tudge 2007).

Problems are even greater in the developing world where the literature on the implementation of learner-centred approaches, '…can make depressing study' (Schweisfurth 2013, 154). The reasons for this are manifold with resource constraints, low teacher expertise, limited epistemological understanding and high staff turnover, all factors which are held to have consistently undermined attempts to change pedagogic practice (Chisholm 2012; Jessop and Penny 1998; Schweisfurth 2013). The problem of resources, both material and human, is very real and the failure of initiatives is often seen to stem from inadequate and insufficient training (Altinyelken 2010; Hardman et al. 2009; Vavrus 2009). Training, often conducted by those with missionary zeal (as seems to have also been the case in Russia) can result in the expression of voiced support by the trained (teachers) for new pedagogic practices, yet long-standing practices often continue largely unchanged (Barrett 2008; Schweisfurth 2013). Crucially, there can be insufficient regard to issues of philosophy, values and belief, and the ways by which these undermine the efforts of those who seek to introduce the new practices. For many comparatively poorly educated teachers in the developing world, traditional forms of teaching and learning locate them as authority figures in possession of important knowledge that they can transmit to their respectful students

(Coe 2005). Approaches in which knowledge is fluid, and where teachers are perceived as facilitators or co-constructors rather than the purveyors of knowledge, may challenge their professional identity. As the present author has noted in his own work in Lesotho, the introduction of cross-age peer tutoring (a practice that would seemingly sit well within the Basotho cultural tradition in which older children routinely guide their younger siblings) may have the negative effect of leaving teachers feeling side-lined and uncomfortable about their status. As a result, long-standing proximal processes operating in the home may not be easily imported into the classroom.

Even before commencing their schooling, children in traditional societies are typically subject to socialisation practices that predispose them to learn passively and unquestioningly [although see, Li and Wegerif (2014) for a more nuanced account of the dynamics of education based on Confucian principles]. As the influence of globalising forces leads to challenges to traditional relationships and greater student desire for individual autonomy (Inglehart and Welzel 2005; Welzel 2011), there appears to be a desire on the part of some sectors in traditional societies that school should act as an important counter-balance for the maintenance of social order and discipline. In such situations, the introduction of Western learner-centred approaches is unlikely to flourish, at least in the short term (Peterson del Mar 2013).

In her examination of learner-centred initiatives in the developing world that seem to have proven effective, Schweisfurth (2013) notes the central importance of sustained and coherent support for teachers by means of ongoing professional development. This begs the question as to whether supportive practices can be established that will persist once the additional input is removed or when the approach is upscaled beyond a narrow range of institutions. The problem of sustaining initiatives is equally evident for industrialised nations. Thus, many of the highly publicised initiatives that followed the call for whole class interactive teaching in the UK and US in the 1990s have faded away as first enthusiasms declined and 'hero-innovators' (Georgiades and Philimore 1975) moved elsewhere. Even the mandatory teaching approaches of the literacy and numeracy strategies, established in the wake of advocacy for whole class teaching by the Reynolds and Farrell (1996) report, were finally shelved in 2010. No doubt their demise was, in part, a consequence of the finding that standards of literacy and numeracy had failed to improve despite earlier claims to this effect (Tymms 2004).

Levels of academic motivation and engagement
There is a well-known anecdote of a man searching for his car keys under a street lamp. When asked whether he is sure that he had dropped them nearby, he replied that he had lost them elsewhere but, 'This is where the light is showing'. In many respects, policymakers will typically fasten onto particular aspects of education systems that they can readily and speedily influence while underplaying more intransigent or challenging factors [for example, the important role of social inequality in educational underperformance (Alexander 2012a; Wilkinson and Pickett 2009)]. By adopting a pick 'n' mix approach to policy borrowing (Morris 2012), factors that do not sit comfortably with governmental strategy may be conveniently ignored [two examples being the highly centralised nature of Japanese education that was anathema to the Reagan administration in the 1980s (Rappleye 2012) and a disregarding of the absence of high-stakes testing in modern day Finland]. Furthermore, a form of projection can operate whereby some policymakers [see, for example, the influence of media accounts of the many virtues of Finnish education (Takayama, Waldow, and Sung 2013)] can

identify features of high-achieving countries that, in actuality, do not exist (Steiner-Khamsi 2012; Takayama 2010; Waldow 2010).

It is hardly surprising that while describing the strong drive for educational success in the Pacific Rim countries, Reynolds followed the publication of his report (Reynolds and Farrell 1996) by high-profile calls emphasising the need for pedagogic reform. Such calls, offering little challenge to politicians, were eagerly embraced by influential members of government and the leaders of the national inspectorate. However, as noted above, pedagogy cannot be divorced from student behaviour and discipline, and these latter factors are underpinned by powerful underlying social, economic, historical and cultural factors (Coffield 2012).

However, even if pedagogy could be imported in the fashion prescribed, it is unlikely to make significant inroads in overall levels of performance. In industrialised nations, if rather less so perhaps in the developing world, the overwhelming reason for comparative international test success is the engagement of students in the educational process. As Elliott et al. (2005) note, the reason why Russian (previously Soviet) children have long been comparatively high academic performers, despite significant social and economic challenges, is because they operate in a culture that expects them to work harder and longer on schoolwork than many children in the West, often at significant cost to their physical and psychological wellbeing (Baranov 1998). Underpinning these efforts was a strong societal belief in the importance of being 'an educated person' who would be widely admired by other children and adults. Such a perspective is rarely found in Anglo-American contexts where education tends to be perceived as having a more instrumental value that may not appear accessible to disadvantaged groups.

It is important to emphasise that anti-intellectual attitudes in the US (Grant and Sleeter 1996; Sedlak et al. 1986) do not spring from the schools in isolation but, rather, grow out of socialising experiences in the wider communities which they serve (Coleman 1961). In a critique of American attitudes to education, Steinberg (1996) reports large-scale parental disengagement from schooling in which acceptance of poor grades is widespread, peer culture is often scornful of academic excellence, and student lifestyles in which a high proportion of time outside of school is spent socialising, engaging in leisure pursuits and/or in part-time employment. Steinberg is scornful of the claims of school reformers which, too often in his opinion, have underplayed the importance of motivational factors:

> No curricular overhaul, no instructional innovation, no change in school organisation, no toughening of standards, no rethinking of teacher training or compensation will succeed if students do not come to school interested in, and committed to, learning. (194)

Learner-centred approaches, where these operate ineffectively, may further undermine levels of engagement. In place of concerted striving, an implicit bargain (Sedlak et al. 1986) may be struck where low-level demands are made characterised by:

> ... relatively little concern for academic content; a willingness to tolerate, if not encourage, diversion from the specified knowledge to be presented or discussed; the substitution of genial banter and conversation for concentrated academic exercises; improvisational instructional adaptation to student preference for or indifference towards specific subject matter or pedagogical techniques; the 'negotiation' of class content, assignments, and standards; and a high degree of teacher autonomy in managing the level of academic engagement, personal interaction, and course content. (7)

Closely allied with a strong desire to work hard is disciplinary climate (i.e. an orderly classroom environment), a factor deemed to be even more important in explaining high levels of achievement in East Asian countries than the extensive time spent on academic learning out of school hours (Ma et al. 2013). Contrary to the impression that is sometimes given in media accounts, however, student behaviour and relationships with teachers are not wholly a consequence of teacher management skill and the influence of school climate but also reflect more deeply culturally held attitudes and beliefs about the nature of authority and personal freedoms (Pace and Hemmings 2007).

In many traditional societies, there are fears that adult authority and student acceptance of teacher legitimacy are being eroded by Western (globalising) influences. Where such pressures occur, teachers are often likely to struggle. Alexander (2000), for example, has reflected upon the tensions resulting from American teachers' professional beliefs (reflecting those embedded in US society) as to the importance of student autonomy and empowerment, and their need to ensure disciplined, hardworking classrooms. He describes in powerful terms how such beliefs, and the classroom interactions and practices that reflected these, led to teacher–student negotiation, confrontation and, ultimately, reduced time on-task. In contrast, his observations of Russian classrooms in the 1990s confirmed those reported by other Western visitors (Elliott et al. 2005; Glowka 1995; Hufton and Elliott 2000; Muckle 1988, 1990) that the high standards of behaviour routinely observed were closely associated with consensual understandings about the nature of knowledge, the authority of teachers, and respect for the educational process.

It can be questioned whether gaining top positions in international league tables such as PISA necessarily indicates superior performance across a broader curriculum and whether, if more subjects were included, the same countries would still occupy the lead positions (Alexander 2012a; Heyneman 2013). Alexander (2012a) also questions whether an ultra-competitive desire to beat other nations is desirable, given the major social and environmental challenges that confront us. The present author would like to pose one further question: even if the league tables do present a valid picture of high educational performance that has important societal value, to what extent is it appropriate to ask our children to make the extensive sacrifices that would be needed? Are the emotional and physical problems that result from the pressures of an unrelenting workload [e.g. in the Soviet Union (Baranov 1998); or in some East Asian countries (Stankov 2010)] an acceptable price to pay for such an outcome? It is likely that the answers to these questions might vary greatly between countries.

Conclusions

Calls to introduce cherry-picked pedagogic practices from other countries have now become less vociferous and the belief in such 'miracle cures' appears not to figure highly on the agendas of policymakers or the influential organisations that advise them. Indeed, the influential McKinsey Report entitled *How the world's best performing systems come out on top* (Barber and Mourshed 2007) chose not to focus on pedagogy on the highly questionable grounds that this was already well debated in the literature.

Rather than having been influenced by the persuasive arguments of those who emphasise the importance of contextual factors, this shift is most likely a consequence of the demonstrated ineffectiveness of simplistic policy borrowing. Notwithstanding this, the 'neocolonial export' (Nguyen et al. 2009a) of Western learner-centred pedagogies to developing societies continues apace despite a lengthy litany of ineffective or unsustained educational outcomes.

Of course, it would be folly to ignore good practice, wherever it is located, and national education systems have always borrowed from each other. However, where this has proven effective, it is because significant elements are shaped and incorporated within models of practice that are appropriate for the host culture. Thus, having noted the seeming paradox that collaborative group practices, seemingly well-suited for collectivist societies, have taken stronger root in individualistic cultures, Nguyen et al. (2009a, 2009b) outline some of the ways by which specific elements of the approach have reflected a Western, rather than an Asian, perspective. To enable collaborative group approaches to take root in Asian schools and colleges, it is necessary to modify various aspects in ways that reflect sensitively to the host culture.

Sadler (1900) observed that the things outside the classroom matter more than those inside the schools, and these ' … govern and interpret the things inside' (310). Unfortunately, governments have too often sought to focus on discrete aspects of schooling and ignored findings such as those demonstrating that socio-economic difference is the single strongest factor in relation to academic performance on PISA (OECD 2001, 2004). Once one strips out broader, but important, explanatory factors such as poverty, economic inequality, racism, health, and social dislocation and alienation, to focus more narrowly upon the specifics of school-related activity, the primary factor that explains high academic success is the degree of student engagement (driven by learner demand), not the operation of particular pedagogies. In order to demonstrate this, one only needs to examine the remarkable educational performance of Asian-American students in the US (Eaton and Dembo 1997; Siu 1992) – the somewhat controversially termed 'model minority' – to see how high levels of achievement motivation and academic engagement impact upon educational performance in classrooms that are typically less successful with other students. In this respect Heyneman (1999, 2013) refers to the importance of student 'demand to learn', ' … a culturally shaped attitude or disposition that places the value of education higher or lower on a scale of socially desirable activities' (2013, 284–285) and which is demonstrably greater in Eastern Asia than England and the US.

Of course, pedagogy and student motivation and engagement are inextricably related and cannot be easily dissociated, with the importance of high teacher knowledge and skills crucial to both. However, to assume that one can import a given set of practices from a seemingly more successful country to one that is less so and rapidly reap educational rewards is a folly that is only now becoming widely understood. Of potentially greater value is a 'policy learning' approach (Raffe 2011) whereby the educational experiences of other countries are examined in order to help us identify the challenges and difficulties that are common to all nation's, understand the strengths and weaknesses of our own educational system, and devise policy strategies that are tailored to our unique needs, goals and circumstances.

In the UK, as in the US, the key educational problem is fundamentally motivational: how can we encourage large swathes of our school population to engage more fully in learning at school and at home. Given the high levels of social and economic inequalities in these countries, and the impact these factors have upon educational performance (Condron 2011), longstanding Anglo-American attitudes about the attainability and value of academic excellence are likely to continue to prove motivationally problematic for many. At least we now understand that importing pedagogy from overseas is not a quick means to circumvent such challenges.

References

Alexander, R. 1996. *Other Primary Schools and Ours: Hazards of International Comparison.* Warwick: University of Warwick Centre for Research in Elementary and Primary Education.

Alexander, R. 2000. *Culture and Pedagogy: International Comparisons in Primary Education.* Oxford: Blackwell.

Alexander, R. 2012a. "Moral Panic, Miracle Cures and Educational Policy: What can We Really Learn from International Comparison?" *Scottish Educational Review* 44 (1): 4–21.

Alexander, R. 2012b. *Improving Oracy and Classroom Talk in English Schools: Achievements and Challenges.* Extended and referenced version of a presentation given at the DfE seminar on Oracy, the National Curriculum and Educational Standards. *20.2.12.* Downloaded from http://www.primaryreview.org.uk/downloads_/news/2012/02/2012_02_20DfE_oracy_Alexander.pdf (19.11.13).

Altinyelken, J. 2010. "Curriculum Change in Uganda: Teacher Perspectives on the New Thematic Curriculum." *International Journal of Educational Development* 30: 151–161.

American Psychological Association. 1997. *Learner-centred Psychological Principles: A Framework for School Reform and Redesign.* Revised ed. Washington, DC: American Psychological Association.

Baranov, A. 1998. "A Real Threat to the Nation's Future." *Russian Education & Society* 40 (1): 6–16.

Barber, M. 1996. *The Learning Game.* London: Victor Gollancz.

Barber, M., and M. Mourshed. 2007. *How the World's Best-performing School Systems Come Out on Top.* Dubai: McKinsey and Company.

Barrett, A. 2008. "Capturing the *Difference*: Primary School Teacher Identity in Tanzania." *International Journal of Educational Development* 28: 496–507.

BBC. 1996. *Panorama: Hard Lessons.* Transmission date 3 June 1996.

Bierhoff, H. J. 1996. *Laying the Foundation of Numeracy: A Comparison of Primary School Textbooks in Britain, Germany and Switzerland.* London: National Institute for Economic and Social Research.

Bierhoff, H. J., and S. J. Prais. 1995. *Schooling as Preparation for Life and Work in Switzerland and Britain.* London: National Institute for Economic and Social Research.

Bray, M. 2010. "Researching Shadow Education: Methodological Challenges and Directions." *Asia Pacific Education Review* 11: 3–13.

Bronfenbrenner, U. 1970. *Two Worlds of Childhood.* New York: Russell Sage Foundation.

Bronfenbrenner, U. 1979. *The Ecology of Human Development.* Cambridge, MA: Harvard University Press.

Bronfenbrenner, U. 2005. *Making Human Beings Human: Bioecological Perspectives on Human Development.* London: Sage.

Burghes, D. 1996. *Education Across the World: The Kassel Project.* Paper presented at conference "Lessons from Abroad: Learning from international experience in education" (London).

Cheng, K. 2011. "Shanghai: How a Big City in a Developing Country Leaped to the Head of the Class." In *Surpassing Shanghai: An Agenda for American Education Built on the World's Leading Systems*, edited by M. Tucker, 21–50. Cambridge, MA: Harvard Education Press.

Chisholm, L. 2012. "Education Policy Borrowing Across African Borders: Histories of Learner-centred Education in Botswana and South Africa." In *World Yearbook of Education 2012: Policy Borrowing and Lending in Education*, edited by G. Steiner-Khamsi and F. Waldow, 206–225. Oxford: Routledge.

Chung, J., and M. Crossley. 2013. "Academic Achievement in Finland." In *International Guide to Student Achievement*, edited by J. Hattie and E. M. Anderman, 462–464. London: Routledge.

Coe, C. 2005. *Dilemmas of Culture in African Schools: Youth, Nationalism, and the Transformation of Knowledge*. Chicago, IL: University of Chicago Press.

Coffield, F. 2012. "Why the McKinsey Reports will not Improve School Systems." *Journal of Education Policy* 27 (1): 131–149.

Coleman, J. 1961. *Adolescent Society: The Social Life of the Teenager and its Impact on Education*. New York: Free Press.

Condron, D. 2011. "Egalitarianism and Educational Excellence: Compatible goals for affluent societies?" *Educational Researcher* 40: 47–55.

Eaton, M. J., and M. H. Dembo. 1997. "Differences in the Motivational Beliefs of Asian American and Non-Asian Students." *Journal of Educational Psychology* 89: 433–440.

Elliott, J. G. 2013. "Some Challenges to Educational Achievement in the Russian Federation Since the End of the Soviet Union." In *The International Guide to Student Achievement*, edited by J. Hattie and E. Anderman, 453–455. New York: Routledge.

Elliott, J., N. Hufton, A. Hildreth, and L. Illushin. 1999. "Factors Influencing Educational Motivation: A Study of Attitudes, Expectations and Behaviour of Children in Sunderland, Kentucky and St. Petersburg." *British Educational Research Journal* 25: 75–94.

Elliott, J., N. Hufton, L. Illushin, and F. Lauchlan. 2001. "Motivation in the Junior Years: International Perspectives on Children's Attitudes, Expectations and Behaviour and their Relationship to Educational Achievement." *Oxford Review of Education* 27: 37–68.

Elliott, J. G., N. Hufton, L. Illushin, and W. Willis. 2005. *Motivation, Engagement and Educational Performance*. London: Palgrave Press.

Elliott, J., and J. Tudge. 2007. "The Impact of the West on Post-Soviet Russian Education: Change and Resistance to Change." *Comparative Education* 43: 93–112.

Foxman, D. 1992. *Learning Mathematics and Science (The Second International Assessment of Educational Progress in England*. Slough: N.F.E.R.

Froumin, I. D. 2005. "Democratizing the Russian School: Achievements and Setbacks." In *Educational Reform in Post-Soviet Russia*, edited by B. Eklof, L. Holmes, and V. Kaplan, 129–152. London: Cass.

Fuller, B., and P. Clarke. 1994. "Raising School Effects While Ignoring Culture? Local Conditions and the Influence of Classroom, Tools, Rules and Pedagogy." *Review of Educational Research* 64 (1): 119–157.

Gaber, S., G. Cankar, L. M. Umek, and V. Tašner. 2012. "The Danger of Inadequate Conceptualisation in PISA for Education Policy." *Compare* 42 (4): 647–663.

Georgiades, N. J., and L. Phillimore. 1975. *The Myth of the Hero-innovator and Alternative Strategies for Organisational Change*. New York: Associated Scientific.

Glowka, D. 1995. *Schulen und unterricht im vergleich. Rusland/Deutschland (Schools and teaching in comparison: Russia and Germany)*. New York: Waxmann Verlag.

Goldstein, H. 2004. "International Comparisons of Student Attainment: Some Issues Arising from the PISA Study." *Assessment in Education* 11 (3): 319–330.

Grant, C.A., and C. E. Sleeter. 1996. *After the School Bell Rings* (2nd edition). London: Falmer Press.

Hardman, F., J. Abd-Kadir, C. Agg, J. Migwi, J. Ndambuku, and F. Smith. 2009. "Changing Pedagogical Practice in Kenyan Primary Schools: The Impact of School-based Training." *Comparative Education* 45 (1): 65–86.

Heyneman, S. P. 1999. "American Education: A View from the Outside." *International Journal of Leadership in Education* 2 (1): 31–41.

Heyneman, S. P. 2013. "The International Efficiency of American Education: The Bad and the Not-so-bad News." In *PISA, Power, and Policy. The Emergence of Global Educational Governance*, edited by H. Meyer and A. Benavot, 279–302. Oxford: Symposium Books.

Heyneman, S. P., and B. Lee. 2014. "The Impact of International Studies of Academic Achievement on Policy and Research." In *A Handbook of International Large-scale Assessment: Background, Technical Issues, and Methods of Data Analysis*, edited by L. Rutkowski, M. von Davier, and D. Rutkowski, 37–74. London: Chapman Hall/CRC Press.

Hufton, N., and J. Elliott. 2000. "Motivation to Learn: The Pedagogical Nexus in the Russian School: Some Implications for Transnational Research and Policy Borrowing." *Educational Studies* 26: 115–136.

Inglehart, R., and C. Welzel. 2005. *Modernization, Cultural Change and Democracy: the Human Development Sequence*. Cambridge: Cambridge University Press.

Jessop, T., and A. Penny. 1998. "A Study of Teacher Voice and Vision in the Narratives of Rural South African and Gambian Primary School Teachers." *International Journal of Educational Development* 18 (5): 393–403.

Li, J. 2012. *Cultural Foundations of Learning: East and West*. New York: Cambridge University Press.

Li, L., and R. Wegerif. 2014. "What Does it Mean to Teach Thinking in China? Challenging and Developing Notions of 'Confucian Education'." *Thinking Skills and Creativity* 11: 22–32.

Liu, J. 2009. "Cram Schooling in Taiwan." *Journal of Youth Studies* 12 (1): 129–136.

Liu, J. 2011. "Does Cram Schooling Matter? Who goes to Cram Schools? Evidence from Taiwan." *International Journal of Educational Development* 32 (1): 46–62.

Liu, J. 2013. "An Overview of Student Achievement and the Related Factors in Taiwan." In *International Guide to Student Achievement*, edited by J. Hattie and E. M. Anderman, 490–492. London: Routledge.

Luxton, R. G., and G. Last. 1997. *Under-Achievement and Pedagogy: Experimental Reforms in the Teaching of Mathematics using Continental Approaches in Schools in the London Borough of Barking and Dagenham* (*Discussion Paper No. 112*). London: National Institute of Economic and Social Research.

Ma, X., C. Jong, and J. Yuan. 2013. "Exploring Reasons for the East Asian Success in PISA." In *PISA, Power, and Policy. The Emergence of Global Educational Governance*, edited by H. Meyer and A. Benavot, 225–245. Oxford: Symposium Books.

Markowitz, F. 2000. *Coming of Age in Post-soviet Russia*. Chicago: University of Illinois Press.

Morris, P. 2012. "Pick 'n' Mix, Select and Project; Policy Borrowing and the Quest for 'World Class' Schooling: An Analysis of the 2010 Schools White Paper." *Journal of Education Policy* 27 (1): 89–107.

Muckle, J. 1988. *A Guide to the Soviet Curriculum*. London: Croom Helm.

Muckle, J. 1990. *Portrait of a Soviet School Under Glasnost*. London: Macmillan.

National Commission on Excellence in Education. 1983. *A Nation at Risk: The Imperative for Educational Reform*. Washington, DC: NCEE.

Ng, P. T. 2008. "Educational Reform in Singapore: From Quantity to Quality." *Educational Research for Policy & Practice* 7 (1): 5–15.

Ng, P. T. 2013. "Academic Achievement in Singapore." In *International Guide to Student Achievement*, edited by J. Hattie and E. M. Anderman, 484–486. London: Routledge.

Nguyen, M., J. G. Elliott, C. Terlouw, and A. Pilot. 2009a. "Neocolonialism in Education: Cooperative Learning, Western Pedagogy in an Asian Context." *Comparative Education* 45 (1): 109–130.

Nguyen, M., C. Terlouw, A. Pilot, and J. G. Elliott. 2009b. "Cooperative Learning that Features a Culturally Appropriate Pedagogy." *British Educational Research Journal* 35 (6): 857–873.

Oakley, A. 2002. "Social Science and Evidence-based Everything: The Case of Education." *Educational Review* 54 (3): 277–286.

O.E.C.D. 2001. *Knowledge and Skills for Life: First Results from PISA 2000*. Paris: O.E.C.D.

O.E.C.D. 2004. *Learning for Tomorrow's World: First Results from PISA 2003*. Paris: O.E.C.D.

Pace, J., and A. Hemmings. 2007. "Understanding Authority in Classrooms: A Review of Theory, Ideology and Research." *Review of Educational Research* 77 (1): 4–27.

Park, H., S. Byun, and K. Kim. 2011. "Parental Involvement and Students' Cognitive Outcomes in Korea: Focusing on Private Tutoring." *Sociology of Education* 84 (1): 3–22.

Peterson del Mar, D. 2013. "Ghana." In *International Guide to Student Achievement*, edited by J. Hattie and E. M. Anderman, 465–467. London: Routledge.

Phillips, D., and K. Ochs, eds. 2004. *Educational Policy Borrowing: Historical Perspectives*. Oxford: Symposium Press.

Polyzoi, E., and E. Dneprov. 2003. "Harnessing the Forces of Change: Educational Transformation in Russia." In *Change Forces in Post-communist Eastern Europe*, edited by E. Polyzoi, M. Fullan, and J. P. Anchan, 13–33. London: Routledge Falmer.

Prais, S. J. 1997. "Whole-class Teaching, School Readiness and Pupils' Mathematical Attainments." *Oxford Review of Education* 23 (3): 275–290.

Prais, S. J. 2003. "Cautions on OECD's Recent Educational survey (PISA)." *Oxford Review of Education* 29 (2): 139–163.

Prais, S. J. 2007. "Two' Recent (2003) International Surveys of Schooling Attainments in Mathematics: England's Problems." *Oxford Review of Education* 33 (1): 33–46.

Raffe, D. 2011. *Policy Borrowing or Policy Learning? How (Not) to Improve Education Systems*. Edinbugh University: CES Briefings, No. 57.

Rappleye, J. 2012. "Reimagining Attraction and 'Borrowing' in Education: Introducing a Political Production Model." In *World Yearbook of Education 2012: Policy Borrowing and Lending in Education*, edited by G. Steiner-Khamsi and F. Waldow, 121–147. Oxford: Routledge.

Reynolds, D. 2010. *Failure-free Education? The Past, Present and Future of School Effectiveness and School Improvement*. Oxford: Routledge.

Reynolds, D., and S. Farrell. 1996. *Worlds Apart? A Review of International Surveys of Educational Achievement Involving England*. London: Her Majesty's Stationery Office.

Roth, K. J., S. L. Druker, H. E. Garneir, M. Lemmens, C. Chen, and T. Kawanaka. 2006. *Teaching Science in Five Countries: Results from the TIMSS 1999 Video Study (NCES 2006-011)*. Washington, DC: U.S. Department of Education, National Centre for Education Statistics. U.S. Government Printing Office.

Ryan, R., and E. Deci. 2000. "Self Determination Theory and the Facilitation of Intrinsic Motivation, Social Development and Well-being." *American Psychologist* 55 (1): 68–78.

Sadler, M. 1900. How can We Learn Anything of Practical Value from the Study of Foreign Systems of Education? Originally published in the Surrey Advertiser (1.12.1900). Reprinted in Bereday, G.Z. (1964) *Comparative Education Review*, 7 (3): 307–314.

Sahlberg, P. 2007. "Education Policies for Raising Student Learning: The Finnish Approach." *Journal of Education Policy* 22 (2): 147–171.

Schweisfurth, M. M. 2013. *Learner-Centred Education in International Perspective: Whose Pedagogy for Whose Development?* New York: Routledge.

Sedlak, M., C. W. Wheeler, D. C. Pullin, and P. A. Cusick. 1986. *Selling Students Short: Classroom Bargains and Academic Reform in the American High School*. New York: Teachers College Press.

Sellar, S., and B. Lingard. 2013. "Looking East: Shanghai, PISA 2009 and the Reconstitution of Reference Societies in the Global Education Policy Field." *Comparative Education* 49 (4): 464–485.

Shin, J. 2013. "Academic Achievement in South Korea." In *International Guide to Student Achievement*, edited by J. Hattie and E. M. Anderman, 487–489. London: Routledge.

Silander, T., and J. Välijärvi. 2013. "The Theory and Practice of Building Pedagogical Skill in Finnish Teacher Education." In *PISA, Power, and Policy. The Emergence of Global Educational Governance*, edited by H. Meyer and A. Benavot, 77–97. Oxford: Symposium Books.

Siu, S. F. 1992. *Toward an Understanding of Chinese American Educational Achievement (Report No. 2)*. Washington, DC: U.S. Department of Health and Human Services, Center on Families, Communities, Schools and Children's Learning.

Song, M. J., and H. P. Ginsburg. 1987. "The Development of Informal and Formal Mathematical Thinking in Korean and US Children." *Child Development* 58: 1286–1296.

Sorensen, C. W. 1994. "Success and Education in South Korea." *Comparative Education Review* 38 (1): 10–35.

Stankov, L. 2010. "Unforgiving Confucian Culture: A Breeding Ground for High Academic Achievement, Test Anxiety, and Self-doubt?" *Learning and Individual Differences* 20 (6): 555–563.

Steinberg, L. 1996. *Beyond the Classroom: Why School Reform has Failed and what Parents Need to Do*. New York: Touchstone Books.

Steiner-Khamsi, G. 2012. "Understanding Policy Borrowing and Lending: Building Comparative Policy Studies." In *World Yearbook of Education 2012: Policy Borrowing and Lending in Education*, edited by G. Steiner-Khamsi and F. Waldow, 3–17. Oxford: Routledge.

Stevenson, H. W., and S. Lee. 1990. "A Study of American, Chinese and Japanese Children." *Monographs of the Society for Research in Child Development, No. 221* 55 (1–2).

Stevenson, H. W., and J. W. Stigler. 1992. *The Learning Gap: Why Our Schools are Failing and what We can Learn from Japanese and Chinese Education*. New York: Summit Books.

Stigler, J. W., and J. Hiebert. 1999. *The Teaching Gap*. New York: Free Press.

Stigler, J. W., S. Lee, and H. W. Stevenson. 1990. *Mathematical Knowledge of Japanese, Chinese and American Elementary School Children*. Reston, VA: National Council of Teachers of Mathematics.

Sung, K. 2006. "A Study on the Middle School Effect of Korea: A Test of the Creemers' Theoretical Model of School Effect." *Korean Journal of Sociology of Education* 16 (4): 93–114.

Tabulawa, R. 2003. "International Aid Agencies, Learner-centred Pedagogy and Political Democratisation: A Critique." *Comparative Education* 39 (1): 7–26.

Takayama, K. 2010. "Politics of Externalization in Reflexive Times: Reinventing Japanese Education Reform Discourses Through 'Finnish PISA Success'." *Comparative Education Review* 54 (1): 51–75.

Takayama, K., F. Waldow, and Y. Sung. 2013. "Finland Has it All? Examining the Media Accentuation of 'Finnish Education' in Australia, Germany and South Korea." *Research in Comparative and International Education* 8 (3): 307–325.

Tan, C. 2013. *Learning from Shanghai: Lessons on Achieving Educational Success*. Dordrecht: Springer.

Tudge, J. R. H. 1991. "Education of Young Children in the Soviet Union: Current Practice in Historical Perspective." *The Elementary School Journal* 92: 121–133.

Tymms, P. 2004. "Are Standards Rising in English Primary Schools?" *British Educational Research Journal* 30 (4): 477–494.

Vavrus, F. 2009. "The Cultural Politics of Constructivist Pedagogies: Teacher Education Reform in the United Republic of Tanzania." *International Journal of Educational Development* 29 (3): 303–311.

Vavrus, F., T. Thomas, and L. Bartlett. 2011. *Ensuring Quality by Attending to Inquiry: Learner-centered Pedagogy in Sub-Saharan Africa*. Addis Ababa: UNESCO.

Waldow, F. 2010. "Der Traum vom 'skandinavisch schlau Werden': Drei Thesen zur Rolle Finnlands als Projektionsfläche in der gegenwärtigen Bildungsdebatte." *Zeitschrift für Pädagogik* 56 (4): 497–511.

Waldow, F. 2012. "Standardisation and Legitimacy: Two Central Concepts in Research on Educational Borrowing and Lending." In *World Yearbook of Education 2012: Policy Borrowing and Lending in Education*, edited by G. Steiner-Khamsi and F. Waldow, 411–427. Oxford: Routledge.

Welzel, C. 2011. "The Asian Values Thesis Revisited: Evidence from the World Values Surveys." *Japanese Journal of Political Science* 12: 1–31.

Wilkinson, R., and K. Pickett. 2009. *The Spirit Level: Why Greater Equality Makes Societies Stronger*. New York: Bloomsbury Press.

Wiseman, A. W. 2010. "The Uses of Evidence for Educational Policymaking: Global Contexts and International Trends." *Review of Research in Education* 34: 1–24.

Wiseman, A. W. 2013. "Policy Responses to PISA in Comparative Perspective." In *PISA, Power, and Policy. The Emergence of Global Educational Governance*, edited by H. Meyer and A. Benavot, 303–322. Oxford: Symposium Books.

Woodhead, C. 1996. Interview in BBC *Panorama* 'Hard Lessons', 3rd June.

Wrigley, T. 2004. "'School Effectiveness'; The Problem of Reductionism." *British Educational Research Journal* 30 (2): 227–244.

Zhao, Y. 2005. "Increasing Math and Science Achievement: The Best and Worst of the East and West." *Phi Delta Kappan* 87 (3): 219–222.

From adult education to lifelong learning and beyond

Peter Jarvis

School of Politics, University of Surrey, Guildford, Surrey, UK

> Over the period of this journal's life the education of adults has been changed and developed in a wide variety of ways: the same phenomenon – adult learning – has been given a variety of meanings and the education of adults has assumed many titles. The aim of this paper is to unravel some of the changes that have occurred in this field during this time

It is a great privilege to contribute to this anniversary issue of *Comparative Education* and to record how the study of the comparative education of adults has emerged: this changing scene was the reason why Edmund King approached me to join the Editorial Board since the journal was beginning to receive submissions which were of an adult education nature. My career has not quite spanned the length of time this journal has been published, since I have only been in higher education for 45 years, but over the past 50 years the education of adults has seen many changes, and most of these have happened during my career in higher education – and so this paper includes a number of personal references and quotes from my own writing. However, this paper is not so much an historical analysis as a comparative reflection of some of these changes which were driven by the forces of globalisation resulting in the global capitalist market. This paper contains seven parts, starting with the situation of adult education from just before I entered it in 1976.

Part 1. Prior to 1976

In the period just before I entered university adult education, modern globalisation was taking off with the growth in Japanese and European productivity, which was causing them to question the United States as the world's global leader and the United States to question its own position as having the dollar as the global 'gold standard'. In August 1971 the USA began the process of withdrawing from the Bretton Woods Agreement (Cohen – Bretton Woods System) which was finalised in 1973 when the monies of all the industrial countries were to be set free to float independently (8) and so the modern global capitalist market was born.

Corporations were free to compete with each other in an open market and so they needed to produce their commodities at the lowest possible cost and to produce new ones, which demanded new research and an educated and up-to-date workforce with new and relevant knowledge and new and efficient production techniques. Hence a demand for a new form of education of adults was being created. Some scholars, looking to the future, predicted that the nature of education would change quite radically. Kerr and his colleagues (1973, 47), who propounded the logic of industrialism thesis, predicted this:

> The higher education of industrial society stresses the natural sciences, engineering, medicine, managerial training – whether private or public – and administrative law. It must steadily adapt to new disciplines and new fields of specialization. There is a relatively smaller place for the humanities and the arts, while the social sciences are strongly related to the training of managerial groups and technicians for the enterprise and the government. The increased leisure time of industrialism, however, can afford a broader public appreciation of the humanities and the arts.

They overplayed industrialism but were completely right about the way that these developments would affect education. The arts and the humanities have been distinguished from the really 'useful' subjects like the sciences and social sciences: they consigned the humanities to leisure time and for them education was to be the handmaiden of industry taking the raw material of humanity and turning it into the human resources that would drive the world. This is precisely what has occurred. Adult educators know that many of the liberal adult education subjects have not only been consigned to leisure time, they have been priced at such an exorbitant fee that few people are able to afford to enrol in them.

But when I joined the Adult Education Department at the University of Surrey in 1976, the conditions were hardly ripe for radical change in the education of adults. There was a major division in thinking about education and training, as reflected in the works of R. S. Peters and P. Hirst and their associates (Dearden, Hirst, and Peters 1972). Education was regarded as fundamentally knowledge based while training was about skills development: the former taught in adult education institutes (AEI) and the Responsible Body (RB) institutions (university adult education departments, the WEA (Workers Education Association) and the WI (Women's Institutes)) and the latter in colleges of further education and the emerging polytechnic sector. The universities co-operated with the adult education institutes and with the other RB institutes in offering university level courses in whatever subjects there was a local demand for, while the AEIs offered non-university level subjects. Adult education departments in universities were on the margins of the universities since they offered no qualifications and did little research: indeed, many academics did not regard adult education as a university subject. Indeed, it was a field of practice but hardly a field of study.

There was only limited adult literacy provision – but I will not focus on this in the following paper; suffice to say that the provision has expanded since the problem was recognised.

Perhaps the most significant advances in liberal adult education in the UK and Europe were the foundation of the Open University in the UK and the University of the Third Age in France. The Open University (OU) was a catalyst for the development of distance education in the wider world – I was employed part-time by the OU for the first 30 years of its existence – and it did offer degree awards from the outset. However, it was not long before the OU began to offer vocational courses as well as liberal ones. As distance education spread throughout the world it became increasingly vocational and large distance educational institutions rapidly emerged[1] being almost entirely vocational.

The University of the Third Age (U3A) spread throughout Europe quite rapidly and initially each separate one was attached to a local university but none offered academic awards. However, with the establishment of the U3A in the UK a different model was created since every U3A was a separate and almost completely independent, local, non-governmental organisation[2] with no formal connection to the university sector. Not being tied to a local university means that the programme in British universities tends not to be entirely academic and, at times, the idea of dropping the term 'university' from its title has been mooted. The European model treated the U3A rather like a separate department since it both appointed the tutors and did a great deal of the curriculum development which meant that each U3A maintained a reasonably high academic standard.

While there was some government funding for RB departments the courses offered were expected to be self-supporting and if the course was not self-supporting it would be closed – usually after three sessions to see if recruitment could be improved.

One distinctive area in liberal adult education was the recognition that teaching adults required different skills to teaching children and the study of teaching adults was to become one of the major routes by which adult education gradually gained acceptance into higher education as it introduced award-bearing courses in the teaching of adults. At the same time a major debate was about to dawn as to whether the teaching of adults and the teaching of children were completely different.

This liberal–vocational distinction was not prevalent in the USA where vocational subjects were taught in universities and the courses were certificated: adult education was an award-bearing discipline although it hardly had a distinctive identity. Adult education in Eastern Europe actually had such an identity and when Malcolm Knowles met Dusan Savicevic – a Serbian adult educator – he learned of the concept of andragogy and by publishing *Androgogy not pedagogy*[3] in 1968 and *The modern practice of adult education* in 1970 he gave the field a distinctive identity and actually sparked a great deal of debate about, and study of, the field, initially in the USA and later in Western Europe.

Part 2. From adult education to the education of adults

Adult education could be defined by the fact that it was adults who were receiving the education which was liberal in nature but adult educators recognised that adults often knew a great deal about the subject they had registered to study and so the teachers of adults had to develop new methods of teaching. This was recognised as early as 1919 when it was suggested that teachers of adults should have more opportunities for training (Smith 1919, para 261). This was a recurring feature in the literature on adult education (Peers 1958, *inter alia*). Peers was the first professor of adult education in the world when the University of Nottingham's Department of Adult Education was founded, which was also the first such department in the world. It is, therefore, not surprising that this university took the lead in the training of adult educators and by the 1970s it had produced its own training programme (Bestwick and Chadwick 1977) which became a model for the government inaugurated report (Haycocks 1978) on the same subject. In this report no distinction was drawn between further education and adult education: adult education was treated as a sub-section of further education but the report recommended that all teachers working in the post-school level should be trained. Significantly, however, the report recommended that this training should be award-bearing leading to a Certificate of Education which should be equivalent to the completion of the first year of a university undergraduate course. Some professions, notably nursing, began to expect that their new tutors should be trained under this scheme and so it was not long before a course was designed that was of the same structure as the one year post-graduate course in school teacher training (Post Graduate Certificate in Education – PGCE) and the University of Surrey launched its PGCEA[4] in the education of adults, from which there was also a rapid rise in Masters degree courses in adult education and eventually doctoral research.[5] However, it was not long before different professions began to train their own tutors and together with different universities and polytechnics offered their own PGCEAs and later Masters degrees and doctorates. Adult education had become the education of adults which was also a field of study, so that the focus was no longer so much on the adult as on the field of practice and study.

Further education was recognised as a major division of education in the same way as initial education and higher education, but the boundaries between these divisions of education did cause some concern: for instance, did adult/further education begin on completion of initial education or at the age of the completion of compulsory education, or even undergraduate education? What rights for further education did individuals have after their completion of full-time education? But it also became very clear that adult/further education should not be regarded as the same as continuing education since education beyond schooling was occurring in many places in the world and other systems than the British one were emerging. But when did continuing education begin – at the end of full-time compulsory education (Venables 1976) or should it be post-initial rather than post-compulsory education, where initial education could stretch into higher education (McIntosh 1979)? This was a similar debate to the andragogy–pedagogy in the USA where Knowles wanted to separate the two since he considered that adults and children actually learn differently but other scholars considered that this was a false divide (see Elias 1979; McKenzie 1977, 1979). Knowles (1980) later revised his thinking.

However, a major moral issue was emerging at this time – what rights did individuals have to education after they had completed compulsory education? The OECD (1973) raised this debate by suggesting that continuing education should be of a recurrent nature and it should be a strategy for lifelong education in which everybody had the right to education for six years at later stages in their life after the completion of compulsory education. However, the practicalities of this scheme were questioned and the cost of such a scheme was recognised as too great, so that it was not long before the rights issue was dropped but the concept was retained and the idea of recurrent education was built into continuing education – and such schemes as paid educational leave began to occur. Indeed, the International Labor Organization had already called on each country in the European Union to produce a policy for paid educational leave (OECD 1973). Continuing education, however, carried none of the moral overtones of recurrent education and was, therefore, a safer term.

Continuing education was a form of lifelong education, and retained its popularity for a few years, during which time the Open University was launched in Britain.[6] The Open University was, at first, mainly a liberal adult education institution but it soon expanded its activities into vocational education. The term 'continuing education' was replacing the term 'education of adults' but at the same time it was recognised that this was a form of lifelong education and *The International Journal of Lifelong Education* was launched[7] in 1981.

About this time UNESCO also adopted a definition for lifelong education, pioneered by Paul Lengrand (1975), a term that had been in the literature since the 1919 report and especially after Yeaxlee (1929). UNESCO also took a major role in placing this growing emphasis on the education of adults into a much wider perspective with the publication of *Learning to be* (Faure 1972) – almost certainly the most influential book on the education of adults in its period. Whilst the book retained UNESCO's traditional humanistic approach to education it did succeed in linking together both liberal and vocational education into a lifelong framework.

Part 3. Other developments in liberal adult education[8]

This was a period of rapid growth and new innovations in adult education and just three of them are discussed here – community education, universities of the third age and retirement education.

Community education has been part of the history of adult education but in a number of different guises. However, occasionally a word appears in the English language that becomes ideologically acceptable for a period of time. 'Community' is such a word that was becoming widely accepted in the United Kingdom in the 1960s and 1970s as something intrinsically good and right. Not surprisingly the idea of community education appeared to have been accepted with almost the same uncritical appraisal as the term *community*. Three distinct forms of community education can be distinguished:

- education for action and/or development;
- education in the community; and
- extramural forms of education.

The first of these forms of adult education seeks to make individuals and community groups and to provide awareness of ways in which they can improve their communities and help them learn how to put change into practice. By its very nature it nearly always assumes a radical form since it is intrinsically a critique of the status quo. Consequently, it has tended to be a minority interest, although there are two major exceptions – Paulo Freire and Myles Horton (see Freire 1972a, 1972b, *inter alia*), who both recognised in many works that such education can never be neutral. Freire formulated his ideas in Latin America, against a background of illiteracy and poverty, and his thinking was a synthesis of Christian theology, existentialism and Marxism – one that underlay liberation theology. While his ideas developed in a Third World context, they are relevant to the United Kingdom and America, as Kirkwood and Kirkwood (1989) showed (see also London 1973). He emphasised that education should make the learners critically aware of their false consciousness and their social condition. Having undergone a process of conscientisation, learners should act upon the world to endeavour to create a better society. Clearly Freire's radical, but moral, approach is one that has been criticised, especially by those who, for varying reasons, wish to see education as a neutral process, but over the years his stature has grown and his thinking has been much admired throughout the educational world.

In America, perhaps the most well-known institution organising radical adult education was, and still is, Highlander, which was founded by Myles Horton in Tennessee. It played a significant role in the civil rights movement in the United States and its work is becoming increasingly well documented (Horton with Kohl and Kohl 1990). In 1987, Horton and Freire came together at Highlander to 'talk a book' (Horton and Freire 1990) in which they exchanged their understandings of radical adult education and produced a most insightful understanding of the place education might play in community development.

Adult education beyond the walls: extra-mural adult education is a term usually restricted to university adult education extension classes where academic staff from the universities teach in the community, or the universities employ part-time staff to teach liberal adult education classes under their auspices in the wider community. But with the advent of neo-liberal economic policies and practices, universities have had their funds curtailed to such an extent that they are ceasing to provide such education.

Perhaps the earliest formal education in the community arose from the work of Henry Morris, who was responsible for the establishment of community colleges in Cambridgeshire before the Second World War (see Jennings n.d.), and whose ideas were influential in their introduction in Leicestershire shortly afterwards (Fairbairn 1978). From these beginnings have grown larger urban educational and social complexes, such as the Abraham Moss Centre in Manchester and the Sutton Centre in Nottinghamshire, in which the school is regarded as the focal point of the community, in a similar manner to that of the parish church in medieval times, and that adults, as well as children, should be able to attend classes in these centres. As a result of his work in Liverpool, Midwinter (1975, 99) concluded that:

> Education must no longer be open to caricature as a few hours at school for a few years in … pre-adult life. It must be viewed as a total, lifelong experience, with the home and the neighbourhood playing important parts, and everybody contributing to and drawing on this educative dimension of the community.

Senior citizens

In this period there has been a tremendous growth in non-formal learning for seniors with perhaps the two most well-known organisations being the University of the Third Age and the Elderhostel Institute Network in North America. People are living longer and Western Europe is now regarded as a 'greying' population, so that it is not surprising that such institutions have emerged.

As early as 1962 the Institute for Retired Professionals was founded in the USA by Hy Hirsch and sponsored by the New York School for Social Research: this was 10 years before the University of the Third Age (U3A) was established by Pierre Vellas at the University of Toulouse in France and it took another 10 years for the latter idea to spread to the United Kingdom. Despite the fact that the founder in the UK, Peter Laslett, was a Cambridge don, the U3A in UK has little connection with the university world. Each U3A in the UK is an independent non-governmental organisation (NGO) and there are well over 700 of these in the UK, although there is a Third Age Trust: this model has also been adopted in some Commonwealth countries, such as Australia. A third form has appeared in other European countries, such as Germany and Spain, the seniors' classroom, where universities are encouraged to open their classes to seniors.

Retirement education

As life expectancy increased people were living longer after they retired and so workers who were about to retire were offered the opportunity of preparation for retirement. Corporations and educational providers both offered courses for older workers.

While there was a statutory retirement age (65 years in the UK) it was possible to offer courses that looked at various aspects of life beyond retirement such as: activities, finance, friendships, health, identity, mental stimulus, opportunities, purpose in life, structuring time (Jarvis 2000a, 67–68). However, two things above all others contributed to the decline in these courses – they were expensive for employers and retirement patterns were changing. For some retirement was a new beginning, for others a disruption, merely a continuation of their lives, and for some it was a transition to old age. Courses, therefore, were different and, depending on what the employing organisation could contribute, the courses were of different lengths of time – some two–three days and others a week, few were residential but most were held locally to the employers. There was no academic certification for these courses.

Part 4. Vocational education

University education was originally regarded as part of initial education in the sense that most students completed their education before they began their vocational training, so that most students completed their initial education by the age of 25 years – only a few students went on to study at Masters level and doctorates – this was regarded as the route taken by those who were to teach and research their subjects in higher education. Vocational training was undertaken by non-university students as apprentices working in employing organisations and attending colleges of further education and polytechnics on a part-time basis – but there was little opportunity to study at degree level, although the polytechnic sector was eventually granted the opportunity to offer degree level courses, validated by a new national body – the Council for National Academic Awards (CNAA). The CNAA was a national council having a number of subject boards which constituted working parties to assess polytechnics' proposals when they applied for validation to offer undergraduate degrees in a variety of subjects.[9]

The universities in the UK were very gradually changing and offering short courses in a variety of vocational subjects on an in-service, part-time basis and the term 'continuing professional education' (CPE) was gradually appearing. However, the dominant philosophy of these courses was that the education being offered was an optional-extra to the initial professional education but another philosophy was emerging – that the workers needed to be developed for the good of the employing organisation rather than for the benefit of the workers. Employing organisations began to develop their own training courses and employees were regarded as human capital.

Schultz (1961) introduced the term *human capital* but he pointed out that economists had shied away from the use of this term because, while individuals actually invested in themselves, they might find it offensive to think of themselves in this manner. He (1961) wrote:

> Our values and beliefs might inhibit us from looking upon human beings as capital goods, except in slavery, which we abhor. We are not unaffected by the long struggle to society on indentured service and to evolve political and legal institutions to keep men free from bondage. These are achievements we prize highly. Hence, to treat human beings as wealth that can be augmented by investment runs counter to deeply held values. (Cited from Jarvis with Griffin 2003, vol. 5: 246)

Schultz's concern was rightly founded since this was the first time that human beings were being treated as means rather than ends in the teaching and learning process. It was a contradiction to Kant's maxim that human beings should always be treated as ends and never as means to an end. Nevertheless, it was not long before the idea of human capital development became commonplace, and corporations felt free to treat their employees in this way and they opened their own human resource departments and training schools (Eurich 1985), some of which eventually sought to become corporate universities (Jarvis 2001a, *inter alia*; Meister 1998). In more recent years competency-based training and National Vocational Qualifications (NVQ) have been introduced, which involve work-based learning and with it systems of mentoring have also been introduced. HRD has rapidly assumed its own place in the learning society (see Brinkerhoff 1987; Hargreaves and Jarvis 2000, *inter alia*). In 1993 the Academy of Human Resource Development was founded in the United States by adult educators who had undertaken a great deal of their research in organisational and vocational settings. The Academy has since run its own conferences and publishes its own books (see Redmann 2000).

CPE soon developed with the introduction of part-time higher degrees with Masters degrees and doctoral research becoming part of the normal programme, and CPE became 'continuing education'. The age profile of universities was changing – indeed, in Canada this happened a lot earlier with Campbell (1984) claiming that from 1974 there were more part-time adult students registered for courses in universities than there were normal undergraduates. Universities were now becoming centres of lifelong education rather than educational institutions for the young adults who were the children of upper and middle class parents, and adult students were now commonplace on university campuses. In addition it was being recognised that workers seeking additional learning in order to keep abreast with the changes in their profession – both in knowledge and practice – did not need a full educational course, although additional qualifications were useful, so that short courses were being offered in both theory and practice and the process of modularisation had begun and appropriate awards were developed. But another change was beginning to occur as it was recognised that a great deal of vocational learning occurred in the workplace, and so the term education was no longer quite so significant as the term 'learning'.

Part 5. From education to learning

The concept of 'lifelong learning' was emerging and really came to prominence in the 1990s with its adoption by the European Union when it sought to influence policy by publishing a number of documents and introducing other policy measures. Lifelong learning differed conceptually in a number of ways from lifelong education as education and learning are different concepts, though at the same time there was considerable confusion and overlap between the two terms.

Education is fundamentally an institutional phenomenon offering learning opportunities to people throughout their lives, as continuing education but in practice the adult learning was of a recurrent nature. There were institutional systems in childhood and young adulthood – but other providers of education than the state also provided many opportunities to learn thereafter.

Learning, however, is a term with many meanings, but it fundamentally refers to the process whereby individuals acquire knowledge and skills (and much more besides)[10] from different sources, either intentionally or not. The sources may be established teaching institutions but need not be; sources can be other people, every situation in life, and so on. Learning is an individual process, although some theorists have suggested that it is a group phenomenon, although the problem with this is that we do not actually have a group brain and so I think it better seen as an individual process. But the fact that learning does not have to be institutionalised and can occur at any time in life was sufficient rationale for the wide acceptance of the term. Since it also places responsibility on the individual to learn and not the state or the employing organisation to provide learning opportunities, it naturally rapidly found favour. However, the terms 'lifelong education' and 'lifelong learning' became confused in as much as lifelong learning was often treated as lifelong education.

Using the term 'learning' rather than 'education' meant that there were other sites for learning than educational institutions – the workplace became the most frequently recognised and many courses have been offered by educational institutions and employing organisations that involve learning in the workplace in both practice and theory, and there has been much research in this form of learning over the past 20 years. Lifelong learning became associated with workplace learning so that other learning sites, such as the community, were not as widely researched.

Lifelong learning was, consequently, the term adopted by the European Union when it began to pronounce its own policies on education. While it employed the term in many policy documents it never actually separated lifelong learning from initial education and training nor did it examine lifelong learning beyond retirement for many years. Indeed, the Commission actually retained three separate divisions throughout this period and each published its own policy documents: education and training, higher education and adult education.

In its first policy document (European Commission 1995) on lifelong learning the EC argued that the aims of lifelong learning were employability and citizenship. This was quite a natural development when it is recognised that the EU countries were competing in a global market in a knowledge economy and at the same time it was recognised that if the EU was to survive it was necessary to devise policies that would draw the separate EU countries together. Nevertheless, the main focus was on employability. In the Memorandum on Lifelong Learning (EC 2000) that followed there were four aims: employability, citizenship, social fulfilment and personal achievement but employability was so dominant that the Commission was forced to stand back a little in the following year and make the point that the Europe of Knowledge threatened to bring about 'greater inequalities and social exclusion' (EC 2001, 6). Consequently it also claimed that lifelong learning

> is much more than economics. It also promotes the goals and ambitions of the European countries to become more inclusive, tolerant and democratic. And it promises a Europe in which citizens have the opportunity and ability to realise their ambitions and to participate in building a better society. (7)

Significantly, the emphasis on the relationship between active citizenship and employability was explicitly downplayed (9). The aims of lifelong learning had become: personal fulfilment, active citizenship, social inclusion and employability/adaptability. Lifelong learning has been the preferred term for the education of adults in many policy documents in many countries of the world since this time, but it was frequently pointed out that it was never actually life long since it did not include the education of children and young people, higher education nor the education of seniors, despite the fact that it was referred to as learning from the cradle to the grave.

Nevertheless, life expectancy has increased over this period and so when the idea of learning in the fourth age began to appear, the idea of a university of the fourth age gained very little support and when provision began to be made it was under the title of 'Learning in the Fourth Age' (L4A). While the idea of providing learning opportunities for the very old has been received favourably, its growth has not been very rapid.

Part 6. Learning and living

Learning from living is another way of looking at lifelong learning and three different approaches to the study of learning through life and from life may be referred to here: biographical learning, experiential learning and learning from life itself. In fact, the basis of these is the assumption that life is a learning experience and, as Faure (1972) has argued, that we are always learning to be – a point that was made again in the Delors Report (1996) on learning.

Two forms of biographical/autobiographical learning may be distinguished – Alheit and a number of other scholars (Alheit et al. 1995, *interalia*, 2012) have concentrated on examining individuals' biographies to better understand the way that they have learned through living, while Dominice (2000) focused on people's educational biographies.

A contrast is experiential learning developed from the work of Dewey (1938) and popularised in this period by David Kolb (1984). Kolb's book was seminal and many writers studied experiential learning after the publication of this book, including Boud, Keogh, and Walker (1983), Brookfield (1986), Jarvis (1987), *inter alia*. Experiential learning has been at the heart of studies of human learning ever since Kolb's study was published although the concept of experience has not been widely studied within educational circles, though it has in philosophy – especially the philosophy of mind (Freser 2005, *inter alia*). The major point that has gone undiscussed in learning studies has been in the area of conscious/unconscious experience and with it implicit learning, although Alheit (2012) does recognise its significance: implicit learning is a concept developed by Reber (1985).[11]

Finally, in this section there has recently been a number of studies that have focused specifically on learning from our lives (Field 2012) in which it is recognised that life itself is the basis of learning and that this learning also occurs outside of the educational framework and in a wider socio-cultural framework and within geographical and historical contexts. Such studies also constitute the major foundation for the development of educational gerontology.

Part 7. And beyond lifelong learning

In one sense it is impossible to go beyond lifelong learning conceptually but, as we have seen, neither the EU nor any individual society has an institutionalised system of lifelong education or learning and so it was widely recognised that the EU documents were not actually referring to lifelong learning and so it was no surprise when it published *Adult learning: It's never too late to learn* (EC 2006) in 2006. Adult learning was defined as 'all forms of learning undertaken by adults having left education and training' (EC 2006, 2). Paradoxically, senior citizens' learning is mentioned in this policy document for the first time, but 'adult learning' did not really escape the conceptual problems since 'learning' was still treated as institutionalised education! Its messages were:

(1) the barriers to adult participation in education and training should be lifted;
(2) the quality of adult learning should be high;
(3) learning outcomes should be recognised and validated;
(4) more investment in the education of an ageing population and in migrants' education is necessary; and
(5) there is a great need for indicators and benchmarks in order to produce evidence-based policies. (EC 2006, 5–10)

Adult learning has remained the preferred term in the latest EU *Council resolution on a European agenda for adult learning* (EC 2011) and its accompanying guide *EC strategies for improving participation in and awareness of adult learning* (EC 2012).

All of these documents treat learning as if it were education and so it is not surprising that the idea of adult learning and education (ALE) is now being mooted in some quarters, and we have nearly reached the full circle since education implies learning!

Conclusion

When I came into adult education as an extra-mural lecturer I organised, ran and taught classes for adults in a variety of subjects in the designated RB area around my university. If the class was not sufficiently large then it would not run as it was not cost effective. This was liberal adult education – there were no academic awards, it was just learning for learning's sake. Now this activity is undertaken nationally by the Open University in co-operation with the British Broadcasting Corporation when series of topics in a wide variety of subjects – in the sciences, social sciences and the humanities – are broadcast throughout the nation – it makes no pretence to be adult education but it is providing opportunities for viewers to learn at a university level and this has almost made the extra-mural adult educator in the traditional sense redundant!

Notes

1. The Open University in Beijing, for instance, has over three million students. I learned this from a conversation with the Principal at the Asian Distance Education Conference in Tianjin, China.
2. It was my privilege to be founding chair of the U3A in my home town.
3. Knowles actually spelt andragogy wrong in his first publication on the subject.
4. When I entered higher education, it was to a College of Education training school for teachers and it was in 1976 that I moved to the University of Surrey where I was involved in planning and teaching this course.
5. The first doctorate in adult education in the world was gained by Basil Yeaxlee for his study *Spiritual values in adult education*.
6. I was employed as a part-time tutor and counsellor in various capacities for the first 30 years of the Open University's existence and still acted as an external examiner for many years thereafter.
7. I was privileged to be the founding editor supported by Michael Stephens and Teddy Thomas, both from the University of Nottingham – Teddy Thomas was my co-editor from the outset.
8. I have relied quite heavily on my own writings here, especially Jarvis (2010).
9. I actually served on two boards for further education and the humanities at different times and a number of working parties for the CNAA over the period of time I entered university higher education. The College of Education at which I taught nominated me after it had gained validation from the CNAA to offer a B.Ed. degree.
10. In my latest writing I have defined learning as 'The combination of processes throughout a lifetime whereby the whole person – body (genetic, physical and biological) and mind

(knowledge, skills, attitudes, values, emotions, meaning, beliefs and senses) – experiences natural and social situations, the content of which is then transformed cognitively, emotively or practically (or through any combination) and integrated into the individual person's biography resulting in a continually changing (or more experienced) person' (Jarvis 2009, 35).
11. See Jarvis – unpublished *Human Learning – Implicit and Explicit*.

References

Alheit, P. 2012. "The Biographical Approach to Lifelong Learning." In *The Routledge International Handbook on Learning*, edited by P. Jarvis with M. Wates, 168–175. London: Routledge.

Alheit, P., A. Bron-Wojciechowska, E. Brugger, and P. Dominicé, eds. 1995. *The Biographical Approach in European Adult Education*. Vien: Verband Wiener Volksbildung.

Bestwick, D. and Chadwick, A. 1977. "A co-operative training scheme for part-time teachers of adults." *Adult Education* 50 (4). Leicester NIACE.

Boud, D., R. Keogh, and D. Walker, eds. 1983. *Reflection: Turning Experience into Learning*. London: Kogan Page.

Brinkerhoff, R. 1987. *Achieving Results from Training*. San Francisco: Jossey Bass.

Brookfield, S. 1986. *Selecting and Facilitating Adult Learning*. San Francisco: Jossey Bass.

Campbell, D. D. 1984. *The New Majority*. Edmonton: University of Alberta Press.

Cohen, B. *Bretton Woods System* (downloaded 19/11/2013).

Dearden, D., P. Hirst, and R. S. Peters, eds. 1972. *Education and the Development of Reason*. 3 vols. London: Routledge and Kegan Paul.

Delors, J., chair. 1996. *Learning: The Treasure Within*. Paris: UNESCO.

Dewey, J. 1938. *Experience and Education*. London: Collier Macmillan.

Dominice, P. 2000. *Learning from our Lives*. San Francisco: Jossey-Bass.

Elias, J. 1979. "Andragogy Revisited." *Adult Education* 29: 252–256.

Eurich, N. 1985. *Corporate Classrooms*. Princeton, NJ: Carnegie Foundation for the Advancement of Teaching.

European Commission. 1995. *Teaching and Learning: Towards the Learning Society*. Brussels: European Commission.

European Commission. 2000. *A Memorandum on Lifelong Learning*. Brussels: European Commission SEC(2000) 1832.

European Commission. 2001. *Making a European Area of Lifelong Learning a Reality*. Brussels: European Commission COM (2001) 678 final.

European Commission. 2006. *Adult Learning: Its Never Too Late to Learn*. Brussels: European Commission COM(2006)614 final.

European Commission. 2011. "Council Resolution on a Renewed Agenda for Adult Learning." *Official Journal of the European Union* 20.12.11.

European Commission. 2012. *Strategies for Improving Participation in and Awareness of Adult Learning*. Brussels: European Commission.

Fairbairn, A. N. 1978. *The Leicestershire Community Colleges and Centres*. Nottingham: Department of Adult Education, University of Nottingham.

Faure, E. 1972. *Learning to Be*. Paris: UNESCO.

Field, J. 2012. "Learning from Our Lives." In *The Routledge International Handbook on Learning*, edited by P. Jarvis with M. Wates, 176–183. London: Routledge.

Freire, P. 1972a. *Cultural Action for Freedom*. Harmondsworth: Penguin.

Freire, P. 1972b. *Pedagogy of the Oppressed*. Translated by M. B. Ramer. Harmondsworth: Penguin.

Freser, E. 2005. *Philosophy of Mind*. Oxford: One World.

Hargreaves, P., and P. Jarvis. 2000. *The Human Resource Development Handbook*. Revised edition. London: Kogan Page.

Haycocks, J. 1978. *The Training of Adult Education and Part-time Further Education Teachers.* London: Advisory Committee of the Supply and Training of Teachers.
Horton, M., and P. Freire. 1990. *We Make the Road by Walking*, edited by B. Bell, J. Gaventa, and J. Peters. Philadelphia: Temple University Press.
Horton, M., with J. Kohl, and H. Kohl. 1990. *The Long Haul.* New York: Anchor Books.
Jarvis, P. 1987. *Adult Learning in the Social Context.* London: Croom Helm.
Jarvis, P. 2001a. *Universities and Corporate Universities.* London: Kogan Page.
Jarvis, P. 2001b. *Learning in Later Life.* London: Kogan Page.
Jarvis, P. 2009. *Learning to be a Person in Society.* London: Routledge.
Jarvis, P. 2010. *Adult Education and Lifelong Learning: Theory and Practice.* London: Routledge.
Jarvis, P., with C. Griffin, ed. 2003. *Adult and Continuing Education: Major Themes in Education.* 5 vols. London: Routledge.
Jennings, B., ed. n.d. *Community Colleges in England and Wales.* Leicester: NIAE.
Kerr, C., J. Dunlop, F. Harbison, and C. Myers. 1973. *Industrialism and Industrial Man.* Harmondsworth: Penguin.
Kirkwood, G., and C. Kirkwood. 1989. *Living Adult Education.* Milton Keynes: Open University Press.
Knowles, M. 1968. "Androgogy not Pedagogy." *Adult Leadership* 16 (10): 350–352.
Knowles, M. 1970. *The Modern Practice of Adult Education: Andragogy Versus Pedagogy.* New York: Association Press.
Knowles, M. 1980. *The Modern Practice of Adult Education: Andragogy and Pedagogy.* New York: Association Press.
Kolb, D. 1984. *Experiential Learning.* Englewood Cliffs, NJ: Prentice Hall.
Lengrand, P. 1975. *An Introduction to Lifelong Education.* London: Croom Helm.
London, J. 1973. "Reflections Upon the Relevance of Paulo Freire for American Adult Education." *Convergence* 6 (1).
McIntosh, N. 1979. "To Make Continuing Education a Reality." *Oxford Review of Education* 5 (2), Republished by ACACE, Leicester.
McKenzie, L. 1977. "The Issue of Andragogy." *Adult Education* 27: 225–229.
McKenzie, L. 1979. "Andragogy Revisited." *Adult Education* 29: 255–261.
Meister, L. 1998. *Corporate Universities.* 2nd ed. New York: McGraw-Hill.
Midwinter, F. 1975. *Education and the Community.* London: Allen and Unwin.
Organisation for Economic Cooperation and Development. 1973. *Recurrent Education: A Strategy for Lifelong Learning.* Paris: OECD.
Peers, R. 1958. *Adult Education: A Comparative Perspective.* London: Routledge and Kegan Paul.
Reber, A. 1985. "Learning, Implicit – Entry." In *Dictionary of Psychology*, edited by A. Reber and E. Reber, 392. London: Penguin.
Redmann, D., ed. 2000. *Defining the Cutting Edge.* Minnesota: Academy of Human Resource Development.
Schultz, T. 1961. *Investment in Human Capital.* Basingstoke: MacMillan, cited from P. Jarvis with C. Griffin (ed) (2003) *Adult and Continuing Education: Major Themes in Education.* 5 vols. London: Routledge.
Smith, A. 1919. Adult Education Committee Final Report reprinted in *The 1919 Report* (University of Nottingham Adult Education Department).
Venables, P. 1976. *Report of the Committee on Continuing Education.* Milton Keynes: Open University.
Yeaxlee, B. A. 1925. *Spirital Values in Adult Education.* 2 vols. London: Oxford University Press.
Yeaxlee, B. 1929. *Lifelong Education.* London: Cassell.

The intellect, mobility and epistemic positioning in doing comparisons and comparative education

Terri Kim

Cass School of Education and Communities, University of East London, London, UK

> This article offers a reflexive analysis and discussion of the relationship between academic mobility and comparative knowledge creation. It argues that what constitutes 'comparative knowledge' is not solely *Wissenschaften* but more often entwined with *Weltanschauungen*, derived from lived experiences – as exemplified in the biographic narratives of some of the major intellects. It reviews the notions of the 'gaze' and the concepts of the Other and Homeworld/Alienworld as epistemic positioning in doing comparative education. In the framework of phenomenological thinking, the paper discusses the intimate relationship between comparative knowledge and positional knowledge.

Introduction

Although there is a field of expertise entitled comparative education, comparative knowledge is not just understandable as the possession of comparativists. Durkheim wrote: 'Comparative sociology is not a special branch of sociology; it is sociology itself' (1983, 157). C. Wright Mills also wrote: 'Comparisons are required in order to understand what may be the essential conditions of whatever we are trying to understand' (Mills 1970, 163). Without necessarily invoking Durkheim or Mills, we do comparative analysis reflexively and much of the works in intellectual history entail comparative inquiries.

From this starting point, this article is concerned with the aims and values of doing comparisons and comparative education. It reviews methodological nationalism agendas as the dominant epistemic positioning that has drawn the boundaries of doing comparative education. Using the concept of the 'gaze', it offers a reflexive analysis and discussion on the relationship between academic mobility and comparative knowledge creation. It argues that what constitutes 'comparative knowledge' is not solely *Wissenschaften* (scientific knowledge) but is more often entwined with *Weltanschauungen* (world view) derived from lived experiences. The paper reviews the biographies of some of the major intellects whose mobile life courses have shaped the intellectual agendas for comparative knowledge creation, and reviews the concepts of the Other and Homeworld/Alienworld as epistemic positioning in doing comparative education.

In the framework of phenomenological thinking, the paper discusses the position of a 'stranger': the inside outsider or outsider within (Kim 2009). This leads to a critical analysis of power embedded in forming and shaping new comparative knowledge to suggest the intimate relationship between comparative knowledge and positional knowledge.

Methodological agendas in comparative education

Ever since I became a student of comparative education more than two decades ago, I have kept thinking about the ways in which our comparative knowledge is produced. This reflective inquiry has made me look at the specific relationship between *Wissenschaft* (scientific knowledge) and *Weltanschauung* (world view); and the relationship between Homeworld (*Heimwelt*) and Alienworld (*Fremdwelt*), in the framework of phenomenological thinking (Husserl 1960; Steinbock 1995).

In the field of comparative education, however, the connection between *Wissenschaft* and *Weltanschauung* (and between *Heimwelt* and *Fremdwelt*) has too often been trapped in 'methodological nationalism' in the social sciences. The centrality of nation-states in comparative education is widely accepted. Historically, the genealogical roots of comparative education can be traced back to the 'modernist' epoch of the European Enlightenment of the late eighteenth and early nineteenth centuries (Kazamias 2009). The conventional founding of 'modern' comparative education is often attributed to the writing of Marc-Antoine Jullien de Paris in 1817 who had a very clear definition of usefulness: i.e. comparative education, as a positive science, will show the correct way to improve national education policy decisions (Fraser 1964). Since the rise of romantic nationalism inspired by the ideas of Rouseau and Herder in eighteenth century Europe, the modern conceptions of nation-states became a collective delusion, which was based on the assumption that the nation-state is a natural social and political form of the modern world. In other words, the modern 'state' entered into a symbiotic relationship with the nationalist political project, which *en passant* framed our cognitive map in doing comparative education during the nineteenth and twentieth centuries, within gradualist notions of social amelioration and the expansion of education. In the national framing of states and societies in the modern age, comparative education has been typically employing 'juxtaposition', 'similarities and differences', 'contexts' and ultimately 'learning from' other nations (Cowen 2011). The title of Sadler's Lecture in 1900 captures the classic motifs of comparative education: 'How far may we learn anything of practical value from the study of foreign systems of education?' (Sadler 1900, in Higginson 1979, 50). He claimed that: 'The practical value of studying, in a right spirit and with scholarly accuracy, the working of *foreign* systems of education is that it will result in our being better fitted to study and to understand our *own*' (italics added, Sadler 1900, in Higginson 1979, 50).

In this way, everyday discourses and educational practices were structured and interpreted according to nation-state principles and became routinely assumed and 'banal' (Billig 1995). In comparative education, this is also true, though the banality of the nation-state as a unit of analysis cannot be just attributed to the early generation of comparative educationalists. Across disciplines in the social sciences, in general, methodological nationalism has continued to serve as a powerful invisible background to both empirical and epistemic worlds (Wimmer and Glick Schiller 2002).

Over a long period of time comparative education gradually developed its own 'methods' literature and has diversified its analytic and epistemic agendas,[1] which have been extended into postmodern, postpositivist approaches[2] in the broad domain of comparative education. The normative agendas of 'international development' with a vision of improving the world have also continued to intersect the field to establish 'international comparative education' institutionally, e.g. CIES and BAICE (Crossley 2009; Masemann, Bray, and Manzon 2007; Unterhalter 2009).

Overall, in terms of academic disciplinary formation, as investigated by Manzon (2011), comparative education has evolved into an interdisciplinary subfield of educational studies, although it 'has been constructed initially on the basis of strong institutional power albeit weak intellectual legitimacy' (Manzon 2011, 101). She argues that structures of power that are external to comparative education have also influenced the history, borders and definition of what the field is. Cowen (2003) captures such epistemic traditions and diverse agendas of comparative education aesthetically in the following sentences:

> As comparative educationalists, our attention flickers and we anguish about ourselves. We cannot make up our minds whether we are hygienic dissectors, like skilled fishmongers; agents of melioration – the politically alert plumbers of educational system improvement; or artistic empathisers, culturally-sensitive florists who examine the exotic in the world's educational gardens. (Cowen 2003, 299)

However, Cowen (2006) also declares clearly what (academic) comparative education is *not*:

> comparative education as an academic subject does not fix educational things, when they are broken; it does not service the needs of Ministries of Education; it is not a branch of policy studies; it is not reducible to sociology, or to political science, or to history; it has not yet succumbed to the one true way of a specified methodology; nor has it accepted the seductive but corrosive position of claiming for itself disciplinary status in the terms defined so carefully by London philosophers of education … (Cowen 2006, 570)

Contemporaneously, the multiple epistemological positionings in comparative education with a dilution in its intellectual identity and institutional status have increased complexity further given the new global contexts where trans-national and territorial cultures are entangled with one another in manifold ways and systemic measures for the international comparisons of educational outputs have become ever more routinised and assuming a new normative force (such as OECD PISA). At the time of writing this article, the 2012 Programme for International Student Assessment (PISA) results have been announced worldwide; and it is a high season for the comparative educationalists who are approached to provide instant comments on the PISA results in the media hype. PISA, administered every three years by the OECD, measures performance on maths, reading and science. It is designed to test whether students can apply what they have learned in school to real-life problems – i.e. 'problem-solving' skills. It was first run in 2000 and since then has rapidly become a strong governing technology, producing the world's most 'trusted' education league tables, with postulates and implications for all these 65 participating countries to base education reforms on them.

As Gita Steiner-Khamsi points out, 'implicitly, the semantics of globalization promotes de-territorialization and de-contextualization of reform, and challenges the past conception of education as a culturally bounded system' (Steiner-Khamsi 2004, 5). Accordingly, comparison in itself has become a mode of governance (Beech 2009; Nóvoa and Yariv-Masha 2003; Rizvi and Lingard 2009), governing narratives (Ozga 2011) and global 'policyscapes' (Carney 2012).

However, a decade ago, two missions of academic comparative education were proffered by Cowen (2006):

one is primarily to continue with theoretical comparative thinking. The other is to retain the tradition of 'comparative education' as a social movement, as a set of possibilities for action-on-the-world, without the leftover vocabularies of colonialism, neo-colonialism, aid and development and so on. (Cowen 2006, 570)

But what are we actually trying to understand? He continues to suggest a permanent academic agenda in doing comparative education that is to understand the intersection of international and domestic politics as they shape 'educational systems' and the compression of social power into educational forms – something that is made real for us in individual biographies and educated identities. 'Understanding those processes would permit us to speak truth unto the State; and a few other people as well' (Cowen 2009, 1287–1291).

Following this line of comparative education tradition and mission in my academic journey, the second theme that has kept my attention is 'positioning', which is crucial in the process of comparative meaning-making and new knowledge creation, as things can (and do) exist independent of our knowledge of them.

Positioning in comparative knowledge creation: the 'gaze'

I employ the concept of the 'gaze' here as a means to understand 'positioning' in the process of comparative knowledge creation. In Las Meninas in *The Order of Things* (1970), Michel Foucault examined the peculiar function of the gaze, and argued that the ensuing relationship between the gaze of the spectator and the gaze of the painting breaks down the usual binary nature of the gaze: i.e. between a viewer-gaze and a viewed-gaze (Foucault 1970). This implies that the positioning becomes a 'relationship' in which someone enters. In this regard, Jean Paul Sartre saw the gaze as the battleground for the self to define and redefine itself. The gaze of the 'Other' is outside our immediate control and the way the gaze objectifies us robs us of our freedom as a subject: 'insofar as I am the object of values which come to qualify me without my being able to act on this qualification or even to know it, I am enslaved' (Sartre 1956, 110, re-quoted from http://lucian.uchicago.edu/blogs/mediatheory/keywords/gaze/).

Foucault extends this almost paranoid notion of the gaze into the realm of surveillance, arguing that the gaze becomes the perfect medium for spreading domination. In *The Birth of the Clinic* (*Naissance de la clinique: Une archéologie du regard medical*), Foucault noted that the gaze becomes the 'speaking eye' that surveys and describes everything at the level of medicine; the eye becomes the 'depository and source of clarity', equated with knowledge, which in turn is equated with power[3] (Foucault 1973, 114). The medical gaze is then extended to power relations. Lacan also took his position on the gaze as he developed his theories in psychoanalysis. Lacan's notion of the gaze is not just a seen-gaze but also a gaze-*imagined* in the field of 'the Other'. The gaze becomes the medium for self-differentiation (Lacan 1978). Accordingly, in the gaze, there is never the Other in and of itself. The Other is always relative, as determined by the gaze, the way in which he/she is accessed.

The paradoxical form of the Other is suggested by Husserl as 'the verifiable accessibility of what is not originally accessible' (Husserl 1960, 114). The Other is established through a kind of order that determines what is 'inside' and what is 'outside' and contributes the meanings of the Other as 'the elsewhere itself' (by Merleau-Ponty) or 'lively absence' (by Waldenfels). The Other is like memory, retaining its impact on the present (Waldenfels 2007). Likewise, the Homeworld is in some mode of lived mutuality with the Alienworld – the world of difference and otherness (Steinbock 1995, 178–185). 'The past is a foreign country' [the title of Lowenthal's (1985) tome] is a useful trope that resonates with the relationships as such, which I think have significant epistemic implications for comparative educationalists. John Urry also used the concept of the gaze in the realm of tourism, asserting that 'To be a tourist is one of the characteristics of the "modern" experience' (Urry 2002, 4).

Overall, all these theories of spectatorship, the gaze and the analyses of its entailed implicit power relations made me think about a specific 'comparative' gaze in doing comparative education, especially in relation to my research inquiries of a specific relationship between academic mobility and new knowledge creation. Academic mobility in that sense cannot just be regarded as a simple physical movement from one place to another. It can be 'secular pilgrimage' – referring to Rupert Sheldrake's metaphor here (Urry 2002, 4). Academic mobility proffers the accumulation of grace by visiting the shrines of high academic culture and sacred centres of learning, and also by cultivating what Honoré de Balzac called 'the gastronomy of the eye', from which one can derive a new 'comparative gaze'.

Academic travels have always been regarded as important among intellectual elites, let alone educationalists with particular aims and uses of comparative inquiries about 'foreign worlds and educations'. Even before the time of Jullien de Paris of 1817, the typical eighteenth-century sentiment was that of the studious observer travelling through foreign lands reporting his findings on human nature for those unfortunate enough to have stayed at home. Foreign travels were considered an inherent part 'to complete the education of an English gentleman' (Shackleton 1971). What was then named the 'Grand Tour' was a phenomenon which shaped the creative and intellectual sensibilities of some of the eighteenth century's greatest artists, writers and thinkers. In other words, foreign travels provided a comparative 'gaze' for both young and established scholars with power networks in both political and intellectual circles of the time.

Adam Smith, for instance, derived much personal philosophical benefit and comparative knowledge creation from the period of journeying on continental Europe. When Smith travelled the Continent as a tutor with his pupil, the young Duke of Buccleuch in 1763, he met Voltaire in Geneva and spent almost a year in Paris, where he discussed political economy with the French Ministers, Turgot and Necker, and various luminaries of the thriving circle of philosophies, including Quesnay, a French economist of the Physiocratic School and also a court physician (Elliott 1990, 10). Adam Smith was exposed to both the English and French political-economic systems of the day; and it was during the time in France that Adam Smith began to write his magnum opus, which he continued to write on his return to Kirkcaldy. Smith devoted himself deeply to his inquiry into the nature and causes of national wealth and it took Adam Smith 10 years to dictate and edit *The Wealth of Nations* (1776), which was conceived as a sequel to *The Theory of Moral Sentiments* published in 1759, for he never ceased analysing human behaviour and moral obligations.[4] He had often discussed it in Edinburgh, often with David Hume, often in London and France. He proceeded to dictate his masterpiece, slowly, haltingly, breaking off from time to time to travel down to London to consult others on special problems.[5] Benjamin Franklin, for instance, provided valuable information about the economy and trade of colonies (Viner 1937) for Adam Smith's comparative knowledge and 'vent-for-surplus' theory of international trade.

As such, a specific comparative gaze taken by an itinerant academic would result in a particular interpretation and theorisation of comparative inquiries. In other words, it can be suggested that mobility affects our positioning and cultivates new perspectives through the comparative 'gaze' taken – both seen and imagined. Highly mobile academics – as I examined in my biographic narrative research on 'mobile academics and knowledge creation' (which received a SRHE Research Award, 2011–12) – have all engaged in taking a comparative 'gaze' in the course of encountering and crossing 'boundaries' – both empirical and epistemic, which accompanies 'voluntary' and 'involuntary' displacement experiences.

Methodological clarification of my research analysis

As a mobile academic, comparative educationalist myself, I have always been interested in the relationship between academic mobility and comparative knowledge creation. My biographic narrative analysis takes a phenomenological approach – as an instance of 're-living' rather than 're-porting' (Madison 2010, 65), concerned with the experience and perspective of the individual, 'bracketing' taken-for-granted assumptions and conventional ways of perceiving. In this regard, Max van Manen reminds us of phenomenology as an experience of humility and depth – combining hermeneutics and inter-subjective heuristics. He warns us that if research writing is conceived as a reporting process, imbued with values of methodological objectivity, we may lose the nuanced fecundity of qualitative insight. Accordingly, 'method can become a "law" and the work sterile, method can kill a piece of qualitative research' (van Manen 1997, 125; recited from Madison 2010, 65).

Given the phenomenological standpoint, my analytic frame of reference draws on C. Wright Mills' Sociological Imagination and Paul Ricoeur's Time and Narrative and Narrative Identity to delineate the intricate connection between the patterns of individual lives and social structures and movements and the course of world history in an attempt to 'understand the larger historical scene in terms of its meaning for the inner life and the external career of a variety of individuals' (Mills 1959, 5). Thus, historical time becomes human time 'to the extent that it is articulated through a narrative mode, and narrative attains its full significance when it becomes a condition of temporal existence' (Ricoeur 1984, 52).

Homo viator: exemplary comparativists

Academic mobility constitutes an intrinsic professional identity of comparativists. We are homo viator – itinerant men and women in perpetual (academic) pilgrim condition both in real life and metaphorically. Many of the early generation comparative educationalists were notably trans-national, either as émigré scholars or with immigrant family backgrounds – e.g. Robert Ulich (German émigré scholar), Nicolas Hans (Russian émigré scholar), Joseph Lauwerys (Belgian British) and George Bereday (Polish American). Here, I would take Robert Ulich's biography and life history as an exemplary émigré comparativist, whose scholarship in comparative education illustrates the very intrinsic relationship between *Wissenschaft* and *Weltanschauung*. The following summary of Robert Ulich's biography is mainly depicted from Harvard Square Library online sources (http://www.harvardsquarelibrary.org/unitarians/ulich.html).

Robert Ulich (1890–1977) was a professor of the history and philosophy of education at Harvard University from 1935 until 1960. During those years, he published ten books whose subjects ranged from comparative education to the history of educational thought to his own philosophy of self-transcendence outlined in his best known book, *The Human Career*. Born in Bavaria to a family with a long tradition of religious and contemplative thinkers, Ulich entered the *Humanistisches Gymnasium* at the age of 9. Over the course of the following decade, he was educated in the Classics as well as English, French and Hebrew. Ulich's classical studies provided him with a profound sense of Western history which proved critical to his academic career. His broad interests and unending curiosity made it difficult for him to specialise until he had a brief but defining experience working in a metal plant. Observing the misery of his working-class colleagues, he conceived of an education that must accommodate the basic human desire for progress and happiness, an education that is commensurate with the dynamics of the society in transformation. Although Ulich's works published during the first two decades of his career are slim in contrast to his later prodigious outpouring, two works published during this era suggest the direction of his later research. Dietmar Waterkamp (1997) has noted that these works demonstrate his ability to analyze the social and political tendencies of the present epoch by comparing them with similar constellations in history. Neither work bore any relation to education.

In 1933, in response to a group firing of colleagues at the Dresden Institute of Technology who were described as 'racially and politically undesirable', Ulich resigned both his professorship there and his position with the Ministry of Education of Saxony. He could easily have been arrested for this act of protest, but his wife's high social standing protected him. Soon after his resignation Ulich was offered a one year position as lecturer in comparative education at the Harvard Graduate School of Education. The lectureship rescued Ulich from an increasingly dangerous political climate in Germany. In 1934, Ulich, a 44-year-old and seasoned academic scholar and administrator, arrived at Harvard. After one year, Ulich was appointed Professor of the History and Philosophy of Education and was soon naturalised as a US citizen.

There is little question that the tragic rise of the Nazi party in Germany, whose ultimate aims Ulich foresaw with uncommon clarity, shaped his approach to educational philosophy. Ulich wrote, 'Nothing is more dangerous to mankind than the divine gift of faith uncontrolled by the equally divine gift of reason'.

As remarked by Francis Keppel, who served as Dean of Harvard's Graduate School of Education at the time of Ulich's 1960 retirement from the faculty, Ulich's departure from Germany in 1933 was not caused by academic ambition. It was rather a magnificent protest against a way of life he could not approve. It was an act of personal courage and intellectual honesty. Once arrived in the United States, he did not take the easier path for which his academic training had fitted him. He joined the faculty of a School of Education, well knowing that it was neither fashionable nor an easy road for a new citizen.

His rich historical knowledge and philosophical training set him apart from most educational thinkers at work in the United States. Education, wrote Ulich, was a long enduring process of cultural self-evolution in which we must discover ourselves as part of a reality that is creative and whose power compels a cosmic reverence. His thinking reflected a secular religiousness. As Ulich explained, 'The most radical and comprehensive thinking leads a person beyond the boundaries of the merely empirical and rational into the sphere of the mysterious'.

Waterkamp (1997) explains that Ulich's religiousness was a spirituality and a belief in belonging to a cosmic totality with no specified contents of belief and an aversion to every dogmatism. This belief may have been nourished by his friendship with Paul Tillich, whom he first met at the Dresden Institute of Technology and knew later when both men were at Harvard University. His philosophy of self-transcendence conformed with the Unitarian faith to which he and one of his favourite educational philosophers, Thomas Jefferson, belonged.

As a scholar of comparative education, Ulich analysed the American school system. In his 1951 book, *Crisis and Hope in American Education*, Ulich outlined the weaknesses of the current system, mentioning as key factors in its failure 'the lack of a coherent curriculum in schools and undergraduate studies, the rule of the credit-system, the widespread application of tests, the broad range of choice for the students – which allowed the avoidance of intellectually demanding courses and impeded coherent and sequential learning – the lack of selection in schools and undergraduate studies, and the clinging to a "single-ladder" school system' (Waterkamp 1997). His preferred model for the US educational system has been described as elitist in that it fell in line with fellow Unitarian Thomas Jefferson's belief in a 'natural aristocracy among men'. Waterkamp (1997) explains that 'it set up a typology of talents in relation to societal needs as a basis for establishing a selective school system'. In such a system, the two social classes would share a mutual understanding, if unequal educational opportunities. Social mobility ought to be a slow process, according to Ulich, in order to prevent 'the half-education of the Hitler type' and 'an uprooted and unemployed academic proletariat of the Goebbels type'. In 1954, Ulich's prolific contributions to the fields of the history of education, philosophy of education and comparative education were recognised with his appointment to the first James Bryant Conant Professorship at Harvard University. He retired from teaching in 1960 and returned to Germany in 1970.

The fact that Ulich's name and philosophy are not commonly known in education today may be related to his intellectual aims for education which resisted concretisation. He did not focus his energies on a dissection of the American system or on the creation of methodology, but strove instead to persuade educational leaders to think critically about educational problems within a historical and philosophical framework. One might have thought then that Robert Ulich would champion the pure tradition of German intellectualism, since a perversion of it was itself in part responsible for some of the tragedies of his own life. Or he might have reacted, as so many have done, by taking the leadership in expounding the popular educational philosophy of the day in America. Characteristically, he did not. He ever sought the strength of both traditions, and struggled to rid them of their weaknesses. He soon found in the America of the 1930s and 1940s that he walked a lonely road. (Harvard Alumni Bulletin 1977: http://www.harvardsquarelibrary.org/unitarians/ulich.html)

Overall, my research, using biographical accounts of distinguished trans-national academic intellectuals, has focused on how mobility has led to a new mode of knowledge creation in the process of becoming 'strangers' and being positioned as academic migrants. The biographies of the selected mobile academics whose knowledge have become trans-national tell us that the whole set of mobility-related experiences – the initial act of crossing territorial boundaries, settling in and adaptation to a new (academic) milieu – are entwined with the process of epistemic transformation. 'Displacement' is a common experience for most migrants, but for some academics, if not many, such experience has led to a new breakthrough and paradigm shifting knowledge creation (Kim and Brooks, 2013).

Zygmunt Bauman, a renowned Polish academic émigré in Britain since 1971 and one of the most prominent academic intellectuals of our time, confirms his ontological position as a 'stranger' here: 'I used to be earlier a citizen of Poland, but my citizenship was later withdrawn. I found refuge in England, but I was only adopted by that country. Here and there, I am a "bloody foreigner" … (laughs)' (JDC International Centre for Community Development, 'Interview with Zygmunt Bauman': http://www.jdc-iccd.org/en/article/42/interview-with-zygmunt-bauman).

Among the mobile academic intellectuals whose academic biographies and life histories I examined, there was a considerable difference in the way the host country was perceived between those enthusiastically welcomed in academic society and those who had to depend, initially, on their own resources. Norbert Elias's biography belongs to the latter case. Norbert Elias's personal biography and his sociological theory came nowhere nearer convergence than in his propositions about established–outsiders' relationships.

Significance of marginality in knowledge creation

With his first-hand experience of the First World War as a soldier in the German army and the subsequent social disorder in the Weimar period and the murderous nature of the Nazi regime, Elias analysed *The Civilizing Process* (1969, 1982) as a specific transformation of human behaviour. Even after he escaped Nazi Germany, however, his career as an academic émigré was unusual and difficult.

> Elias (1897–1990) initially studied both medicine and philosophy in Breslau and later sociology in Heidelberg where he learned from Karl Jaspers and did Habilitation under Alfred Weber (the brother of Max Weber). In 1930 Elias chose to follow Karl Mannheim to become his assistant in Frankfurt. After the Nazi takeover in 1933, Mannheim's sociological institute was forced to close and Elias fled to Paris. In Paris, although he was soon able to move into French intellectual circles, there was no prospect of academic employment in France. After two years in poverty in Paris, he moved to London, accepting the invitation from Karl Mannheim who was already at LSE. Elias was 38 years old by then, had published very little, and did not speak English. Therefore, his career prospects in Britain were also very limited. Whilst working as Senior Research Assistant to Karl Manheim at LSE, he completed the two volumes of his magnum opus, *The Civilizing Process* (*Über den Prozeß der Zivilisation*, 1939). Elias argues that the process of civilisation in not linear and consistent. The multiplicity of social groups, as well as the varying and uneven sources of change, have created a variety of social behaviors and formations. However Elias does not see this as a source of legitimate social heterogeneity but rather a different phase in the course of the hegemonic formation of the Western habitus. These large scale and broad processes, Elias explains, have permeated into the consciousness of the individual. Elias terms this process as 'sociogenetic'. The civilising process described by Elias is a constant process of self-restraint and impulse

> management that were developed and established since the sixteenth century and that were eventually spread world-wide (Elias 1969, 1982, 2000).
>
> When the German invasion of Britain appeared imminent in 1940, Elias was detained at internment camps on account of his being German, even though he was a Jewish academic émigré (Kim and Brooks, 2013). After his release in 1941, he taught evening classes in an adult learning organisation in Cambridge, and towards the end of the war, Elias also worked for British intelligence. It was only in 1954 that Elias had his first secure academic post at the University of Leicester, Sociology Department. He was then 57 years old. And it was only in his late seventies and eighties that Elias came at last to be regarded by many social scientists as being 'one of the world's most original and penetrating sociological thinkers' (Mennell and Goudsblom 1998).
>
> Elias's biography suggests that critical incidents in his lifetime and the experiences of crossing boundaries – epistemic, academic culture and territorial boundaries – have intimately interwoven and led to new knowledge creation. Elias' writing reflects his powerful sympathy for outsiders of every kind and, in retrospect, Elias remarked that personal experiences and the events of his time influenced his thinking at least as much as any book he read (Mennell and Goudsblom 1998).

As exemplified in Elias' life and scholarship, what academics carry is not just expertise (knowledge as science) but also a mode of thinking – the overall orientation toward structures of meaning (Gouldner 1979; Hannerz 1990). They are engaged in reflexive knowledge creation. Their world views derived from lived experiences (*Weltanschauungen*) are an integral part of their knowledge creation (*Wissenschaften*).

There are some common characteristics of trans-national mobile academics and their mode of knowledge creation, as examined in my SRHE research (Kim and Brooks 2013). For instance, academics become mobile through discipline-based networks. Secondly, mobile academics in crossing many borders and boundaries often assume the role of international 'knowledge broker', 'knowledge trader' as well as become institutionalised 'local career adapter'. And thirdly, mobile academics tend to employ interdisciplinary, comparative approaches.

In terms of new comparative knowledge creation, however, I would stress the importance of 'nomadic imagination' exercised by free floating thinkers in pursuit of intellectual emancipation through knowledge creation, which is transcending the territorial confinement of knowledge bound to the nation-state as a unit of analysis. The biographies and life histories of Robert Ulich and Norbert Elias illustrated above confirm this epistemic positioning.

Position of a 'stranger': becoming a trans-national comparativist

Further, I would suggest that this is possible by assuming the position of a 'stranger' (invoking Simmel) or the 'consecrated heretic' (invoking Bourdieu). Simmel confirms that

> to be a stranger is naturally a very positive relation … It is a specific form of interaction … He [the stranger] is not radically committed to the unique ingredients and peculiar tendencies of the group, and therefore approaches them with the specific attitude of 'objectivity'. (Simmel 1908; Wolff, trans.Ed. 1950, 402–408)

Objective here, according to Simmel, is a 'particular structure composed of distance and nearness, indifference and involvement' (Simmel 1908; Wolff, trans. Ed. 1950, 402–408).

I argue that becoming a trans-national comparativist is like assuming the position of a stranger – as conceptualised by Georg Simmel: 'His position within it, is fundamentally affected by the fact that, he does not belong in it initially, and that he brings qualities into it, that are not, and cannot be, indigenous to it' (404).

Also, the description of 'consecrated heretics' in Pierre Bourdieu's book, *Homo Academicus* (1988) matches the importance of marginality that I consider an attribute to comparative knowledge creation, which I have found often among trans-national academic intellectuals.

> ... even when they are not entirely estranged from the 'normal' career pattern – as is the case with those of them who were not born in France, without being totally alienated from the university order, they [transnational academic intellectuals] are often those who have accomplished a more or less decisive detour from the 'normal' trajectories which lead to simple reproduction and from the psychological and social security which these trajectories guarantee. (Bourdieu, *Homo Academicus* 1988, 107)

Drawing upon the sociology of Georg Simmel and the philosophy of Jacques Derrida, Bauman (1991) also discussed the position of a 'stranger' who is present yet unfamiliar, society's undecidable. In Bauman's analysis, the Jews became 'strangers' *par excellence* in European history. In *Modernity and the Holocaust*, Bauman (1989) argued that the Holocaust should not simply be considered to be an event in Jewish history, nor a regression to pre-modern barbarism. Rather, he argued, the Holocaust should be seen as deeply connected to 'modernity' and its order-making efforts – procedural rationality, taxonomic categorisation and the tendency to view rule-following as morally good. Similarly, Bernhard Waldenfels (1997) also suggested in his *Topography of the Alien* [*Topographie des Fremden*] that modern Europeans used to assume 'the standpoint of universality' but they blindly turned it into 'the universal standpoint'. The latter standpoint/positioning leads to the 'pressure of universalization', which pushes the self and the other under its compulsion (Waldenfels 1997; re-quoted from Yu 2005, 29).

Dénouement

As reviewed earlier, the geneaology of comparative education entails the ideology of usefulness framed by methodological nationalism, which 'has helped to permit a whole range of intellectual, quasi-intellectual, and rather practical activities to be gathered together under the umbrella name, "comparative education" to the point where serious epistemological, ethical and political confusions are occurring' (Cowen 2006, 561). There are many versions of comparative education after all, as Cowen (2009) pinpoints that, 'what we call comparative education, in its growth, in its shape-shifting, is itself part of international, political, economic, cultural and educational relations' (Cowen 2009, 1289).

Contemporaneously, in the age of academic mobility and migration, comparative research involves crossing and bridging boundaries more frequently than ever before, and The idea of boundaries is suddenly becoming itself at the centre of a number of 'comparative' fields. In this regard, it is suggested that mobile academic comparativists should take on the position of a 'stranger'; and their embodied travelled knowledge reflects the notion of a dialectical third, which creatively escapes from the binary division between Homeworld and Alienworld in the framework of phenomenological comparative thinking.

Meanwhile, the global expansion of neoliberal market-framed university regimes may indicate that what used to be the idiosyncrasies of 'colonial' higher education – which I depict as pragmatic and problem-solving approaches to knowledge – has become a global trend contemporaneously. Such trends leave very little space for free floating mobile academic intellectuals as comparativists, who hold positions as an inside outsider, or outsider within, whose work produces *new* comparative knowledge. I would suggest it is essential for comparativists "to see a riddle, a problem, or a paradox, not previously seen by anyone else", which is, according to Popper, "a greater achievement than resolving the riddle". Popper suggested: "The philosopher who first sees and understands a new problem disturbs our laziness and complacency... He opens out a new horizon before us." (Popper, 1963).

Similarly, Daniel H. Pink argues, in his recent book *To Sell is Human* (2012), that the premium has already moved from 'problem solving' to 'problem finding' as a 'skill' in the business world. School superintendents rated problem-solving as the top capability they wanted to instil, whereas corporate executives rated problem-solving as seventh on their list of attributes in employees, but rated problem identification as the single most important skill. Pink says,

> Right now, especially in the commercial world, if I know exactly what my problem is, I can find the solution to my own problem. I don't need someone to help me. Where I need help is when I don't know what my problem is or when I'm wrong about what my problem is. Problem solving is an analytical, deductive kind of skill. The phrase 'problem finding' comes out of research on artists. It's more of a conceptual kind of skill. (Rose, 13 January 2013)

I would suggest the same logic could be applied to the role of mobile academic intellectuals as the Schumpeterian entrepreneur (Schumpeter 1934, 2008) in the world of comparative education. For many of us, as mobile academics engaged in comparative knowledge creation, problem-finding would be a more appropriate job than problem-solving, especially nowadays as education itself is on the verge of a new paradigm shift. We can leave the old mantras of comparative education now.

Notes

1. E.g. research on education policy transfer (Phillip 1989; Phillips and Ochs 2004; Phillips and Schweisfurth 2008); policy borrowing and lending (Steiner-Khamsi and Waldow 2012) and the new meta-theorisation of transfer, translation and transformation (Cowen 2006, 2009); and 'transitologies' (Cowen 1999; Larsen 2010).
2. E.g. Postmodernism and its Comparative Education Implications (Rust 1991); and Postpositivist Theorizing and Research (Ninnes and Mehta 2000; Unterhalter 2009).
3. Foucault's intellectual project was to analyse the *longue durée* of formation and use of these discourses within the context of specific historical practices. In *The Order of Things* (*Les Mots et les choses*), published three years later in 1966, Foucault presented a comparative study of the development of economics, the natural sciences and linguistics in the eighteenth and nineteenth centuries, which can be claimed as the first 'postmodern' history of ideas. Foucault wrote his next major work, *The Archaeology of Knowledge* (*L'Archéologie du Savior*) during the period when he was residing in Tunisia (1966–1968). This period of writing was a turbulent time for Tunisia with serious political violence and demonstrations aimed primarily at Israel. It is said that Foucault's experience in Tunisia had an effect on his work and thought. In the *Archaeology of Knowledge*, Foucault argued that in addition to the classical unities of the existing human sciences, there are discursive unities that underlie them and are often not evident (The Foucault Society, 2010: http://foucaultsociety.wordpress.com/about-michel-foucault/).

4. Adam Smith wrote his 'economics' as part of his work as a philosopher. He was the Chair Professor of Moral Philosophy at the University of Glasgow. In the days of Adam Smith, much of the study carried out at universities was history and philosophy; a course in philosophy would include a study of jurisprudence. A study of justice leads naturally to a study of the various legal systems, which of course leads to the study of government, and, finally, to a study of political economy (http://martinfrost.ws/htmlfiles/adam_smith.html).
5. Dugald Stewart states that Hume wrote out his books with his own hand, and Adam Smith dictated his to a secretary. (Account of the Life and Writings of Adam Smith LL.D. by Dugald Stewart, 1793, from the Transactions of the Royal Society of Edinburgh. Read by Mr Stewart, 21 January and 18 March 1793. Printed in the Collected Works of Dugald Stewart, vol. 10, pp. 1–98 (http://www.adamsmith.org/sites/default/files/resources/dugald-stewart-bio.pdf).

References

Bauman, Z. 1989. *Modernity and the Holocaust*. Ithaca, NY: Cornell University Press.
Bauman, Z. 1991. *Modernity and Ambivalence*. Ithaca, NY: Cornell University Press.
Beech, J. 2009. "Who is Strolling Through the Global Garden? International Agencies and Educational transfer." In *International Handbook of Comparative Education*, edited by R. Cowen and A. Kazamias, 341–358. Springer.
Billig, M. 1995. *Banal Nationalism*. London: Sage Publications.
Bourdieu, P. 1988. *Homo Academicus* (Peter Collier, Trans.). Stanford, CA: Stanford University Press.
Carney, S. 2012. "Imagining Globalisation: Educational Policyscapes." In *Policy Borrowing and Lending n Education, World Yearbook of Education 2012*, edited by G. Steiner-Khamsi and F. Waldow, 338–353. Abingdon, Oxon and New York: Rougledge.
Cowen, R. 1999. "Late Modernity and the Rules of Chaos: An Initial Note on Transitologies and Rims." In *Learning from Comparing New Directions in Comparative Educational Research, Vol.1, Contexts, Classrooms and Outcomes*, edited by R. Alexander, P. Broadfoot, D. Phillips, 73–88. Oxford: Symposium Books.
Cowen, R. 2003. "Agendas of Attention: A Response to Ninnes and Burnett." *Comparative Education* 39 (3): 299–302.
Cowen, R. 2006. Acting comparatively upon the educational world: puzzles and possibilities In *Oxford Review of Education*, Vol. 32, No. 5, p. 561–573.

Cowen, R. 2009. "Then and Now: Unit Ideas and Comparative Education." In *International Handbook of Comparative Education*, edited by R. Cowen and A. Kazamias, 1277–1294. Springer.

Cowen, R. 2011. "Edging Closer to the Hero, the Barbarian, and the Stranger." In D. Daniel Tröhler and R. Barbu (Eds). Education Systems in Historical, Cultural, and Sociological Perspectives, The Future of Education Research Volume 1, pp 21–36.

Crossley, M. 2009. "Rethinking Context in Comparative Education." In *International Handbook of Comparative Education*, edited by R. Cowen and Kazamias, 1173–1187. Springer.

Durkheim, D. 1894; 1983. *Les Règles de la Méthode Sociologique; The Rules of Sociological Method*, translated by William D. Hall, New York: Free Press.

Elias, N. 1969. *The Civilizing Process, Vol.I. The History of Manners*. Oxford: Blackwell.

Elias, N. 1982. *The Civilizing Process, Vol.II. State Formation and Civilization*. Oxford: Blackwell.

Elias. N. 2000. *The Civilizing Process. Sociogenetic and Psychogenetic Investigations*. Revised edition. Oxford: Blackwell.

Elliott, N., ed. 1990. *Adam Smith's Legacy*. London: Adam Smith Institute.

Foucault, M. 1970. *Las Meninas In The Order of Things*. New York: Pantheon Books.

Foucault, M. 1973. *Seeing and Knowing In The Birth of the Clinic: An Archaeology of Medical Perception*. New York: Pantheon Books.

Foucault Society. 2010. Biography of Michele Foucault: http://foucaultsociety.wordpress.com/about-michel-foucault/.

Fraser, S. 1964. *Jullien's Plan for Comparative Education 1816–1817*. New York: Teachers College, Columbia University Bureau of Publications.

Gouldner, A. 1979. *The Future of the Intellectuals and the Rise of the New Class*. London: Macmillan.

Hannerz, U. 1990. "Cosmopolitans and Locals in World Culture." *Theory, Culture & Society* 7: 237–251.

Higginson, J. H. (Ed.) 1979. *Selections from Michael Sadler: Studies in world citizenship*. Liverpool: Dejall & Meyorre.

Husserl, E. 1960 *Cartesian Meditations: an introduction to phenomenology*. Trans. Dorion Cairns. M. Nijhoff: The Hague.

Kazamias, A. 2009. "Comparative Education: Historical Reflections." In Cowen, R. and Kazamias, A. (eds). Op. cit., pp. 139–157.

Kim, T. 2009. "Transnational Academic Mobility, Internationalisation and Interculturality in Higher Education." *Intercultural Education* Special Issue on Interculturality and Higher Education. Edited by Terri Kim & Matthias Otten. 20 (5): 395–405.

Kim, T., and R. Brooks. 2013. Internationalisation, Mobile Academics, and Knowledge Creation in Universities: a Comparative Analysis. SRHE Research Award (2011/12) Final Report.

Lacan, J. 1978. Four Fundamental Concepts in Psychoanalysis, ed. Jacques-Alain Miller and trans. Alan Sheridan. New York: Norton.

Larsen, M., ed. 2010. *New Thinking in Comparative Education: Honouring the Work of Robert Cowen*. Rotterdam: Sense Publishers.

Madison, G. 2010. *Existential Migration: Voluntary migrants' experiences of not being-at-home in the world*. London: LAP Lambert Publishing.

Manzon, M. 2011. *Comparative Education: The Construction of a Field*. Hong Kong: Comparative Education Research Centre, The University of Hong Kong & Springer.

Masemann, V., M. Bray, and M. Manzon, eds. 2007. *Common Interests, Uncommon Goals: Histories of the World Council of Comparative Education Societies*. Hong Kong: CERC.

Mennell, S., and J. Goudsblom, eds. 1998. *Norbert Elias: On Civilization, Power and Knowledge, Selected Writings*. Chicago: University of Chicago, 1998.

Mills, C. W. 1959. *The Sociological Imagination*. New York: Oxford University Press.

Mills, C. Wight. 1970. *Sociological Imagination*. Harmondsworth: Penguin.

Ninnes, P., and S. Mehta. 2000. "Postpositivist Theorizing and Research: Challenges and Opportunities for Comparative Education." *Comparative Education Review* 44 (2): (May), 205–212.

Nóvoa, A., and Yariv-Mashal, T. 2003. "Comparative Research in Education: A Mode of Governance or a Historical Journey." *Comparative Education* 39 (4): 423–438.

Ozga, J. 2011. "Governing Narratives: "Local" Meanings and Globalising Education Policy." *Education Inquiry* 2 (2): May 2011, 305–318.

Phillips, D. 1989. Neither a Borrower not a Lender Be? The Problems of Cross-national Attraction in Education. Cross-National Attraction in Education, Special Issue, *Comparative Education* 25 (3): 267–274.

Phillips, D., and K. Ochs, eds. 2004. *Educational Policy Borrowing: Historical Perspectives*. Oxford Studies in Comparative Education. Oxford: Symposium Books.

Phillips, D. and Schweisfurth, M. (2008). *Comparative and International Education: An Introduction to Theory, Method and Practice*, London: Continuum.

Pink, D. H. 2012. *To Sell is Human*. New York: Riverheads Books (Published by the Penguin Group).

Popper, K. 1963. *Conjectures and Refutations: The Growth of Scientific Knowledge*. London: Routledge.

Ricoeur, P. 1983. Temps et récit, Paris: Editions du Seuil; (1984) Time and Narrative vol. 1, trans. by Kathleen McLaughlin and David Pellauer, Chicago: University of Chicago Press.

Rizvi, F., and Lingard, B. 2009. The OECD and Global Shifts in Education Policy In Cowen, R. and Kazamias (Eds). Op. cit.

Rust, V. 1991. "Postmodernism and Its Comparative Education Implications." *Comparative Education Review* 35 (4): (November), 610–626.

Sadler, M. 1900. 'How Far can we Learn Anything of Practical Value from the Study of Foreign Systems of Education?' Address of 20 October. In J.H. Higginson (Ed.), Selections from Michael Sadler (pp.48–51). Liverpool: Dejall & Meyorre.

Sartre, J. P. 1956. *The Look In Being and Nothingness*. New York: Philosophical Library.

Schumpeter, J. A., 1934 (2008), *The Theory of Economic Development: An Inquiry into Profits, Capital, Credit, Interest and the Business Cycle*, translated from the German by Redvers Opie, New Brunswick (U.S.A) and London (U.K.): Transaction Publishers.

Shackleton, R. 1971. "The Grand Tour in the Eighteenth Century." In *Studies in Eighteenth Century Culture 1*, edited by Louis T. Milic, 127–142. Cleveland: The Press of Case Western Reserve University.

Simmel, G. 1908; 1950. *The Sociology of Georg Simmel*. Translated, edited and with an introduction by Kurt H. Wolff, Glencoe, Illinois: The Free Press.

Smith, A. 1776; 1964. *An Inquiry into the Nature and Causes of the Wealth of Nations*. London and New York: The Everyman's Library edition, Random House.

Steinbock, A. 1993. Homeworld/alienworld: Towards a Generative Phenomenology. Front Cover. Anthony Joseph Steinbock. State University of New York at Stony Brook.

Steinbock, A. 1995. *Home and Beyond: Generative Phenomenology after Husserl*. Evanston, IL: Northwestern University Press.

Steiner-Khamsi, G., ed. 2004. *Lessons from Elsewhere: The Politics of Educational Borrowing & Lending*. New York: Teachers College Press.

Steiner-Khamsi, G., and F. Waldow. 2012. *World Yearbook of Education 2012: Policy Borrowing and Lending in Education*. London and New York: Routledge.

Unterhalter, E. 2009. Social Justice, Development Theory and the Question of Education In Cowen, Kazamias and Unterhalter (Eds) Internaional Handbook of Comparative Education Part Two, Springer, pp. 781–802.

Urry, J. 2002. *The Tourist Gaze*. London: Sage.

van Manen, M. 1997. *Researching Lived Experience: Human Science for an Action Sensitive Pedagogy* (2nd ed.). Canada: The Althouse Press.

Viner, J. 1937. *Studies in the Theory of International Trade*. New York: Harper and Brothers Publishers.

Waldenfels B. 1997. *Topographie des Fremden*. Frankfurt am Main: Suhrkamp.

Waldenfels, B. 2007. *The Question of the Other*. New York: SUNY.

Waterkamp, D. 1997. Robert Ulich: Ideal Universalism: A German Emigrant's Contribution to Education Studies in the USA. Dresdner Universitätsverl. & Universitätsbuchhandlung.

Wimmer, A., and N. Glick Schiller. 2002. "Methodological Nationalism and Beyond: Nation-state Building, Migration and the Social Sciences." *Global Networks* 2 (4): 301–334.

Yu, Chung-Chi. 2005. "Between Homeworld and Alienworld: Waldenfels on Interculturality." *Philosophy, Culture and Traditions* 3: 25–38.

'Comparatography', history and policy quotation: some reflections

David Phillips

St Edmund Hall, Oxford, UK

> This paper revisits the question of the importance of a historical dimension in comparative inquiry and reflects on some problems in what is termed 'comparatography', the writing of comparative education.

There is one particular tradition in work in comparative education that seems to be increasingly under-represented. The early exponents who can be described as comparativists (though rarely primarily as social scientists) wrote from perspectives rooted in history and philosophy. It was natural for them to approach the topics they were investigating from a starting point of historical analysis and understanding, what Kazamias has termed the 'historical–philosophical–cultural and liberal humanist motif in comparative education' (2009, 37) and what Watson called 'historical and cultural analysis' in the context of his arguing for a rediscovery of the roots of the subject (1998, 28). The fiftieth anniversary of *Comparative Education* provides an opportunity to reflect afresh on the under-representation of a 'historical dimension' in comparative inquiry and at the same time on some of the problems identifiable in the many papers submitted to the journal each year. And so there is a dual purpose in what follows: to argue for more consideration to be given to historical inquiry generally and to the inclusion of a historical dimension in comparative studies generally; and to identify some aspects of writing in comparative education that cause papers to be rejected.

Writing within comparative inquiry in education is and should be a complex undertaking. Despite the criticism I shall make of unnecessary neologisms (rehearsed below), I shall use the term 'comparatography' (by analogy with historiography, the writing of history) as a shorthand for everything that constitutes the methods educationists employ to write comparatively. Editors and others concerned with reading papers submitted to comparative education journals see a huge range of texts from around the world, written from an extraordinary variety of perspectives. We can easily gain some idea of what work judged to be successful looks like: a reading of recent issues of *Comparative Education* or one of the other leading journals in the subject will provide evidence of what has been deemed acceptable through the various processes of peer review. It is clear that the subject is outstandingly rich in terms of what it sets out to cover. What is not so evident, outside of the editorial boards of the journals concerned, is what kind of writing is judged less successful, what causes papers not to be accepted for publication. These 'absences' from the published record have failed to satisfy the criteria for publication on a number of counts, some of which are implicit in the reflections that follow, but my main focus will be on the neglect of history – what Kazamias has lamented as 'the virtual abandonment of one of the unifying elements of the field' of comparative education (Kazamias 2001, 440) – and on the desirability of framing comparative investigation in historical understanding.

Starting points

Those engaged in educational inquiry involving comparison will bring to their investigations a variety of expertise emerging for the most part from the disciplines in which they have principally been trained. On the whole they will not be comparativists by origin, unless – exceptionally and somewhat implausibly – they have been able to 'major' in the subject as undergraduates. There is in effect no ideal foundation discipline on which comparativists might build to establish themselves as investigators with a claim to appropriate expertise, though some might clearly be judged more potentially useful than others. (While it might seem intuitively the case that, say, a base in sociology would be more useful than, for example, one in engineering or biochemistry, the two latter fields would at least involve a disciplined training in methodology that might be transferred, in terms of rigorous research styles, to social science investigation.)[1] Two prominent British academics, Edmund King (1914–2003) and Brian Holmes (1920–1993), came from polarised academic backgrounds: King was a classicist, Holmes a physicist, and they brought to their work skills embedded in the traditions of their respective disciplines. Their disagreements about the nature of comparative studies and research methods owe much to their opposite starting points as scholars. The lenses through which they saw the world were obviously focused differently. Neither, of course, was by origin a social scientist. But King brought the multifaceted skills of the humanist researcher to his work in comparative education, while Holmes's contribution was informed by his training in rigorous scientific method. Both of them used their disciplinary origins effectively to inform their approaches to comparative education evident in their substantial writings.

A contemporary of King and Holmes, George Bereday (1920–1983), demonstrated a broad range of credentials as a comparativist. Born in Poland, he was multilingual; he was trained both as a historian and as an educationist/sociologist in three distinguished universities in two countries, and he spent time as a visiting professor in yet other places, including Moscow and Tokyo. His demands as to what constitutes the basic requirements for competence as a comparativist (among them a substantial period of residence in the country to be investigated and knowledge of foreign languages) were clearly rooted in his own experience and accomplishments and in his secure disciplinary foundations. So secure was he in the breadth and depth of his own knowledge and skills that he could go so far as to argue that '[a]ll of the humanities and social sciences should be used to broaden the vistas of comparative education' (Bereday 1964, 21).

Bereday's multiplicity of skills and experience was egregious, but many of the early investigators had expertise approaching his, among them Isaac Kandel (1881–1965) and Nicholas Hans (1888–1969), both of whom were proficient linguists and trained historians. So too – to delve further back into the origins of comparative education – were Matthew Arnold (1822–1888) and Michael Sadler (1861–1943), both of whom studied *literae humaniores* at Oxford and demonstrated in their pioneering work profound historical understanding as well as an ability to read untranslated documents and to engage with others in foreign languages (both were competent in German and French). Scholars like W.D. Halls (1918–2011), historian of education in France and a speaker of French, German and Dutch, and Nigel Grant (1932–2003), *inter alia* historian of Soviet and Eastern European education (whose knowledge of other languages, including a proud fluency in Scots, was extensive), continued this tradition and approached Bereday's requirements. Indeed, among the qualifications that might be demanded of a competent comparativist, intimate and expert knowledge of another society and its historical development – can this be seriously contested? – and acquired foreign language competence have arguably counted among the more useful.

What unites the comparativists I have cited so far is a style of investigation that relies on the philosophical–historical and culturalist traditions in scholarship. While they can usually be 'placed' in terms of a firm foundation in a discipline (history, philosophy, classics, principally), they had an established competence as generalist scholars, able to draw on a variety of contributing disciplines with confidence. They could move with ease between disciplines without appearing to dabble.

The first point I wish to make here is that while it is desirable for researchers to demonstrate that they have a foundation discipline that informs their investigations, so that readers know – to use the colloquial term – where authors are coming from (as psychologists, sociologists, economists, historians, geographers, etc.), comparativists need also to work within broader parameters, to have a wider perspective, and one which should benefit from historical insight into both the development of comparative education and its styles and the topics they set out to investigate.

History of comparative education

Epstein and Carroll (2005) have written convincingly of 'abusing ancestors'. A basic problem is that contemporary discussion about the nature of comparative inquiry in education can sometimes occur as if from a *tabula rasa* starting point, presenting issues as if they have never been considered before and are not woven into the historical fabric of the subject. This is a failing identifiable in many papers that do not get published. Of course, many of the fundamental questions about the nature of comparison emerge at least from the writings of the nineteenth-century investigators, especially from the French philosopher Victor Cousin's inquiries, from the administrator Horace Mann's reporting in the United States, from Matthew Arnold's investigations in England and – at the turn of the century – from the extensive output of Michael Sadler, who is still one of the most frequently cited comparativists.

Through examining the writings of these 'ancestors' we can exemplify most of the issues that are of continuing significance for the activities of comparativists today. Their approaches to comparative education should be widely known: they were not merely representative of and locked into their time. What might be termed 'comparatography' – the accumulated wisdom culled from the considerable literature of comparative education and its methods as a guide to how work within the subject might be written – is still profitably informed by the work of earlier generations. They should still have a place in the syllabuses of comparative education courses; as too should the systemic studies (which many of them undertook with full academic rigour), now curiously absent from such courses as if studying education systems is mere *Auslandspädagogik* (literally 'pedagogy of foreign countries', viz. the study of foreign systems of education) of no significance. Studying an education system involves using a variety of approaches rooted in several contributing disciplines, not least in historical analysis, and it should be a matter of concern that such study is so often replaced by 'issues', which, while of enormous importance, cannot be properly addressed without considerable knowledge of systems in which they are manifest.

When Noah and Eckstein (1969) posited a historical periodisation of comparative education they pointed out that the periods they suggested to characterise the main thrusts of comparative studies overlapped: that is, one approach did not replace another but added to it, so that comparative education as a field of inquiry could develop as an accretion of approaches/dimensions/theories and would consequently be the richer for it. Their periodisation looked like this:

(1) Travellers' tales;
(2) Travellers with a specific educational focus; learning through example; improving circumstances at home;
(3) Understanding of other nations; detailed accumulation of information; educational exchange;
(4) Study of 'national character' and its deterministic role in shaping national systems of education;
(5) Quantitative research; explanation of educational phenomena. (4–7)

Phillips and Schweisfurth (2014) developed the notion in an overlapping 'chain of emphases' (see Figure 1).

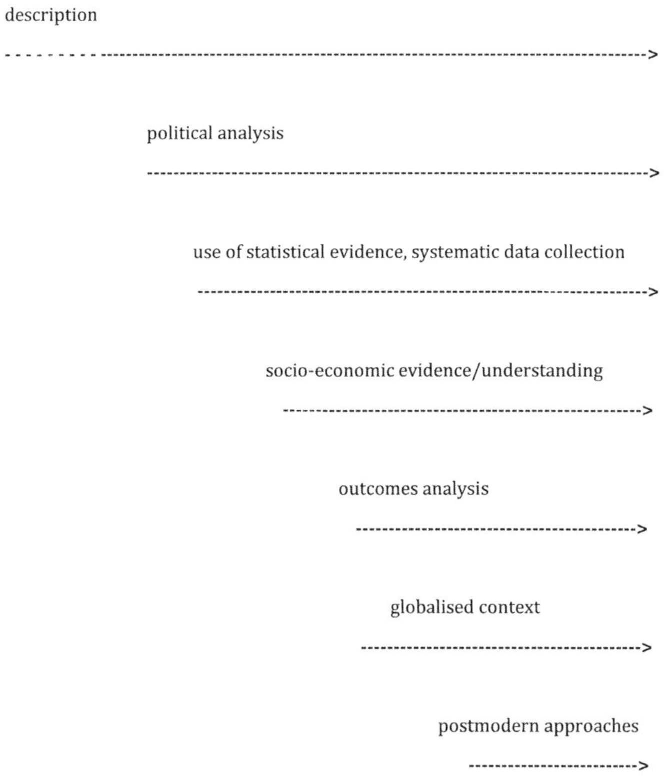

description
-->

political analysis
-->

use of statistical evidence, systematic data collection
-->

socio-economic evidence/understanding
-->

outcomes analysis
------------------------------------>

globalised context
------------------------------->

postmodern approaches
-------------------------->

Figure 1. Historical emphases in comparative analysis. *Source*: Phillips and Schweisfurth (2014, 27)

These descriptors can of course be challenged, but the simple point is that if, say, in the context of what we describe here as 'outcomes analysis', a large-scale investigation of pupil attainment is undertaken, it should not ignore, for example, the political and socio-economic analysis that will illuminate the data. But clearly this does not always happen. The league table approach to analyses of learners' ability focuses on statistical evidence and how it has been produced, on outcomes rather than the complex processes that have led to them, so that the historical/cultural/sociological/economic/geographical (etc.) factors that might account for the results are not fully taken into account, if at all. Comparative studies should be informed by the rich interdependence of approaches to comparison that have evolved over a long period – developed by a succession of significant researchers – and should not become trapped in one single tradition, imagining others to be somehow surpassed and so redundant.

Theory

A tendency to use overarching theory *as a starting point* of comparative inquiry has become increasingly evident in much of the comparative work presented at conferences and submitted to journals. In the second edition of our introduction to comparative and international education, Michele Schweisfurth and I have sketched the problem as follows:

> [In] a field of intellectual inquiry as diverse as comparative education there is no 'one size fits all' device with universal explanatory power. Instead the comparativist is better served by an appreciation of ways in which a variety of theoretical perspectives might be drawn upon to elucidate particular issues/problems/methodological approaches – essentially an eclectic approach not dissimilar from Edmund King's embracing of the concept of 'tools for the job'. (Phillips and Schweisfurth 2014, 37)

If a Weberian approach is to be adopted, if Foucault is going to guide the research, if Bourdieu provides the parameters for an investigation, then we might expect that the work of these theorists will be properly used on the basis of close reading of their writings, such as would be undertaken by a philosopher. Let us suppose, for example, that there are researchers in comparative education who assert that their work is rooted in Hegel (not an implausible supposition). We would then have to be convinced that a specialist Hegel scholar would readily sanction the particular interpretation of Hegel's thought and the use made of it. Reliance on second- or third-hand accounts of the work of leading thinkers will not do for philosophers and it should not do for comparativists. This is not an especially tendentious point; it is certainly one with serious implications for our subject. Theory should of course be used critically and on the basis of a thorough reading and interpretation of the original texts behind it. Nothing less should do – otherwise the criticism from outside of our subject will be that of dilettantism or the shortcut approaches of journalism.

In an earlier paper I used the anecdote of relatives of a deceased elderly lady finding among her possessions a box labelled 'pieces of string too short to be of any use':

> This is a nice image for comparativists who must of necessity know about a wide range of contributing disciplines while inevitably not knowing as much about any one of them as a specialist within any of them would be required to know. The danger is that their knowledge would be, as it were, a collection of pieces of string, each of which, when tied together, would form a not very strong rope. (Phillips 2006, 291)

The potential strength of comparative inquiry is to weave together a substantial rope of analysis, with each part demonstrably not too short or insubstantial or misreported to be of any use. To begin with theory is to do things the wrong way round: studies should serve to lead to theory, to test existing theoretical approaches, to confirm or refute them, to contribute to and build on them in various ways.

A note on jargon

Another problem identifiable in much of the unsuccessful work seen by journal editors revolves around the language used in the social sciences. A common and obvious criticism is that it is too jargon-ridden, too introspective, far too arcane for a general readership. It lends itself easily to parody. The common defence is that complex ideas are involved in serious work in the social sciences, and that complex ideas require complex language: sometimes only neologisms or new meanings assigned to existing vocabulary will suffice to convey ideas with the required precision. Yet in a language as rich in vocabulary as English this seems a weak argument. Just reading a chapter or two of Isaiah Berlin, or Karl Popper, or Bertrand Russell, will demonstrate how simple language – what is called 'ordinary' language in philosophers' terms – is very capable of expressing complex thought. Papers written in impenetrable jargonese are directed most obviously only at others who write in the same style, to the (conscious? deliberate?) exclusion of a general readership seeking enlightenment. Writings in comparative education – especially journal articles in English designed to be read around the world – serve such a readership best when written in language that is transparent and accessible. Most writing in mainstream history – from whose styles a lot may be learnt – is refreshingly jargon-free.

History in comparative education

Study of the history of education used to be an essential part of university courses, the obvious and accepted justification for devoting time to historical understanding being that without it an appreciation of present-day educational issues would lack a significant explanatory dimension. To have a full understanding of current education policy in England, for example, would require investigation of the complex historical development of 'maintained' education (i.e. provision with central or local government funding) since the 1870 Education Act. To appreciate the political agonising in Germany following the so-called *PISA-Schock* would need at least a knowledge of the historical origins of federalism in German politics, of the German constitution and the juridification of education, and of the reforms of the tripartite system. To examine properly the present-day situation in education in Japan would need knowledge of the influences on the system from abroad at critical stages in the nation's development. Nóvoa and Tariv-Mashal conclude in a paper on comparative research and history that the deeper historical perspective they advocate is a 'history that enables us to understand the problems of the present through an analysis of the way they have been and are constituted throughout the past and present, enabling a constitution of the future' (2003, 436).

A historical dimension would require a careful analysis of how educational periods might be determined and the extent to which different societies have experienced similar trends in educational development over similar or dissimilar time spans. Comparative periodisation poses particular challenges which need to be addressed as a structure for historical analysis is formulated for any particular comparative study (Cowen 2002; Phillips 1994, 2002; Sweeting 2007).

A recent publication by a distinguished British historian devotes considerable space to discussion of comparative history, which he describes as 'the Cinderella among approaches to the past'. Sir John Elliott (Elliott 2012), writing from his long experience as a historian of Spain, identifies the main problems with a clarity that will be of considerable value to educationists engaged in historical investigation.

Elliott quotes at the outset the distinction made by the historian Otto Hintze (1861–1940) between the sociologist's use of comparison and that of the historian: the sociologist seeks generalisations, while the historian looks for singularities. This dichotomy – effectively the divide between 'nomothetic' and 'idiographic' approaches – has been described by Guenter Lewy as follows (though he goes on to argue that as a contrast it is 'overdrawn'[2]):

> Historians, according to one widespread view, deal with the unique while social scientists look for generalizations. The historian tries to describe and explain specific events such as the Puritan or French revolutions, while the social scientist is interested in the causes of revolution in general. (Lewy 1968, 103)

Crook and McCulloch argue that it is precisely because the history of education 'gravitates most naturally toward the study of the particular and individual context or case' that a comparative approach to the history of education is essential (2002, 397), and they also expect comparative approaches to history 'to generate or inform overarching theory and general patterns', citing examples of research that has achieved 'generalizability and theoretical advances' (398–399). In this connection, Kazamias identifies a strength in what comparative historians can achieve: 'Most historians are not theoretical, but most comparative historians and, by extension, most comparative educational historians use theoretical insights, often derived from other disciplines' (Kazamias 2001, 446). This ability to profit from a strength in approaches relatively neglected by mainstream historians deserves to be exploited by the comparativist-social scientist. Historians, Elliott argues, have been sceptical of general laws; their training – traditionally in narrative rather than the analysis that comparative history demands – has caused them to concentrate on the unique quality of what they investigate. Social scientists have clearly led the way in comparative inquiry, however, with historians trailing, despite the fact that '[e]very general law propounded by a social scientist somehow has a way of bumping up against an inconvenient fact' (170). Comparisons are clearly implicit in much of the work of historians, despite a reluctance to be explicit in ways with which social scientists are comfortable (172).

Elliott's elegant chapter is invaluable as an example of an eminent historian's analysis of his own experience; he concludes by calling for 'a more generous response' to Marc Bloch's argument in favour of comparative history (195). His account is of course written from a historian's perspective rather than that of a social scientist, but it can usefully be accommodated by the educationist-comparativist seeking to understand why history and specifically why comparison in history might be regarded as an essential element of/contributor to analysis and theory construction in education.[3]

Educational transfer; 'policy quotation'

The work of Cousin (on Prussia), of Mann (on Germany and Britain), and of Arnold (on Germany and France, especially) are implicitly concerned with the possibility of policy transfer in its basic form: what might be learnt from the experience 'elsewhere'? Sadler's multifarious inquiries also focussed on the notion of 'borrowing', with caveats now firmly established in the literature of comparative education. Researchers looking at the phenomenon of policy transfer today can profit from revisiting the thoughts on 'borrowing' of these early investigators.

'Educational transfer' is the umbrella term for ways in which ideas and practices move [and 'morph', as Cowen (2009) puts it] from one – usually national – setting to another. Often the term employed is 'borrowing', though – despite its established usage – this has always been unsatisfactory, as have alternatives such as 'copying' or 'assimilation'. (There might be a lesson to be learned here from music. When a composer uses themes from another composer's work, the process of incorporating the material into a new work is known as musical 'quotation'. When the themes are amended/developed, so that they differ from the originals, they are known as 'variations'. 'Policy quotation' and 'policy variations' might more readily describe the processes involved in the transfer of educational ideas/practice.)

In terms of comparatography, describing and analysing processes of policy transfer/ 'quotation' can be especially challenging, as the now extensive literature on the subject testifies. (The literature has grown exponentially over the past decade.) And a historical approach to the topic is particularly revealing, and in a sense inescapable, since it is completed processes that provide the best evidence for the phenomenon of transfer.

In writing about the British (specifically English) attraction to educational provision in Germany over a long historical period (Phillips 2011), as an exemplar of policy quotation with varying degrees of impact, I had to contend with a number of challenges of the kind that Elliott summarises:

> Historians are reluctant to embark on attempts at comparison until they have succeeded in corralling what appear to be all the relevant facts, Since this takes time, the process of synthesizing can be endlessly prolonged. Once a satisfactory synthesis is achieved, it is still necessary, for purposes of comparison, to identify an area or a period for which a roughly similar level of synthesis makes the exercise feasible. In the circumstances, it is understandable that all too often the game does not seem worth the candle. (Elliott 2012, 170–171)

The research involved needed to be grounded in factual knowledge of historical development in two countries, depended on an ability to read a huge range of material (both published and archival) in two languages, involved analysis of policy at various levels, attempted to devise a comparative periodisation of educational development in England and Germany, and tried to juggle much conflicting evidence from very diverse sources. Sometimes, the game did, indeed, not 'seem worth the candle'. And yet it is only when a researcher is thus deeply immersed in the unravelling and understanding of a complex historical chain of events that something approaching full understanding of present-day phenomena can be reached and, in this case, of the nature of policy transfer. It becomes inconceivable that, say, the German model of vocational training could be properly examined in terms of policy borrowing without a thorough appreciation of its historical origins, or that the particular concept of state provision in education in England could be fully appreciated without knowledge of the historical arguments which enshroud it and without contrasting it to the state's role in other nations (here the contrast with Germany is especially informative). And while it was possible to identify some processes in ways that policy was both quoted and used, as between Germany and England, that fitted with the so-called

Oxford models designed to assist in their analysis, nothing that could be described as generalisable theory could be implied from the research – though were a series of such studies to be completed the work on Germany might not unreasonably contribute to future theorising. The longstanding research on world systems theory, of fundamental importance in the context of policy quotation, is clearly rooted in historical understanding and analysis and demonstrates the efficacy of the historical dimension in creating significant theory.

Policy quotation as a research topic in comparative education essentially provides rich opportunity for historical approaches. We can only know whether a policy has been 'borrowed' and whether the borrowing has been successful or not, by examining historical examples and attempting to explain the processes involved which in turn might serve to inform any present-day attempts to import educational policy from elsewhere.

Conclusions

Comparatography inevitably draws on a very wide range of traditions, disciplines and methods. It would be disproportionate to argue for any one paradigm over another, but there is a present danger that measurement and the theory, generalisation, and nomothetic prediction it engenders, have become dominant and that there is a style of writing that rejects or at best neglects historical–philosophical approaches as irrelevant. This is particularly regrettable in an field of inquiry that is intrinsically 'broad church' in its beliefs. It would be inconceivable for many writing within the historical–philosophical tradition to be so easily dismissive of, say, the work of positivists who undertake large-scale international investigations of pupil attainment. Rather, such work can be drawn upon within historical contexts and so becomes part of the explanatory power of historical investigation.

It is not fashionable in academic life to celebrate scholarship. There was a time when it was the *sine qua non* of the activities of university teachers. Now a particular interpretation of 'research' is what determines recognition and status, and research is interpreted by the managers who now control university life in ways that do not presuppose scholarship. Breadth and multi- or interdisciplinarity are less valued in terms of research recognition. Most of the earlier generations of comparativists cited at the beginning of these reflections could rightly be described as scholars.

In an earlier paper with a focus on the need for a historical dimension in comparative inquiry I concluded that:

- Historical analysis is central to the concerns of comparativists and provides invaluable historical functions;
- Historical understanding is essential in any plans for reform and development, even if it is agreed that prediction and lesson learning are not possible on the basis of historical antecedents;
- It is necessary to absorb the methods of historical inquiry alongside other methodological skills, as every comparativist is to some extent a historian. (Phillips 2006, 291)

What I have urged in these present discursive reflections is that a historical dimension to comparative investigation should be an essential ingredient and not something to be gratuitously dismissed as an irrelevant approach rooted in earlier traditions. And that writing in comparative education, 'comparatography', would benefit from authors taking a broad scholarly approach rather than one from within a narrow theoretical framework and on the basis of non-specialist understanding of the theories espoused. As an editor of longstanding experience I would welcome something of a return to the style of the comparativists who helped to establish our field and to make it, actually and potentially, so intellectually rewarding.

Notes

1. Bereday suggests that 'should a rigorous training in one parent discipline, such as political science, be accepted as a prerequisite for comparative education, this would give its researchers strength to explore related disciplines in the manner of social scientists' (1964, 21).
2. 'We recognize a historical event because it has certain characteristics in common with other events, and while each such historical event is unique in some respects, it is also similar in other respects to other historical events' (Lewy, 1968, 103).
3. Of importance in this connection is the short study by McCulloch and Richardson (2000), aimed at the historian working on education and the educationist working on history.

References

Bereday, George. 1964. *Comparative Method in Education*. New York: Holt, Rinehart and Winston.
Bray, Mark, Bob Adamson, and Mark Mason, eds. 2007. *Comparative Education Research: Approaches and Methods*. Hong Kong: Comparative Education Research Centre & Springer.
Cowen, Robert. 2002. "Moments of Time." *History of Education* 31 (5): 413–424.
Cowen, Robert. 2009. "The Transfer, Translation and Transformation of Educational Processes: And Their Shape-Shifting?." *Comparative Education* 45 (3): 315–327.
Cowen, Robert, and Andreas M. Kazamias, eds. 2009. *International Handbook of Comparative Education*. 2 vols. Dordrecht: Springer.
Crook, David, and Gary McCulloch. 2002. "Comparative Approaches to the History of Education." *History of Education* 31 (5): 397–400.
Elliott, J. H. 2012. *History in the Making*. New Haven: Yale University Press.
Epstein, Erwin, and Katherine Carroll. 2005. "Abusing Ancestors: Historical Functionalism and the Postmodern Deviation in Comparative Education." *Comparative Education Review* 49 (1): 62–88.
Kazamias, Andreas M. 2001. "Re-Inventing the Historical in Comparative Education: Reflections on a *Protean Epistome* by a Contemporary Player." *Comparative Education* 37 (4): 439–449.
Kazamias, Andreas M. 2009. "Forgotten Men, Forgotten Themes: The Historical-philosophical-cultural and Liberal Humanist Motif in Comparative Education." In *International Handbook of Comparative Education*, Vol. 1, edited by R. Cowen and A. M. Kazamias, 37–58. New York: Springer.
Lewy, Guenter. 1968. "Historical Data in Comparative Political Analysis." *Comparative Politics* 1 (1): 103–110.
McCulloch, Gary, and William Richardson. 2000. *Historical Research in Educational Settings*. Buckingham: Open University Press.

Noah, Harold, and Max Eckstein. 1969. *Toward a Science of Comparative Education*. London: Macmillan.

Nóvoa, António, and Tali Tariv-Mashal. 2003. "Comparative Research in Education: A Mode of Governance or a Historical Journey?." *Comparative Education* 39 (4): 423–438.

Phillips, David. 1994. "Periodisation in Historical Approaches to Comparative Education: Some Considerations from the Examples of Germany and England and Wales." *British Journal of Educational Studies* 42 (3): 261–272.

Phillips, David. 2002. "Comparative Historical Studies in Education: Problems of Periodisation Reconsidered." *British Journal of Educational Studies* 50 (3): 363–377.

Phillips, David. 2006. "Comparative Education: An Approach to Educational Inquiry." In *The Sage Handbook for Research in Education*, edited by Clifton F. Conrad and Ronald C. Serlin, 279–294. Los Angeles: Sage.

Phillips, David. 2011. *The German Example: English Interest in Educational Provision in Germany Since 1800*. London: Continuum.

Phillips, David, and Michele Schweisfurth. 2014. *Comparative and International Education: An Introduction to Theory, Method, and Practice*. 2nd ed. London: Bloomsbury.

Sweeting, Anthony. 2007. "Comparing Times." In *Comparative Education Research: Approaches and Methods*, edited by M. Bray, B. Adamson, and M. Mason, 145–163.

Watson, Keith. 1998. "Memories, Models and Mapping: The Impact of Geopolitical Changes on Comparative Studies in Education." *Compare*, 28 (1): 5–31.

Neither orthodoxy nor randomness: differing logics of conducting comparative and international studies in education

Jürgen Schriewer

Philosophische Fakultät IV, Humboldt University, Berlin, Germany

The issue of the presumed 'identity' of Comparative Education as a field of study or a discipline has been discussed for decades. Yet what remains open to question is a kind of systematic structure that provides the basic principles for a coherent exposition of the field. After conceptualising and rejecting almost a dozen possible outlines for such an exposition over recent years, my contention is that 'Comparative Education' can no longer be conceived in terms of an imaginary field's coherence – let alone consistency – but, rather, in terms of distinct branches of comparative and international studies in education and their underlying *problématiques*. Such an understanding is fostered through a deepened awareness of the basic problems, and successive solutions, constitutive of the emergence and further conformations of the comparative approach in education and the social sciences. This requires analyses informed by the sociology and the history of the sciences. Thus, drawing some inspiration from the thought-provoking theses formulated by historical sociologist Friedrich H. Tenbruck, and building on some of my earlier works concerning the history and theory of comparative study, I shall try, in this essay, to untangle the structural distinctions accounting for what I propose to call the '*epistemo*-logic' of comparative social enquiry proper, the '*socio*-logic' of reform-orientated international studies on education, and the '*globo*-logic' of investigating inherently trans-national and/or world-spanning educational phenomena and organisations.

'What was cross-cultural comparison before cross-cultural comparison came into existence?' This paradoxical question titles an incisive article published in the early 1990s by Friedrich H. Tenbruck (1992), a then widely known German sociologist. However, while contrasting 'scientific cross-cultural comparisons' [wissenschaftliche Kulturvergleiche] with 'socially involved cross-cultural comparisons' [gesellschaftliche Kulturvergleiche], Tenbruck not only reveals his confusing question as being just a play on words; he also endeavours, in this article as well as in two earlier essays (Tenbruck 1981; 1989), to point out the socio-historical conditions and ontological visions giving rise to styles of doing comparative and international studies that are governed by profoundly differing logics. In what follows, I would like to use Tenbruck's somewhat provocative theses as a welcome trailblazer, as it were, suited to facilitating the discussion, in novel terms and by means of different conceptual tools, of an issue which has been debated for decades, namely Comparative Education's presumed 'identity' as a field or a discipline. My contention is that this issue can no longer be discussed in terms of 'boundaries', consolidated 'disciplinary traditions', or accumulated 'corpora of authorised knowledge' [cf. among others, Cook, Hite, and Epstein (2004)]. Nor can it adequately be discussed in solely methodological terms. This issue requires, instead, historical analyses as well as analyses in terms of the anthropology and sociology of knowledge and the sciences. Thus, the challenge set to this essay is to highlight the central *problématiques* underlying differing branches of comparative and international studies in education, and, in doing so, to untangle the structural distinctions accounting for what I propose to call the '*epistemo*-logic' of comparative social enquiry proper, the '*socio*-logic' of reform-orientated international studies on education, and the '*globo*-logic' of investigating inherently trans-national and/or world-spanning educational phenomena and organisations.[1]

I. The long route towards social-scientific comparisons: epistemo-logic

An appropriate appreciation of the uncommon distinction introduced at the beginning of this article requires an additional note. Friedrich H. Tenbruck's considerations – more precisely his incisive critique – in essence targeted Emile Durkheim's conception of sociology (influenced by contemporary ideals of positivist science) and his notion of 'society' (moulded upon the pattern of nineteenth-century nation states). In consequence of this critique, however, Tenbruck was also led to debate Durkheim's method of comparison (defined according to scientific models). This methodology, which conceived the comparative approach as 'rules for the demonstration of sociological proof' par excellence (Durkheim [1895] 1982, 147), has been a decisive turning point in the development of comparative social research.

On the one hand, this methodology built on the *grand programme* of developing comparative social and human sciences that emerged in the late eighteenth and early nineteenth centuries. Following the example set by comparative anatomy, this programme sought to transform into distinct fields specialising in the comparative study of language, religion, mythology, law, government, and education the bodies of heterogeneous knowledge that had been accumulated since the age of discovery, and particularly through the extensive late eighteenth-century expeditions led by naturalist explorers and officers. Durkheim's often quoted statement, according to which 'comparative sociology is not a special branch of sociology; it is sociology itself, in so far as it ceases to be purely descriptive and aspires to account for facts' (Durkheim [1895] 1982, 157), reconfirmed the wide-ranging expectations on both the methodically driven scientification of these fields and their transformation into increasingly autonomous disciplines. Scientification and discipline-formation, however, made it indispensable that the new fields of comparative study had to conform to the specific requirements of knowledge production that had become prevalent in the emerging system of modern science. They had to define, in other words, adequate methods and theories.

In both respects, Durkheim was able to build on the achievements brought about by illustrious predecessors. With regard to methods, this meant acknowledging a distinction already made in the eighteenth-century French *Encyclopédie* and demonstrated by Montesquieu's *Esprit des Lois*, namely the distinction between 'simple' and 'complex' comparisons or, coined in more graphic twentieth-century terms, between 'considering institutional-*cum*-organisational patterns' and 'ascertaining regular relationships under varying contextual conditions as observable in different socio-cultural settings' (Robinsohn 1970, 456). This distinction is all the more important as it provides the very basis for differentiating between comparison as a 'universal mental operation' practised in everyday social life and comparison transformed into a specific 'method of the social sciences'. As developed in greater detail elsewhere [cf. especially Schriewer (1990; 2007)], comparison as a social-scientific method does not consist in 'establishing relations between observable facts' but, rather, in 'establishing relations between relationships or whole patterns of relationships'. Only in the latter form, and due to its more abstract approach, did it become possible to make use of the comparative method to investigate, informed by theoretical concepts and models or by morphological types amenable to variation, the multiple interrelations assumed to exist between the phenomena of interest – be these different myths and religious representations or varying patterns of legal, educational, or political organisation – and their formation by, and impact upon, different socio-historical settings.

With respect to theories, Europe-wide processes of scholarly and intellectual exchange from the late eighteenth century onwards generated concepts and models – such as 'function', 'organisation/organism' or 'culture' – that on their part came towards meeting the requirements of the method of comparison (Eggers and Rothe 2009; Luhmann 1995b). These concepts were suitable not only for structuring operations of 'establishing relations between relationships'; of no less importance was the fact that they had increasingly incorporated into their meaning mental attitudes and corresponding cognitive styles that had taken a long time to fully unfold. While presupposing that the emotionally binding force of an observer's social group interests, value systems and social orientation patterns be suspended, the styles of 'detachment' and 'perspectivism' invited scholars to explore the phenomena of interest not in disjointed isolation, but always in terms of their structural elaboration over time as well as of their interrelations with more encompassing societal and socio-political contextual conditions. In varying proportions, therefore, these cognitive styles and the corresponding concepts of 'function', 'organism' and 'culture' combined the posture of cultural relativism with forms of perceiving, comprehending and interpreting things in historical and sociological perspectives. By leading the comparative scholar to systematically understand the phenomena under study by means of grasping their embeddedness in, and interrelationships with, distinctive socio-historical contexts, this 'culturalist' or 'contextualising' mode of looking at subjects and articulating *problématiques* gained virtually research-framing significance for the further development of the comparative social and human sciences.

On the other hand, in spite of these methodical, conceptual and cognitional advances, a central problem directly related to the late eighteenth-century *grand programme* of increasing scientification through comparative research still remained unresolved. The promise of achieving a higher degree of scientificalness by way of comparative enquiry implied – and continues to imply – that the comparative approach had to fulfil, couched in the graphic terms of modern epistemology, methodically arranged 'bridging' functions (Albert 1972, 13ff.). This involved bridging the gap between spatio-temporally specific observations and more generalised models, concepts and assumptions, or between propositions regarding empirical findings (gathered in particular areas, societies, nations or wider socio-historical regions) and propositions pertaining to some strand of theorising (in education and the social sciences). Attempts at solving the comparative 'bridging' problem, however, were reliant upon far-reaching presuppositions. These included not only assumptions concerning the ontological constitution of social reality and the degree to which the social would be susceptible to theorisation, but also the epistemological preferences given to either an inductive or a deductive approach as well as the underlying understanding of the 'scientific method' as such. Moreover, these were presuppositions that, for their part, were to be explicated only during the later nineteenth century in reaction to, or by way of critical discussion of, the all-embracing progress achieved by the natural sciences. In this situation, it was the particular achievement of Durkheim to take up the aforementioned methodical, conceptual and cognitional advances, and to closely combine them with the logic of scientific induction worked out by John Stuart Mill (1843) and the logic of scientific experimentation successfully demonstrated by French physiologist Claude Bernard (1865). From the former, Durkheim adopted the rules of inductive reasoning, i.e. the method of difference, the method of agreement and the method of concomitant variations to which he attached particular importance. From Bernard, Durkheim borrowed more than the epistemological approach of a hypothetical-deductive life science. Together with the transfer of this approach from living nature to social life, in other terms from physiology to sociology, he also transformed the natural sciences experiment into the only substitute form that seemed to him appropriate for macro-social research: the comparative method [cf. in greater detail, Schriewer (2003, 5ff.)]. This transformation had considerable consequences. From that point on, social-scientific comparison was insufficiently defined if it was labelled merely a 'method'. Durkheim's transformation, worked out further by his successors, made something different of comparison than a 'method' in the sense of a specific technique of data collection or the drawing up of a survey. The connection of the epistemic components mentioned so far – an elaborated method of establishing relations between relationships, innovative theoretical concepts specifically adapted to this way of establishing relations, cognitive styles leading over to a central research-framing *problématique*, and an analytical logic equivalent to experimentation – resulted, rather, in a distinctive research approach tending toward acquiring, structuring, and analysing data in a creative way. According to varying theoretical orientations, then, this research approach was introduced into subsequent methodologies as a 'meta-method' (Strodtbeck 1964, 223ff.), as a 'quasi'- or 'ex-post-facto' experiment (Berstecher 1970, 29ff.), or as a 'complex research approach' (Lijphart 1971, 683).

The Durkheimian appreciation of the comparative method as the 'high road' of macro-social research delineated the starting point for the numerous comparative methodologies that were developed in increasingly sophisticated forms, and mostly in the framework of epistemological positions rooted in the orthodox philosophy of science (e.g. Nagel 1961), especially after World War II. Initially worked out within the framework of comparative sociology and political science (Lijphart 1971; Mayer 1989; Przeworski and Teune 1970; Smelser 1976), this mainstream methodology of comparative social inquiry met with general acceptance in other fields of study as well, such as cross-cultural psychology, cultural anthropology, and comparative education [cf. among others: Berstecher (1970), Niessen and Peschar (1982), and Noah and Eckstein (1969)]. Nonetheless, this strand of methodological thinking entailed a serious legacy. The repeated borrowing of epistemological and methodological models from the natural sciences – first, towards the late eighteenth century, from comparative anatomy, then, due to the Durkheimian redefinition of the comparative method, from experimental physiology – explains the long-lasting commitment of this strand's underlying assumptions to the understanding of causality prevailing in the natural sciences. Just as Durkheim declared in his *Rules*, and as present-day methodological considerations did not fail to confirm, comparison as a quasi-experimental mode of analysis makes sense only under the condition that the validity of the principle of causality is taken for granted. While Karl Popper in his epistemological considerations was more cautious when declaring the 'belief in causality' a 'typical metaphysical hypostatization of a well justified methodological rule', namely 'the scientist's decision never to abandon his search for laws' (Popper 1968, 248), up to a very recent past, comparative educationalists committed to the social-scientific mainstream tradition were much more direct in voicing their ontological belief, as it were:

> It is assumed that there exists a certain degree of order and uniformity in the world, that events are not random but are connected in a regular and constant way. As Einstein's famous aphorism put it, 'the lord is subtle, but he isn't simply mean'. (Farrell 1986, 205)

Not surprisingly, then, even outstanding comparative historians subscribed to the view that comparative research strategies directed at explanation be grounded on the postulate of the validity of unambiguous and regular causal relationships between causes and effects. Formulations by Marc Bloch or Fritz Ringer, stating that 'a general phenomenon can only be the result of equally general causes' (Bloch 1963, 24ff.; Ringer 1979, 1), seem like a late replication to Durkheim's dictum that 'to the same effect there always corresponds the same cause' ([1895] 1982, 150).

The social-scientific mainstream methodology of comparative research and its presuppositions have not gone unchallenged, though. Several decades of practising this style of comparative enquiry, and its often unconvincing explanations, have led to a radical questioning of its basic theoretical, methodological, and ontological assumptions. Moreover, diverse strands of so-called post-Newtonian science have stimulated wide-ranging processes of 'unthinking social science' (Wallerstein 1991) and conceived the contours of an ontology in which the notion of 'linear causality' is substituted by altered visions both of the natural world and of the social world of man. Thus, the natural sciences as well have increasingly been confronted with an unstable and unpredictable world, a world characterised by the predominance of 'nonlinearity over linearity [and] complexity over simplification', by the impossibility of removing the measurer from the measurement and, most importantly, by the crucial role played by the 'arrow of time' (Gulbenkian Commission 1996). By extension, from the 1970s and 1980s onwards, and with reference to such developments, divergent paradigms in social theorising have evolved, fostering, in correspondence with novel frames of insight, altered forms of realising the 'epistemo-logic' of comparative social enquiry. Such are, to name but a few, (i) a 'functional-*cum*-configurative' approach to comparative analysis, defined in the framework of the theory of self-referential social systems, and bringing to fruition its underlying principles of 'complex causality' and 'functional alternatives' (Schriewer 2003); (ii) comparative-historical approaches referring to self-organisation theories, and aiming to reconstruct the 'morphogenetic character of socio-cultural systems' which are assumed to build up through time in the form of reiterated sequences of structure–social interaction–structural elaboration (Archer 1982, 5 ff.; 1995, 165ff.); (iii) comparative analyses rooted in historical institutionalism and its presuppositions of 'self-reinforcing feedback mechanisms', 'national trajectories', and 'path-dependency' (e.g. Thelen 1999; 2004).

The differences between these theories and their underlying assumptions notwithstanding, however, in comparative research designs conceptualised in the framework of any of these paradigms, the integral components debated so far work together in combination: (a) the phrasing, in the framework of a developed social theory, of a guiding *problématique*; (b) the cognitive styles of 'detachment' and 'perspectivism'; (c) the particular sensitivity to socio-cultural differences, and the exploration of these differences with regard to assumed relationships, whole interrelationship patterns, or distinctive systems configurations amenable to variation; and, finally, (d) the complex techniques of establishing relations between relationships. The combined operation of these components makes up the 'epistemo'-logic of comparative enquiry in education and the social sciences, which is geared towards methodically arranging – with a view to critically examining theories and ideologies, cautiously constructing explanations, or contributing to grounded theory building – the confrontation of theoretical propositions, models, or *problématiques* with socio-historically specific data, conditions, or configurations.

II. The resilience of socially involved comparisons: socio-logic

Unsurprisingly, 'socially involved comparisons' according to the term coined by Friedrich Tenbruck follow a logic that is definitely opposed to the previous one with regard to all components discussed so far. Nevertheless, Tenbruck neither depreciated nor downgraded this genre of comparisons to earlier historical stages in the development of an emerging field as a good many textbooks would do, not to mention treatises rooted in the orthodox philosophy of science (e.g. Noah and Eckstein 1969). Rather, he wanted to highlight the omnipresence, the ongoing resilience, and the social impact of a style of describing socio-cultural otherness that can be traced back in history for centuries, if not millennia. In so doing, he called to mind the ubiquitous reality of varied processes of encounter with, interaction between, or interpenetration of different ethnic tribes, social groups, whole societies, nations, and larger socio-historical contexts defined by religion or common culture. Obviously, such processes have included – and continue to include – the most varied forms of migration, mission, or colonisation, of competition, warfare, and conquest as well as of large-scale population expansion, and of intense relations of exchange both of commodities and of technologies, skills, and learning. Likewise, such processes not only included a multitude of dissemination and adaptation processes, and of operations of lending and borrowing, but also – a fact that matters particularly in this context – varying kinds of observing, reporting about, and assessing other peoples, societies, and socio-cultural configurations. As developed in greater detail elsewhere (Schriewer 1990), these observations and the attendant reports were not primarily intended to provide undistorted analyses of other groups or peoples. Rather, they usually resulted in biased forms of describing and interpreting strangers and newcomers, and of evaluating them subject to the observers' own socio-cultural frames of reference, concerns for self-assertion, and vital group interests. As a rule, therefore, the mental attitudes governing these descriptions were those of 'involvement' and 'socio-centrism' (giving preference to the comparative style of 'establishing relations between observable facts'), not the attitudes of 'detachment' and 'perspectivism' (correlating with the style of 'establishing relations between relationships'). Furthermore, it was in consideration of these descriptions' and interpretations' commitment to a social group's or society's concerns, value systems, and collective self-assertion that Tenbruck had coined the term 'socially involved cross-cultural comparisons', clearly contrasting it to the 'scientific' style of comparisons.

Clearly, just as the proponents of the rising fields of social science-oriented comparative enquiry had felt compelled to conform, from roughly 1800 onwards, to the specific requirements of knowledge production that had become prevalent in the emerging system of modern science, so the practitioners of 'socially involved comparisons' for their part had to conform to a changing environment. In the course of nineteenth-century modernisation processes, they had to conform to the demands formulated by the politicians and administrators of the emerging nation states who were preoccupied with shaping an increasing range of fields of public policy, including the judiciary, railway and communication systems, public health, and, particularly, national education. Accordingly, the problems raised by the organisation of these fields were not theoretical in nature, but practical and technical. In other words, the expectations associated with 'socially involved comparisons' were not directed towards theoretical *problématiques* that need processing with regard to claims to scientific truth, but towards social and political problems that call for answers suited to meeting requirements of practicality, policy relevance and justification. The role that the endless series of international reports, comparative surveys, and meticulous descriptions of other countries' educational organisation – associated with the names of, among others, Victor Cousin, Horace Mann, Domingo Faustino Sarmiento, Matthew Arnold, and Mori Arinori – came to play throughout the nineteenth century was meant to correspond to such expectations. In the course of the twentieth century, these reports, surveys, and descriptions considerably enlarged both their scope and their impact due to a broadened infrastructure (such as specialised institutes and improved facilities for travel), growing collections of data (as a consequence of the activities of international exhibitions and organisations), and new techniques (such as international statistics). Over the last decades, then, the recognition of purportedly common problems in different countries and the identification of apparently transnational issues have even increased the political weight of new styles of reform-orientated reports and surveys advocating definitely international arguments, models, and policies. While these reports and surveys could not simply deny their 'involvement' in pressing social, national, and even trans-national concerns, the primordial stance of unfiltered 'socio-centrism' became tamed, as it were, and sublimated into a social system's relations with itself – in other words into educational systems' committed self-reflection and reform discourses. According to a somewhat intricate, yet exacting, sociology-of-knowledge phrasing, the descriptions, reports, and surveys in question turned into 'descriptions of otherness bound to a system's self-descriptions, and informed by notions proper to that system' (cf. Schriewer 1990, 51ff.; Stichweh 2008, 46ff.).

Traditionally, although to varying degrees, these 'committed' descriptions assumed the form of largely descriptive, a-theoretical, and methodologically weak studies on the educational systems and/or policies in a range of different countries. In this sense, a research report established by recognised experts, and covering various fields of so-called 'comparative policy research', is highly revealing. The concluding chapter, the purport of which has been confirmed by numerous other state-of-the-art reviews, states:

> One of the most serious conclusions to be drawn across the board in this review is that too many comparative research projects are *a-theoretical in their design* or that their *theoretical basis is largely underdeveloped*. They remain *descriptive* rather than *analytical*, and they are thus *unable to provide a basis for more general understanding and prediction*. (Berthoin Antal 1987, 500 – emphasis added)

Unsurprisingly, then, the vast corpus of expert reports, descriptions of foreign systems of education, and surveys of the putative 'major problems of world education' successively accumulated over nearly 100 years constituted a momentous legacy that did not fail to affect the comparative studies in education institutionalised in universities and colleges of education from the 1900s onwards. Moreover, the unfolding of these studies in terms of an academic field was also complicated by the fact that educational studies more generally, i.e. the new field's umbrella subject, had not emerged as a 'discipline' proper, similar for instance to physics, biology or sociology, but – according to a committed view from inside – as a 'composite area of study' (Hirst 1983) or – according to a sociological view from outside – as an 'inter'- respectively 'trans-disciplinary subject' (Luhmann and Schorr 1988, 363ff.). Analyses carried through in the framework of a historical sociology of science have reconstructed in greater detail the reasons for this 'hybrid' status of the subject (Stichweh 1994, 278ff.). These analyses have actually shown how the rise of the modern research university entailed a new, and increasingly clear-cut differentiation between 'disciplines' (oriented towards research and theory-building) and 'professions' (initially meaning only the traditional professions trained in the faculties of law, medicine and theology) as well as, within the latter, a differentiation between the 'core roles of professional practitioners' and 'professional elites' or 'establishments' who do not practise themselves but are in charge of elaborating and teaching profession-related knowledge. Usually placed in academic positions, these elites or establishments on their part had to come to terms with divergent commitments: the commitment to a professional field and its ongoing improvement and the commitment to scientific research and academic values. Imbalances and conflicts that did not fail to ensue were counterpoised by yet another differentiation, which in turn repeated the differentiation between disciplines and professions within a professional establishment itself. Such is the difference between 'basic research' and 'clinical disciplines', long established in the faculties of medicine. In a similar yet slightly different way, professional establishments that developed more recently, such as educational studies, opted for strategies that, in a loosely coupled interdisciplinary context, leave room for both growing scientification and the maintenance of a strong focus on profession-related issues and knowledge, in other words for 'scientific theories' and 'reflection theories' (Luhmann and Schorr 1988).

Structural conditions of this kind explain, then, the dichotomy, repeatedly noted in state-of-the-art reviews, between well-conceptualised social-scientific types of comparative enquiry and methodologically informal types of socially involved comparison. Couched in the sociology-of-knowledge terms mentioned earlier on, this dichotomy between 'systems analyses from outside informed by social science constructs' and 'descriptions of otherness bound to a system's self-descriptions, and informed by notions proper to that system' (cf. Schriewer 1990, 51ff.; Stichweh 2008, 46ff.) can be traced to almost every aspect that is instrumental in defining a comparative research design, namely:

- the specification of the research *problématique* (in terms of a theoretical versus a social and/or political problem);
- the style of comparative relational operations involved (i.e. 'complex' versus 'simple' operations, or, technically speaking, establishing relations between relationships versus establishing relations between observable facts);
- the choice of adequate units of comparison (according to the theoretical fruitfulness of distinctive units of analysis or the policy pertinence of 'significant' reference units); and finally
- the type of relevance implied for evidence-supported advice or policy-formulation (by way of deepened insight into the workings of particular educational arrangements and their structural conditions for change or by constructing 'international standards' and 'perspectives' amenable to politico-ideological interpretation).

However implicitly or explicitly analysed, dichotomous structures of this kind have not remained unnoticed in the methodological debates regarding comparative studies in education. For some time already, critics have established distinctions between, for example, 'comparative education research' and 'international development education', or, more succinctly, between 'academic comparative education' intending explanatory propositions by way of cross-national analysis and 'interventionist comparative education' intending to 'constrain educational decision-making [and] to act upon the educational world'. Likewise, authors have underscored the logical gap and methodological tensions that exist between contrasting objectives such as 'scientificity' and 'practicality'; between 'academic interests' in 'objective research' and 'melioristic interests' in 'professional practice and remedy'; or between the 'search for truth' in accordance with social science models of comparative enquiry and comparative education's 'reformist purpose [rooted in] the normative or reform tendencies' of that field [cf. for corresponding source materials, Schriewer (1990)]. Such distinctions are far from being peculiar to educational studies. A cleavage between divergent intellectual orientations can be shown to pervade those comparative (sub-)disciplines that – to speak in terms of Luhmannian differentiation theory (Luhmann [1997] 2012–2013) – are structurally committed to describing, and theorising about functionally specific sub-systems of society, and entrusted with assisting these systems' professions. Contrasting modes of perceiving and thinking, shaped in accordance with different frames of reference – with scientific search for truth or with a sub-system's needs for self-description and guidance – transform one and the same object domain into distinct subject-matters of study. Thus, from the first perspective, the families of law and legal systems of the past and present, the great religions that have crystallised in the course of history, or the systems of education built up all over the world are explored in terms of context-bound, essentially contingent socio-historical phenomena and of the long-term social and cultural effects they engender. From the second perspective, in contrast, they become the subject of involved forms of analysis tending to affirmatively appraise, to criticise from value-laden standpoints, or to reformulate in melioristic terms the institutional practices under study as well as the patterns of dogmatic, moral, or spiritual meaning these convey.

What needs to be determined, finally, beyond identifying the structural conditions of 'hybrid' fields of study, is the 'socio'-logic peculiar to those styles of comparative study, which are involved in the self-descriptions, and committed to the self-steering of functionally specific sub-systems, but which, as a rule, are weak in terms of comparative methodology and questionable in terms of explanatory power. What is at issue, in other words, are the specific arguments to be gained through 'methodological informal types of [comparative] research […] often characterised by a combination of a descriptive approach and a rather pronounced normative commitment' (Hüfner, Meyer, and Naumann 1987, 192ff.). As argued in greater detail elsewhere (Schriewer 1990), the theory of self-referential social systems developed by Niklas Luhmann proffers a framework suited for this kind of analysis (Luhmann 1995a; Luhmann and Schorr 1988). In particular, the Luhmannian concepts of 'reflection', 'interruptions in relations of interdependence', and 'externalisation' offer the analytical tools which make it possible to decipher – with regard to contextual conditions, prevailing rationales, relevant topics, and reference societies (or model states) selected – those bodies of literature which may be termed, not as comparative enquiry proper, but as international reform-orientated reflection or international policy studies. Corresponding analyses have to start from the self-referential nature of the core components of educational studies, i.e. reflection theories. Like any form of self-reference, reflection theories embedded in, and focusing on particular social sub-systems need to interrupt the relations of interdependence caused by the circular nature of the reflection process. Such interruptions typically take the form of the reflection and communication process opening itself to its external environment, however selectively this may be done, for it is through the incorporation of 'supplemental meaning', as extractable from external points of reference, that circular self-reference becomes amenable to specification (Luhmann 1995a, 466).

Typical patterns of externalisation used in educational theory in general are the recourse to values and value-laden ideologies as well as to organisation (Luhmann and Schorr 1988, 338ff.). But they are far from being the only forms of externalisation. Rather, a good many operations of resorting to history ('traditionalisation') or to internationality ('externalisation' in a restricted sense) are no less significant nor less widespread. Thus, the strands of conventional comparative study found to be weak in terms of methodology and questionable in terms of theorisation perfectly comply with the structural need for externalisation intrinsic to reform-orientated reflection theory on education or policy-related educational discourse. From a perspective internal to a national education system, and from within a discourse constellation committed to this system's reform issues and practical concerns, references to 'examples abroad', to 'international experience', or to 'world situations' are actually understood as providing something more than objectively researched analyses of the contemporary situation in other countries. Rather, such references are expected to serve as 'lessons', to provide 'stimulating ideas' and 'new impetus to policy definition', or to supply a 'frame of reference' for the specification of reform options. The act of 'looking beyond one's frontiers at comparable countries' is thus conceived, in terms particularly indicative of the intended absorption of supplemental meaning through externalisation, as a 'system opening itself outwards [...] to external stimuli' [for these quotes and more source materials, cf. Schriewer (1990, 65ff.)]. Regarding their potential for sifting out supplemental meaning, all these and related references to 'model states' and 'examples abroad', to 'world situations', and to a supposed level of 'international standards' represent forms of selectively resorting to the external environment of reform-oriented educational reflection that provide justification (of values or value-based ideologies), legitimisation (for reform measures, innovations or administrative regulations), self-affirmation (for maintaining idiosyncratic models or practices), or inspiration (for conceiving of novel models and policy solutions).

From a sociology-of-knowledge point of view, therefore, externalisations to international reference horizons are not devised to generate social-scientific knowledge by means of comparative investigation into distinct cultural configurations. They involve, rather, the selective interpretation of international data, structures, or issues with a view to sifting out arguments that are 'relevant' in terms of educational policy and practice. A distinction once introduced by one of the founding fathers of comparative studies in education in the German-speaking countries is particularly instructive in this respect. In fact, Friedrich Schneider clearly rejected contemporary attempts at establishing a 'science of comparative education' patterned, for instance, on examples from comparative religion, and drawing on 'scientific cross-cultural comparison' [*komparative Methode*] in the sense of a methodologically defined approach to scrutinising socio-cultural differences. Drawing, instead, on Paul Monroe and his predecessors and associates at Teachers College, Columbia University, Schneider no less clearly preferred the more implicit procedures of 'considering international organisation patterns' [*vergleichende Betrachtung*], practised with a view to 'synthesising educational problems, ideas, and currents common to all nations' (Schneider 1931–1932, 243 and 403ff.). From such a perspective, then, distinct nations, societies, or civilisations are not used as units of analysis relevant in terms of both their theoretical fruitfulness and the range of variation they represent for comparative enquiry. They rather serve as arbitrarily selected reference units which may be brought into play subject to the policy arguments of current interest. They turn into carriers of 'trans-national standards', or of a supposed 'superiority' and 'progressiveness' which are vested with a quasi-normative character (Waldow 2010). Such were the 'países que están al frente de la civilización del mundo' [countries at the forefront of world civilisation] so characteristically evoked by a nineteenth-century Spanish author (in Pedró 1987, 163ff.), and so are – in no less typical terms – the 'world class countries' or 'world class initiatives and practices' constructed by present-day educational reformers (Boyle Swiniarski 2014; Chalker and Haynes 1994). As the last quotations indicate, the world-encompassing web of cross-system observations and externalisations woven over the past decades has been supplemented, more recently, both by new forms of externalisation and by new agencies of reform discourse. Among the new forms of externalisation, international benchmarking and the comparative ranking of (highly selective and decontextualised) performance indicators in the form of league tables have become prominent in an increasing number of public policy fields, in education and health services as well as in telecommunication markets, employment services, or social security systems. Among the new agencies, international organisations – be they governmental or non-governmental – have dramatically increased their number and their impact. In some instances, such as the OECD, new agencies and new forms of externalisation even go hand in hand. With good reasons, therefore, have the enormous proliferation of international organisations, and the increasing role they play in generating, legitimating, and disseminating both international models for reform and world-level cultural principles based on normative ideas of progress and universalism, become a major research topic for world-systems analyses (Boli and Thomas 1999).

III. Analysing trans-societal structures and world-systems: globo-logic

In addition to its distinctive understanding of causality, the social-scientific mainstream tradition of comparative enquiry had left yet another serious legacy. This legacy was related to the fact that the discipline-formation processes of most of the human and social sciences coincided with the full realisation of the modern nation state, at least in the sense of an institutionalised model (Meyer and Hannan 1979). As a consequence, these disciplines were increasingly constituted with reference to a national context: as political economy; as *Staatswissenschaften* (i.e. political and administrative sciences committed to a particular polity); as historiography of a distinctive nation; as philological and literary disciplines specialising in the study of national languages and literatures; or, finally, as educational studies meant to legitimise, and provide professional knowledge for, a national system of education. Inevitably, then, nation states and national societies became the self-evident subject-matter of study for the comparative branches or sub-fields of those disciplines. Well into the second half of the twentieth century, an international environment defined by nation states and their rivalries, conflicts, and alliances – in other words, the 'interstate system' (Meyer and Hannan 1979) – constituted a political-*cum*-historical setting thought to be virtually without alternative for the development and ongoing practice of comparative study. The uncontested dominance of cross-*national* – and, at best, cross-*cultural* – comparisons even found expression in the conceptual focus of methodological treatises and discussions (e.g. Berstecher 1970; Kohn 1989; Kriesi 2007; Lijphart 1971). Moreover, this dominance was additionally reinforced by the logical premises of experimental science which, as outlined above, played a crucial role in shaping the mainstream methodology of comparative social enquiry. These premises for their part implied the unequivocal distinction between units of comparison conceived as mutually independent and virtually autarchic entities, suited, exactly because of this, to meeting the quasi-experimental logic of analysis. Accordingly, these premises tended to ignore the manifold relations of influence, joint filiation, interference, and interdependency which have, to varying degrees, always been in existence between historically concrete units of analysis. Therefore, due to its very epistemological presuppositions, the elaborate scientific approach of comparative social enquiry reinforced the reductive vision of a world that, as laid down by methodological nationalism, seemed to consist of clearly distinguishable entities defined as nation states and thought to be intrinsically coherent due to internal homogenisation processes.[2]

It was against reductive visions of this kind that Friedrich Tenbruck, in the series of essays introduced at the beginning of this article, levelled his criticisms. He emphatically insisted on the time-bound character of the concepts of nation state and national society. He claimed that their taking as immutable what was merely a transient state of affairs was a serious misconception of the comparative social sciences:

> Namely the self-image of nineteenth-century nations concerned about their cultural individuality and political sovereignty, for which [...] the identity of the people, culture, nation and state was an obvious lesson to be learnt from history. (Tenbruck 1981, 348)

From the vantage point of macro-history, and in contrast to the premises of quasi-experimental analysis, Tenbruck moreover maintained, any form of inter-cultural encounter as well as of 'socially involved comparisons' attendant on such encounters have always made up the essential forces fuelling processes of social change and societal modernisation. Hence his intriguing apology, mentioned earlier, of the 'socially involved' style of comparison, which he considered more universal and more powerful with regard to its impact on ongoing social processes than 'scientific cross-cultural comparisons'. Tenbruck therefore proposed to replace the 'single-society model' that had come to dominate in the wake of Durkheim – the model of a multiplicity of clearly distinguishable, autonomous societies thought to develop by virtue of essentially endogenous forces – by a 'multi-society model' defined as such in order to put the emphasis on the ubiquity and effectiveness of encounters, interactions, and interconnections between a multitude of different societies. Likewise, he rejected the 'dogma of internal causation' of social change, which relied on the assumption of specific development potentials intrinsic to every society, maintaining, instead, that it have always been inter-cultural encounters that have acted – and continue acting – as the 'real driving force of history'. Tenbruck accordingly declined the genetic conception of development, which presupposes a 'general law of endogenous development' purportedly to be discovered by way of comparing its parallel manifestations in different national societies and cultures, and replaced it by an inter-actionist understanding of social processes, thereby emphasising the 'real significance [...] of inter-societal relations and processes' (Tenbruck 1992, 16). Finally, he drew conclusions of a twofold nature for a non-reductionist social research. He definitely relegated – in method – the quasi-experimental model of comparative social enquiry in favour of wide-ranging socio-historical analyses of inter-societal and inter-cultural interactions.

And he no less definitely advocated – in theory – replacing the concept of 'national history' or 'history of a society' by that of 'world history'. As the latter concept indicates, Tenbruck extrapolated inter-societal processes of the past into the present and future in order to open his analyses – well before 'globalisation' became a fashionable catchword for interpreting an increasingly complex social reality – to the dynamism of world-level interrelations and interconnections indicative of an emerging world society.

From the last third of the twentieth century onwards, several lines of innovative research have taken up, empirically substantiated, and conceptually developed, the theoretical and methodological challenges contained in Tenbruck's argument. These lines of research include, for instance, new approaches to transfer analysis (cf. Espagne 1999; Steiner-Khamsi 2004); analyses of dissemination and adoption processes – of institutions, models, and ideas – ranging widely over long periods of time and distant civilisations (e.g. Badie 1992); the empirical elucidation of the emergence of definitely trans-societal institutions, models, and organisation patterns from the nineteenth century onwards (Thomas et al. 1987); and, finally, in response to ideas once developed by Fernand Braudel, analyses of the emergence of a global world system (cf. Wallerstein 1974–2011). Each of these strands definitely puts the emphasis on *trans*-national, *trans*-cultural, or *trans*-societal relations, transfers, and interconnections and sees itself, thus, as a conceptual alternative to the social-scientific mainstream of comparative enquiry traditionally conceived as *cross*-national, *cross*-cultural, or *cross*-societal analysis. Each of the new approaches espouses explicit criticisms – just as Tenbruck did – not only of the presuppositions underlying the mainstream tradition of comparative social research (e.g. the assumption that nations or societies constitute virtually autarchic entities provided with endogenous development potentials), but also of this tradition's epistemic possibilities (e.g. of offering macro-causal explanations and facilitating quasi-experimental theory building). And each of these approaches consequently focuses on units of analysis that are given, not in the form of entities clearly delimited from one another as distinct nations, societies, or socio-cultural settings, but in the form of definitely '*trans*-societal structures' (McMichael 1990, emphasis added). Trans-societal structures in this sense can be tailored in various ways so as to be located on different levels of analysis:

- on the level of cross-border relations, migration movements, or exchange and transfer processes between territorially bound nation states and societies (e.g. Alarcón 2014; Cowen and Klerides 2009; Rappleye 2012; Robertson 2013; Schriewer and Caruso 2005);
- in the form of regions that have taken shape both at the *infra*-national level, such as *Länder*, *autonomías,* cantons, or interlinked areas of trans-border cooperation, and at the *supra*-national level, such as rims – for example the Baltic or the Pacific Rim – or continent-wide mega-regions interconnected by economic exchange relations and/or specific socio-cultural traditions (e.g. Blatter 2000; Cowen 1997; Jules 2012);
- on the level of 'world cities' working as global trendsetters and communication hubs or of cosmopolitan elites whose range of activity extends world-wide (e.g. Hartmann 1999; Sassen 1994);
- on the level of definitely trans-national social groups, networks, and organisations (Boli and Thomas 1999; Charle, Schriewer, and Wagner 2004; Roldán Vera and Schupp 2005); or

- on the level of international relations and the formation and re-formation of successive interstate systems (Buzan and Little 2000).

Finally, trans-societal structures of the kinds just itemised are yet surpassed by definitely global structures which – numerous precursor trends and phenomena notwithstanding – have grown into a dominant feature of the modern world (Bayly 2004). They have become the subject of impressive strands of world-systems theories and globalisation research which draw on concepts, models, and analytical approaches stemming from strands of thought as different as economic history, political economy, social geography, and theories of communication, social differentiation and organisation [cf. the overview by Rossi (2007)]. The common *problématique* in these theories and strands of research is directed at explaining the emergence of the one interconnected world system and exploring the degree to which its all-encompassing nature acts as a global reality exogenous to, and impinging on, the distinct societal, national, and socio-cultural entities it embraces. Thus, although differing as regards their theoretical focus, 'globo'-logic explanations are at the centre of some of the most prominent world system theories. Immanuel Wallerstein, for instance, drawing largely on economic history in conjunction with critical politico-economic schemes of interpretation, defines the world system in terms of an irrevocably interwoven 'world capitalist economy' (Wallerstein 1974–2011), while John W. Meyer and his associates, drawing on neo-institutional theory combined with the sociology of knowledge, conceive the globalised world not primarily in structural, but in cultural terms as a 'transnational cultural environment' or 'world culture' (Meyer 2009). The conceptualisation of 'world society' by Niklas Luhmann, finally, rests on his theory of the functional differentiation of society, which is seen as an irreversible pattern of modernity as such, and on the assumption of a world-encompassing dynamics of communication inherent in this pattern (Luhmann [1997] 2012–2013). Inevitably, then, these theories also tend to favour forms of investigation thought to be commensurate with the 'globo'-logic they involve, such as macro-historical analyses or large-scale quantitative surveys including data from all nation states or state-like organised entities existing in the world at a given period in time.

Especially in conjunction with arguments developed along Wallersteinian lines or with reference to the neo-institutionalist 'world society' model, such methodological approaches have found tremendous response in comparative and international studies in education. These arguments and models have stimulated numerous analyses of the emergence of global patterns of educational governance, of economy-driven transnational policies in education, or analyses seeking to demonstrate the increasingly global homogenisation of patterns of schooling, content and instruction, and educational organisation more generally (cf., e.g. Baker and Wiseman 2007; Dale 2005). Nonetheless, these models, analyses, and findings have not remained uncontested. Thus, the neo-institutionalist 'transnational cultural environment' argument is being challenged by theoretical alternatives assuming, for instance, a more inter-actionist approach towards explaining world-level interconnectedness (e.g. Schwinn 2012). Likewise, the theses positing the purportedly unavoidable world-level standardisation of educational organisation patterns, models, or policies are contested on their part by empirical – particularly historical-*cum*-comparative – research throwing into relief the deviation-generating impact of varying processes of the adoption, appropriation, and re-contextualisation on the local or regional level of the patterns, models, ideas, and policies disseminated internationally (Bruno-Jofré and Schriewer 2012; Schriewer 2004).

In this sense, world systems theories on their part, as well as their extensions into the field of educational studies, are subject to the test of empirical counter-evidence and theoretical challenge. They participate, with a view to ascertaining their scope, their inspirational power, and their potentials for explanation, in the reiteratively arranged confrontation of theoretical models and analyses with empirical evidence characteristic of any theory-informed social research (Schriewer 2012).

Notes

1. Sincere apologies are addressed to the *aficionados* of correct English style for the neologisms I thus introduce.
2. The logical problem resulting from the fact that such entities nonetheless stood in historically evolved relations of interaction and interconnection and that, accordingly, the conclusiveness of explanatory arguments based on comparative analysis remained questionable was occasionally discussed as 'Galton's problem', to be sure. Essentially, however, this problem was pushed back into anthropology, and has aroused little, if any, serious attention among comparativists in fields such as education or politics (Kleinschmidt 1991).

References

Alarcón, C. 2014. *Modelltransfer im Schatten des Krieges: 'Deutsche' Bildungs- und 'Preußische' Militärreformen in Chile, 1879–1920 [Model Transfer in the Shadow of War: 'German' Educational and 'Prussian' Military Reforms in Chile, 1879–1920]*. Frankfurt am Main etc.: Peter Lang.

Albert, H., ed. 1972. *Theorie und Realität. Ausgewählte Aufsätze zur Wissenschaftslehre der Sozialwissenschaften [Theory and Reality. Selected Essays on the Epistemology of the Social Sciences]*. Tübingen: Mohr.

Archer, M. S., ed. 1982. *The Sociology of Educational Expansion. Take-off, Growth and Inflation in Educational Systems*. Beverly Hills: Sage.

Archer, M. S. 1995. *Realist Social Theory: The Morphogenetic Approach*. Cambridge, Cambridge University Press.

Badie, B. 1992. *L'Etat importé. Essai sur l'occidentalisation de l'ordre politique [The Imported State. Essay on the Westernisation of Political Organisation]*. Paris: Fayard.

Baker, D. P., and A. W. Wiseman, eds. 2007. *The Impact of Comparative Education Research on Institutional Theory*. Bingley, UK: JAI Press.

Bayly, C. 2004. *The Birth of the Modern World 1780–1914. Global Connections and Comparisons*. Oxford: Blackwell.

Bernard, C. 1865. *Introduction à l'étude de la médecine expérimentale [Introduction to the Study of Experimental Medicine]*. Paris: Baillière.

Berstecher, D. 1970. *Zur Theorie und Technik des internationalen Vergleichs [Theory and Methodology of Cross-national Comparison]*. Stuttgart: Klett.

Berthoin Antal, A. 1987. "Comparing Notes and Learning from Experience." In *Comparative Policy Research. Learning from Experience*, edited by M. Dierkes, H. N. Weiler, and A. Berthoin Antal, 498–515. Aldershot: Gower.

Blatter, J. 2000. *Entgrenzung der Staatenwelt? Politische Institutionenbildung in grenzüberschreitenden Regionen in Europa und Nordamerika [Dissolution of Political Boundaries? Political Institution Building in Cross-border Regions in Europe and North America]*. Baden-Baden: Nomos.

Bloch, M. 1963. *Mélanges historiques [Miscellaneous Historical Writings]*, vol. 1. Paris: SEVPEN.

Boli, J., and G. M. Thomas, eds. 1999. *Constructing World Culture. International Nongovernmental Organizations Since 1875*. Stanford: Stanford University Press.

Boyle Swiniarski, L., ed. 2014. *World Class Initiatives and Practices in Early Education*. New York & Heidelberg: Springer.

Bruno-Jofré, R., and J. Schriewer, eds. 2012. *The Global Reception of John Dewey's Thought: Multiple Refractions Through Time and Space*. New York & London: Routledge.

Buzan, B., and R. Little. 2000. *International Systems in World History. Remaking the Study of International Relations*. Oxford: Oxford University Press.

Chalker, D. M., and R. M. Haynes. 1994. *World Class Schools*. Lancaster & Basel: Technomic.

Charle, C., J. Schriewer, and P. Wagner, eds. 2004. *Transnational Intellectual Networks*. Frankfurt am Main & New York: Campus.

Cook, B. J., S. J. Hite, and E. H. Epstein. 2004. "Discerning Trends, Contours, and Boundaries in Comparative Education: A Survey of Comparativists and Their Literature." *Comparative Education Review* 48 (2): 123–149.

Cowen, R. 1997. "Late Modernity and the Rules of Chaos: An Initial Note on Transitologies and Rims." In *Learning from Comparing. Volume 2 – Policy, Professionals, and Development*, edited by R. Alexander, M. Osborn, and D. Phillips, 73–88. Oxford: Symposium.

Cowen, R., and E. Klerides, eds. 2009. *Mobilities and Educational Metamorphoses*, special issue no. 38 of *Comparative Education* 45(3), 313–455.

Dale, R. 2005. "Globalisation, Knowledge Economy, and Comparative Education." *Comparative Education* 41(2): 117–149.

Durkheim, E. [1895] 1982. *Les règles de la méthode sociologique* (Paris, Félix Alcan); *The rules of sociological method*, translated by W. D. Halls. New York: Free Press.

Eggers, M., and M. Rothe, eds. 2009. *Wissenschaftsgeschichte als Begriffsgeschichte. Terminologische Umbrüche im Entstehungsprozess der modernen Wissenschaften [The History of Science Pursued as History of Concepts. Terminological Changes during the Origination Process of Modern Sciences]*. Bielefeld: transcript.

Espagne, M. 1999. *Les transferts culturels franco-allemands [Cultural Transfers Between France and Germany]*. Paris: Presses Universitaires de France.

Farrell, J. P. 1986. "The Necessity of Comparisons in the Study of Education: The Salience of Science and the Problem of Comparability." In *New Approaches to Comparative Education*, edited by P. G. Altbach and G. P. Kelly, 201–214. Chicago & London: The University of Chicago Press.

Gulbenkian Commission. 1996. *Open the Social Sciences. Report of the Gulbenkian Commission on the Restructuring of the Social Sciences*. Stanford: Stanford University Press.

Hartmann, M. 1999. "Auf dem Weg zur transnationalen Bourgeoisie? Die Internationalisierung der Wirtschaft und die Internationalität der Spitzenmanager Deutschlands, Frankreichs, Großbritanniens und der USA [Towards a Trans-national Bourgeoisie? Economic Internationalisation and the Internationality of Top Managers in Germany, France, Great Britain, and the USA]." *Leviathan* 27: 113–141.

Hirst, P. H. 1983. "Educational Theory." In *Educational Theory and its Foundation Disciplines*, edited by Idem, 3–29. London: Routledge & Kegan Paul.

Hüfner, K., J. W. Meyer, and J. Naumann. 1987. "Comparing Education Policy Research: A World Society Perspective." In *Comparative Policy Research. Learning from Experience*, edited by M. Dierkes, H. N. Weiler, and A. Berthoin Antal, 188–243. Aldershot: Gower.

Jules, T. D. 2012. *Neither World Polity nor Local or National Societies: Regionalization in the Global South – the Caribbean Community*. Frankfurt am Main: Peter Lang.

Kleinschmidt, H. 1991. "Galtons Problem: Bemerkungen zur Theorie der transkulturell vergleichenden Geschichtsforschung [Galton's Problem: Remarks Concerning the Theory of Cross-cultural Historical Research]." *Zeitschrift für Geschichtswissenschaft* 39(1): 5–22.

Kohn, M. L., ed. 1989. *Cross-national Research in Sociology*. Newbury Park: Sage.

Kriesi, H. 2007. *Vergleichende Politikwissenschaft [Comparative Politics]*. Baden-Baden: Nomos.

Lijphart, A. 1971. "Comparative Politics and the Comparative Method." *American Political Science Review* 65 (3): 682–693.
Luhmann, N. 1995a. *Social Systems*. Stanford, CA: Stanford University Press.
Luhmann, N. 1995b. "Kultur als historischer Begriff ['Culture' as a Historical Concept]." In *Gesellschaftsstruktur und Semantik. Studien zur Wissenssoziologie der modernen Gesellschaft [Structures of Society and Semantic Patterns. Contributions to the Sociology of Knowledge of Modern Society]*, Vol. 4, edited by N. Luhmann, 31–54. Frankfurt am Main: Suhrkamp.
Luhmann, N. [1997] 2012–2013. *Die Gesellschaft der Gesellschaft* (Frankfurt am Main: Suhrkamp); *Theory of Society*, translated by R. Barrett. Stanford: Stanford University Press.
Luhmann, N., and K. E. Schorr. 1988. *Reflexionsprobleme im Erziehungssystem [Reflection Theory within the System of Education]*. Frankfurt am Main: Suhrkamp, 2nd enlarged edition.
Mayer, L. C. 1989. *Redefining Comparative Politics*. Newbury Park etc: Sage.
McMichael, P. 1990. "Incorporating Comparison within a World-historical Perspective." *American Sociological Review* 55: 385–397.
Meyer, J. W. 2009. *World Society: The Writings of John W. Meyer*, edited by G. Krücken and S. Gili Drori. Oxford: Oxford University Press.
Meyer, J. W., and M. T. Hannan, eds. 1979. *National Development and the World System*. Chicago: University of Chicago Press.
Mill, J. S. 1843. *A System of Logic, Ratiocinative and Inductive*. London: John W. Parker.
Nagel, E. 1961. *The Structure of Science: Problems in the Logic of Scientific Explanation*. London: Routledge & Kegan Paul.
Niessen, M., and J. Peschar, eds. 1982. *International Comparative Research. Problems of Theory, Methodology, and Organization in Eastern and Western Europe*. Oxford etc: Pergamon.
Noah, H. J., and M. A. Eckstein, 1969. *Toward a Science of Comparative Education*. London etc: Macmillan.
Pedró, F., ed. 1987. *Los precursores españoles de la Educación Comparada. Antología de textos*. Madrid: Universidad Nacional de Educación a Distancia.
Popper, K. R. 1968. *The Logic of Scientific Discovery. Revised English edition*. London: Hutchinson.
Przeworski, A., and H. Teune. 1970. *The Logic of Comparative Social Inquiry*. New York etc: Wiley-Interscience.
Rappleye, J. 2012. *Educational Policy Transfer in an Era of Globalization: Theory – History – Comparison*. Frankfurt am Main: Peter Lang.
Ringer, F. 1979. *Education and Society in Modern Europe*. Bloomington: Indiana University Press.
Robertson, S. 2013. *Transnational Student-Migrants and the State. The Education-Migration Nexus*. Basingstoke: Palgrave-Macmillan.
Robinsohn, S. B. 1970. "Erziehungswissenschaft: Vergleichende Erziehungswissenschaft [Educational Studies: Comparative Education]." In *Handbuch pädagogischer Grundbegriffe [Handbook of Basic Educational Concepts]*, edited by J. Speck and G. Wehle, 456–492. Munich: Kösel.
Roldán Vera, E., and T. Schupp, 2005. "Bridges Over the Atlantic. A Network Analysis of the Introduction of the Monitorial System of Education in Early-independent Spanish America." In *Nationalerziehung und Universalmethode. Frühe Formen schulorganisatorischer Globalisierung [National Education and Universal Method. Early Forms of the Globalisation of Patterns of Schooling]*, edited by J. Schriewer and M. Caruso, 58–93. Leipzig: Leipziger Universitätsverlag.
Rossi, I. ed. 2007. *Frontiers of Globalization Research: Theoretical and Methodological Approaches*. New York: Springer.
Sassen, S. 1994. *Cities in a World Economy*. Thousand Oaks: Pine Forge Press.
Schneider, F. 1931–1932. "Internationale Pädagogik, Auslandspädagogik, Vergleichende Erziehungswissenschaft [International Education, Foreign Education, Comparative Education]." *Internationale Zeitschrift für Erziehungswissenschaft/ International Education Review/ Revue Internationale de Pédagogie*, 1, 15–39; 243–257; 392–407.
Schriewer, J. 1990. "The Method of Comparison and the Need for Externalization: Methodological Criteria and Sociological Concepts." In *Theories and Methods in*

Comparative Education, 2nd ed., edited by J. Schriewer and B. Holmes, 25–83. Frankfurt am Main: Peter Lang.

Schriewer, J. 2003. "Comparative Education Methodology in Transition: Towards a Science of Complexity?" In *Discourse Formation in Comparative Education*, 2nd rev ed., edited by J. Schriewer, 3–52. Frankfurt am Main: Peter Lang.

Schriewer, J. 2004. "Multiple Internationalities: The Emergence of a World-Level Ideology and the Persistence of Idiosyncratic World-Views." In *Transnational Intellectual Networks*, edited by C. Charle, J. Schriewer, and P. Wagner, 473–533. Frankfurt am Main: Campus.

Schriewer, J. 2007. "Reference Societies and Model Constructions: Questioning International Policy Studies." In *The Public Sector in Transition. East Asia and the European Union Compared*, edited by J. J. Hesse, J.-E. Lane, and Y. Nishikawa, 85–102. Baden-Baden: Nomos.

Schriewer, J., ed. 2012. *Re-Conceptualising the Global/ Local Nexus: Meaning Constellations in the World Society*, special issue no. 45 of *Comparative Education* 48 (4): 409–543.

Schriewer, J., and M. Caruso, eds. 2005. *Nationalerziehung und Universalmethode. Frühe Formen schulorganisatorischer Globalisierung [National Education and Universal Method. Early Forms of the Globalisation of Patterns of Schooling]*. Leipzig: Leipziger Universitätsverlag.

Schwinn, T. 2012. "Globalisation and Regional Variety: Problems of Theorization." *Comparative Education* 48 (4): 525–543.

Smelser, N. J. 1976. *Comparative Methods in the Social Sciences*. Englewood Cliffs: Prentice-Hall.

Steiner-Khamsi, G., ed. 2004. *The Global Politics of Educational Borrowing and Lending*. New York: Teachers College Press.

Stichweh, R. 1994. *Wissenschaft, Universität, Professionen. Soziologische Analysen [The Sciences, the University, and the Professions. Sociological Analyses]*. Frankfurt am Main: Suhrkamp.

Stichweh, R. 2008. "Selbstbeschreibung der Weltgesellschaft [Self-Descriptions of the World-Society]." In *Selbstbilder und Fremdbilder [Self-Images and Images of the Other]*, edited by J. Baberowski, H. Kaelble, and J. Schriewer, 21–51. Frankfurt am Main: Campus.

Strodtbeck, F. L. 1964. "Considerations of Meta-Method in Cross-Cultural Studies." *American Anthropologist* 66 (3): 223–229.

Tenbruck, F. H. 1981. "Emile Durkheim oder die Geburt der Gesellschaft aus dem Geist der Soziologie [Emile Durkheim or the Birth of Society out of the Mind of Sociology]." *Zeitschrift für Soziologie* 10 (4): 333–350.

Tenbruck, F. H. 1989. "Gesellschaftsgeschichte oder Weltgeschichte? [History of Societies or World History?]." *Kölner Zeitschrift für Soziologie und Sozialpsychologie* 41 (3): 417–439.

Tenbruck, F. H. 1992. "Was war der Kulturvergleich, ehe es den Kulturvergleich gab? [What was Cross-cultural Comparison Before Cross-cultural Comparison Came into Existence?]." In *Zwischen den Kulturen? Die Sozialwissenschaften vor dem Problem des Kulturvergleichs [Among Different Cultures? The Social Sciences Considering the Problem of Cross-Cultural Comparison]*, edited by J. Matthes, 13–35. Göttingen: Otto Schwartz & co.).

Thelen, K. 1999. "Historical Institutionalism in Comparative Politics." *Annual Review of Political Science* 2: 369–404.

Thelen, K. 2004. *How Institutions Evolve. The Political Economy of Skills in Germany, Britain, the United States, and Japan*. Cambridge: Cambridge University Press.

Thomas, G. M., J. W. Meyer, F. O. Ramirez, and J. Boli. 1987. *Institutional Structure. Constituting state, society, and the individual*. Newbury Park: Sage.

Waldow, F. 2010. "Der Traum vom 'skandinavisch schlau Werden.' Drei Thesen zur Rolle Finnlands als Projektionsfläche in der gegenwärtigen Bildungsdebatte [The Dream of Becoming 'Smart the Scandinavian Way.' Three Theses Regarding the Use of Finland as a Projection Screen in the Current Educational Debate]." *Zeitschrift für Pädagogik* 56 (4): 497–511.

Wallerstein, I. 1974–2011. *The Modern World-system*, Vols. I to IV. New York: Academic Press, & Berkeley, University of California Press.

Wallerstein, I. 1991. *Unthinking Social Science. The Limits of Nineteenth-Century Paradigms*. Cambridge: Polity Press.

Among the comparativists: ethnographic observations

Michele Schweisfurth

Robert Owen Centre for Educational Change, University of Glasgow, Glasgow, UK

> This article imagines the comparative education community as a tribal grouping. Using traditional anthropological categories, it explores how tribal membership is established and the rites and rituals that bind the tribe; questions of kinship among the larger family groupings within the tribe; belief systems; questions of social stratification in relation to the tribal hierarchy; and the persistence of warfare in this relatively peaceful group. While the article's approach and tone are lightly spoofing, the conclusion raises more serious questions about this tribe and its place in the contemporary world.

Comparative Education, it has been variously argued, is a field, a synthetic field, not a field at all, a discipline, a quasi-discipline and a way of life.[1] Such questions are, literally, academic, and for the purposes of this article, a footnote to other concerns. Regardless of how comparative education is defined, one thing is certainly true: it is an area of human inquiry into human activity and as such it only exists because people consider it worth doing, and do it. There is, therefore, another set of questions of potential interest to the curious and observant: who is doing it, and what do we know about them and their lives as comparativists? If we look at this group of people in its broad cultural configuration, what do we see? Comparative education is a scholarly pursuit of some debatable category and status, but behind this is a group of scholars who have enough in common and spend enough time in each others' (selective) company to be considered a community of sorts. What if we thought of this community as what anthropologists used to call a tribe?[2] And if an ethnographer spent a couple of decades among them as a participant observer, what might she note?

The analysis below is based on a study of the comparativists in their natural habitats over an extended period of immersion. It draws on traditional anthropological categories to consider their socio-cultural habits and patterns of existence. Specifically, it considers: how tribal membership is established and the rites and rituals that bind the tribe; questions of kinship among the larger family groupings within the tribe; belief systems; questions of social stratification in relation to the tribal hierarchy; and the persistence of warfare in this relatively peaceful group.

Membership: identification, initiation and boundaries

There are three main routes to membership of the comparativist tribe: a period of specialist training; sponsorship by a tribal elder; or various initiation rites. Some new members endure all three, and while this is not essential this does secure their status in a shifting tribal configuration. When potential initiates shun or avoid some rites of passage they sometimes, as a consequence, operate on the fringes of tribal life. As the most formal route, specialist training takes place at a narrow range of institutions where courses are offered leading to qualifications signalling tribal affiliation (if not full acceptance). The decision to follow the training route to tribal membership is often delayed until after the study of more foundational courses, and sometimes after personal experiences of education in an international context, and so the courses are usually specialist and serious, and the initiates mature.

These courses are often led by tribal elders and the resultant relationships are one route of introduction to the sponsorship pathway to membership. There are many observable examples of prominent tribal elders taking as informal apprentices one or more of the initiates taking part in specialist training, often a high achiever with an interest and growing expertise in a theme of particular concern to the tribal elder. While there is no doubt that altruism and a desire to help both individuals and the tribe is one set of motivators, it is in the interests of the elders to choose and nurture these initiates carefully in order to ensure that their own learnings are set down in the tribal records and that their work lives on in the tribal memory and sacred texts.

Ceremonies of initiation vary among different tribal kinship groups but there are a number which are common across such boundaries. They are not particularly ritualistic, colourful or celebratory as rites of passage go, but they reflect the sombre nature of the tribe's collective purpose. Paying to join a 'society' or 'association' of comparativists is common, and creates a discernible and verifiable tribal marking. These markings do not, however, guarantee full acceptance. These credentials may be enhanced by further public declarations such as putting unique learnings in one of the tribal records (such as *Comparative Education*, *Compare* or *Comparative Education Review*). Each of these deposits is scrutinised by at least two fully-initiated judges, sometimes including the tribal elders themselves, ensuring that the tribe's values are reinforced but that the learnings grow in directions perceived to be positive, even when new learnings challenge traditions. It is also noteworthy that the quality of the tribal records needs to keep the tribe in good standing among related and rival tribes; without this standing the tribe's resources would be threatened. Learnings which are about the tribe's own activities (i.e. 'the field', see above) seem to be particularly welcome.

The oral tradition is strong amongst the tribe members. Questions of comparative education's status and history are widely discussed and debated within the tribe at their tribal gatherings, and have become a form of shibboleth between established tribal members and a test of the mettle and understanding of initiates. These gatherings, some of which attract hundreds or even thousands of people, are often associated with the 'societies' and 'associations'. It is a formal rite of initiation and occasionally an ordeal for the new or hopeful member to tell their learnings to some of the assembled at one of these meetings. This ritual is presided over by a chairperson who ensures that the storytelling is not too long and that other members of the tribe have opportunities to test the worthiness of the prospective member with questions and comments. It is important to note that both membership payments and the scribing and telling of learnings, while initiation rites in themselves, usually continue through the lifetime of the individual comparativist.

Beyond this more formally-inducted and self-proclaimed group of members, most of whom research, teach or study as members of a wider academic community, there is, however, a parallel category of people of less certain status who complicate efforts to study in meaningful depth the culture of the comparativists. If anyone who does comparative and international education is a comparativist, the tribe is potentially enormous, and growing exponentially. However, there are a great many significant people and groups who collect some or all of their learnings about education in the international domain, or who create or use information generated through comparative studies of education inputs, processes or especially outcomes, but many of these are not self-proclaimed comparativists.[3] Comparative activity has gained global prominence but many of those involved do not identify with the mainstream tribe. Are they then members? Or are they a separate but related group, competing for some of the same resources? Tribal boundaries are blurred.

Consider, for example, the legend of the PISA. The learnings that form the basis for this legend are vast, and for outsiders to the tribe who are unaware of the tribe's inner workings, PISA is comparative education and comparative education is little else. Its lair is an international organisation which refers not to comparative education the field or community but to 'comparative education statistics'.[4] The lure, magnitude and simple beauty of the legend obscures even many of the tribe's most sacredly-held learnings. Such is its influence that powerful elders of nation state tribes invoke the legend in forming the laws of the land and speak its name in reverence when communicating with their tribal followers.[5] But most of the guardians of the PISA legend have not followed any of the routes to comparativist tribal membership as outlined above, and few declare themselves to be active tribal members. Comparativists are quick to raise questions about the legend and while not doubting the existence of the PISA they are sceptical about the spectacle associated with it, and the fanfare that accompanies its cyclical appearances. They especially abhor its wide-reaching and profound influence, which many of them regard as crude and based on superficial inferences. However, compared to some texts celebrating the legend of the PISA, tribe members' more complex and nuanced learnings remain relatively less noticed beyond the inner tribal circle, much to their occasional frustration.

Membership of the comparativist tribe is not linked to geography or space; tribe members are found around the world and have roots in various centres where their activities are nurtured. Clusters proliferate usually around key academic institutions where their learnings and sacred texts are generated, stored and disseminated, and where initiates following the formal training route are first immersed in the tribal traditions. Over time, these institutions change and the loci of tribal life shift. In recent years, for example, Greater China has been a growth point while elsewhere other members of the tribe experience a more threatened and defensive existence. Some of these less secure tribespeople are driven out of their lands by the pressures of resources and the vagaries of policy. These in turn are shaped by understandings of what education systems require in order to improve and what training teachers need in order to meet professional standards. The tribe therefore, while not exactly diasporic in nature, is on the move. This is partly about individuals following the prevailing winds of policy and resource, and partly about new members joining where the homeland hearths are most welcoming and the watering holes most fertile.

Kinship and consanguinity

Within the larger tribal group, kinship networks operate on the basis of a range of relationships. Consanguinity (in the intellectual sense understood by this tribe) is established through varied means. Some of these groupings are based on divisions consecrated in the tribal records, while others are based on demarcations imported from beyond the scope of the tribe. Some groupings are more formal than others.

For example, various versions of the tribal history set out distinctions between those who are comparative educationists and those who are international educationists. While some have argued that these are symbiotic and often difficult to tease apart,[6] in notable key institutions these divisions are marked with strict boundaries and the groups effectively function as separate tribes. This is often a result of historical divisions initiated by tribal elders with strong views on the uniqueness of their learnings and in some noteworthy cases personality clashes between strong-willed and territorial tribal elders have entrenched the divide (see warfare, below).[7] While neither group, comparative or international, is purebred or pedigreed in any verifiable sense, the 'international' group in particular is fraught with challenges of definition and identity and is linguistically diverse, culturally pluralistic, and members are relatively active in their engagement and identification with other tribes. Among the internationalists, the most clearly-definable kinship group is the group of tribespeople concerned with education in developing countries, and their work stretches their kinship ties to the tribes of aid agencies and nation states. Within the comparative kinship circles we also find sub-groupings based partly on belief systems, including those who believe the educational world is converging and those who believe that local cultures and resource realities will or should always prevail (see belief systems and also warfare, below). Kinship groups among the comparativists are in some contexts known colloquially as 'sigs', and these hold their own family gatherings within the larger yearly, biennial or triennial tribal festivals.

Some of these are the kinship groupings which are unique to the comparativists, but there are also sub-groups which resonate beyond the tribe. As in other tribes within the world of academia, we find boundaries established between tribal members who see their research paradigms as mutually exclusive, and there are status fluctuations associated with these differences. The relative value of words or numbers is particularly significant to these divisions and to their status. The use of polysyllabic words ending in the suffix 'ology', or, by contrast, a pre-occupation with how learnings may be practically applied beyond the tribal boundaries, are further markers of difference signalling particular kinship affiliations. And, as with all human tribal or kinship groupings, there are relationships which are based on personal feelings of kinship rather than ontological, epistemological or professional consanguinity. Food, drink, music, humour, charm, intercultural competences, collective loyalty to particular tribal elders or tribal ancestors,[8] and shared feelings of persecution all have roles to play in creating and perpetuating these more fluid and interpersonal networks.[9]

For reasons not readily discerned, with rare exceptions, comparativists do not generally intermarry. Where this does occur, particularly among those who already are or who are destined to be tribal elders, the synergy created by the combined forces has been known to be highly productive and in some cases to generate something of a cult following.

Belief systems

Like the Zoroastrians of the Persian Gulf, the belief system of the comparativists is dualistic with a sustained tension between two powerful and opposing forces. In the case of the comparativists, these two forces are The Global and The Local. Most comparativists perceive this dualism as constructive and dialogic, and seek to understand the interplay of the two as part of their purpose. They document and celebrate this cosmic dance in their learnings, and more contemporary sacred texts often feature this narrative tension. Calls to intervene in this conflict by tribal members are usually a matter of attempts to correct imbalances where they appear (as in recent times a perceived bullying of The Local by The Global in the arena of some poorer nation state tribes).

However, as with many cultures with dualistic belief systems there are cults which worship one of the two forces more-or-less exclusively with the other reduced to a minor role. The Universalists, for example, believe that there is progress occurring in similar ways across tribes and boundaries, which is ultimately consensual, beneficial and uniting for people globally. Within their belief systems, The Local occupies a trickster-like role, upsetting the inexorable flow of The Grand Global Unfolding with annoying but occasionally exotic or amusing antics. In contrast, those who hold Context as sacred are dismissive of The Global as a positive agent in at least two different ways. Some believe The Global to be a myth whose existence has been wildly exaggerated by believers who look for the wrong things in the wrong places and find the patterns they want to find by blurring their detailed vision. On the other hand, there are those who see The Global as a more sinister figure, motivated by power and greed. This evil spirit is believed to tamper with sacred traditions, sucking life from them, and to grant resources and power in its name to agents of oppression and chaos (see warfare, below).

Social stratification

As in virtually all social groupings, there are hierarchies within the comparativist tribe. Some of this is in relation to the status of tribal elder. This is not a mark of age, but a sign of respect. Not all tribal members achieve this status, and not all tribal elders are of advanced age (although it does take time to accrue the legitimation that this recognition requires). The members of this distinguished but unofficial group achieve their status in a range of ways, some more formal and structural than others. Although there is no official list of tribal elders or duties for them, it can be assumed from observation that there is a more-or-less common understanding of who is and who is not an elder, verifiable for example by their being in demand to tell their learnings to the whole assembly at tribal gatherings, or by observing the behaviour of initiates in their presence. While the list is arguably tribal in scope, inevitably the members of a given nation state tribe are most familiar with their own elders.

The elders include many exceptionally highly respected women. However, despite long years of fighting for equality, as in many related tribes, the overall gender balance leans slightly toward the male elders, despite the predominantly female initiate class. This is probably explained by the politics of institutions rather than by the nature of the tribe and its cultural practices themselves.[10]

One common route to elder status is through leadership of one of the training programmes for initiates at an established tribal induction centre. Holding such a position is not only a sign of the standing of the individual in the tribe, it creates opportunities to shape the thinking of initiates and to gain their loyalty. Wisdom and productivity in the creation and dissemination of learnings is perhaps the most significant route, despite the fact that what constitutes 'wisdom' is one of the recurrent murmurings of dissent among members. However, it is important to note that neither of these routes is a guaranteed pathway to tribal elder status. It is essential that respect and loyalty are garnered through these activities being done in a manner that raises the esteem of the elder, their followers, their institutional centre, and of course their learnings; charm, charisma, kindness to initiates and dogged determination all have key roles to play. Obvious attempts at self-promotion are largely unwelcome among the comparativists, who generally value interest in others more than interest in one's self, as is fitting for a tribe devoted to the study of others in its broadest sense. So, unless attempts at self-promotion are combined with more subtle personal qualities, these are often counterproductive and they do not bring the weight of respect demanded for elder status to be conferred.

Another set of hierarchies exists around measurable indicators established from outside the tribe but widely and inevitably employed within it. Comparativists who achieve success on these competitive parameters, regardless of whether they have tribal elder status, have an eminence within the tribe and are the members most likely to have standing outside of its boundaries as well. One noteworthy marker of status is the accrual of material resources through successful appeals to powerful councils able to grant coveted resources to supplicants who present their cases convincingly. As well as conferring wealth and status, these councils have a role in dictating the activities of the tribe, as their resources shape priorities. Unreliable counting games also have surprisingly high importance in determining the value of individual learnings, which are ranked in eagerly-awaited public records and indices.[11] There are similarly dubious but highly influential rankings of the institutions where comparativists do their work and being associated with an institution of high ranking can be a source of status for the individual comparativist as well. These various forms of ranking are treated with some suspicion by the discerning but are given credence by those who covet them or whose standing has been positively affected by them.

The associations that comparativists have created to organise their tribal meetings have their own hierarchies. Official positions are generally gained by democratic election, and an unpredictable mix of tribal elders, self-promoters, and the lesser-known but very committed put themselves forward for what are essentially voluntary posts of considerable responsibility. It is an indication of the comparativists' collective self-belief that these are sustained in the current competition for time and resources. Tribal archives and sacred texts are also held and produced by the collective effort of groups of volunteers who ensure that standards, traditions and values are upheld in their creation, evaluation and dissemination.[12]

Conclusions

Part of the point of this article has been to bring a little gentle humour to the perennial and sometimes doggedly serious questions of who we as comparativists are, what we do, and why. I hope that is obvious and that its good-humoured intent has not been misconstrued, when so many hotly-contested and subtle distinctions have necessarily been glossed for the sake of hyperbole.[13] But beyond the goal of instilling a bit of comic relief into the customary gravitas of the tribal records/academic journals, this piece also begins to raise some more serious and important questions: what is unique about this tribe, and is it thriving?

I would argue that the field is thriving but I fear that the tribe is suffering for its very tribalism. My concerns, while signalled here obliquely and with a smile, are not without weight or foundation. Cowen (2003) has argued that 'we anguish about ourselves', and I agree – and I would add to this that we anguish about ourselves, to ourselves, in ways that are of interest really only to ourselves. In the humble view of this participant observer, the greatest risk to the long-term health of the tribe is incremental banishment to the esoteric hinterlands. The tribe is not the only population doing comparative education (although the others may shun the label) and there are those who believe that in contexts of globalisation and academic mobility, everyone is doing it. There is some truth to this but we, the tribe, know that we do it with a more sophisticated repertoire of learnings and sacred and modern texts which comprise an impressive and eclectic body of theory, evidence and practice that speaks with authority. Histories and reflexive engagements with the field are important and laudable, but we also need to learn to speak the language of the other: not in this case a cultural other in the local or national sense, but the *other* cultural others who make key political and resource decisions that affect our welfare and the impact of our work. The challenge to our sustained existence is to demonstrate that we are not just pandering to the survival instincts of a minor and self-interested population. We need to make our rich repertoire meaningful and accessible to that *other* other, and to document the ways in which we interact with that *other* other in influencing their theoretical repertoires, and in impacting on their policy arenas. As a participant observer I have seen in more than one institution how easily the 'we're all comparativists' narrative can take hold and marginalise those of us who make it our life's work and see its distinctive value, however we might define it.

We are, I believe, unique in the nuances of our learnings and in our ways of learning about that trinity of 't's – transfer, translate and transform (Cowen 2006). We also have ethical principles that drive us, and which are derived from sustained and reflexive engagement with the other in the local or national sense, as a tribe and as individual members. However, whether we believe ourselves to be unique and important is of very little consequence to our *other* other colleagues in nearby tribes or on the periphery of our own, who, to paraphrase Carney (2010), are quite happy to let the world move on without us.

Comparative Man (Rappleye 2014) needs to evolve to adapt to the changing environment in our habitats. Communicating amongst ourselves around the tribal campfires binds us and moves the field forward intellectually and methodologically. But the field needs promoting beyond its own tribal boundaries so that the important messages about our ways of working and what our learnings might mean for others actually reach them. The tribal elders of nation states and higher education institutions need to understand what we do, and to learn from it, or they (with our accidental complicity) will allow 'the field' to be the domain of those who do not comprehend the best of its traditions and intentions.

As a tribe, we have the capacity to act. A field, or even a synthetic quasi-disciplinary way of life, cannot.

Acknowledgements

I am very grateful to two members of the journal's International Advisory Board, Stephen Carney and Jeremy Rappleye, for generous feedback on a draft of this article. If I had followed all of their advice, it would have been bolder and more detailed, but their comments have enriched the contents and helped to reassure me that the perspectives offered are not without foundation.

Notes

1. Manzon (2011) uses the term 'field' in the title of her analysis of comparative education, and discusses in some detail her choice of that term in relation to other academic endeavours.

However, not all commentators agree, and there is some debate at conferences for example as to whether this label is suitable for such a diverse area of inquiry with differing contents, objects and purposes (Manzon 2011) and Mason (2008) categorises it as a sub-field of educational studies with a particular methodology rather than a field in its own right. It has a multi-disciplinary base and a complex history (Crossley, Broadfoot, and Schweisfurth 2007) and sets of actors (Bray, Adamson, and Mason 2007); Rust et al. (1999) have addressed this complexity by labelling it a 'synthetic field'. While some have used the word discipline in relation to comparative education (e.g. Higginson 1999), because it has some characteristics of a discipline but does not have an agreed canon, Phillips and Schweisfurth (2006, 2009, 2014) have described it as a 'quasi-discipline'. In line with the emphasis on people and their lived experiences of doing comparative and international education, fitting for the purposes of this article, Broadfoot (1999) emphasises its place as 'a way of life'.
2. Tribe is in less common usage than in the past due to its association with ethnocentric judgements classifying some ethnic groups as primitive. However, some have argued that it should be reclaimed, not least due to its prevalent and untainted usage in Africa for example (http://www.tolerance.org/magazine/number-19-spring-2001/feature/trouble-tribe). The term tribe has also been used in the context of academic territories (Becher and Trowler 1989).
3. See for example, Bray (2007), who outlines some of the different actors and different purposes on the fringes of the scholarly field.
4. http://www.oecd.org/
5. See, for example, Meyer and Benavot (2013) for analyses of PISA's global reach and power.
6. See, for example, Phillips and Schweisfurth (2006, 2009, 2014).
7. One of the best-known examples of this phenomenon can be found at the University of London's Institute of Education, where taught programme components and research projects do not overlap despite there being a critical mass of tribal members from both comparative education and education and international traditions. The tribal members, while in the same institute and building and ostensibly the same 'field', are not in the same faculty. This has been attributed to historical divisions dating back to the middle of the last century emanating at least in part from personal differences between two powerful tribal elders, which these elders constructed as epistemological and irreconcilable but which more recent analyses have interpreted as complementary (Nicholls 2006).
8. Individual ancestors may be worshipped or reviled (Epstein and Carroll 2005; Larsen 2009), and in fact, where one starts the tribal history is also contested terrain.
9. For an illustrative example of how the interpersonal and professional intersect in the field, see the CIES Presidential address of Levin (2009).
10. For a discussion of higher education management and its relationship to gender equality, see Teelken and Deem (2013).
11. For a discussion of the prevalence and pitfalls of 'rank scholarship' see Post (2012).
12. Some have also argued that the tribe still suffers from divisions – and potentially stratifications – along geo-cultural lines, with UK and North America-centric tendencies persisting despite recent changes in the scale and importance of the tribal groups based, for example, in East Asia. For insider reflections on how the 'Western' tribe continues to exoticise the 'East', see Takayama (2011).
13. And yes, despite all of these deeply-felt contestations and occasional ruptures, and the teasers in this article, there is not really a section on warfare. Sorry. That would have been fun but potentially damaging to people, the field and myself. The battle lines are many: from the status, nature and purpose of the field (e.g. Heyneman 2009; Klees 2010) to questions of the place of post-modernism (e.g. Epstein and Carroll 2005; Rust 1991) and, as intimated above, the debates regarding world culture (e.g. Carney, Rappleye, and Silova 2012). But the tales of battle that extend these beyond academic discussion I will leave to those with insider knowledge or vivid imaginations.

References

Becher, Tony, and Paul B. Trowler. 1989. *Academic Tribes and Territories: Intellectual Enquiry and the Cultures of Discipline*. Milton Keynes: Open University Press.

Bray, Mark. 2007. "Actors and Purposes in Comparative Education." In *Comparative Education Research: approaches and methods*, edited by Mark Bray, Bob Adamson, and Mark Mason, 15–38. Hong Kong: Comparative Education Research Centre and Dordrecht: Springer.

Bray, Mark, Bob Adamson, and Mark Mason, eds. 2007. *Comparative Education Research: Approaches and Methods*. Hong Kong: Comparative Education Research Centre and Dordrecht: Springer.

Broadfoot, Patricia. 1999. "Not so Much a Context, More a Way of Life? Comparative Education in the 1990s." In *Learning from Comparing: New Directions in Comparative Education Research*, edited by Robin Alexander, Patricia Broadfoot, and David Phillips, Vol. 1. 21–31. Oxford: Symposium Books.

Carney, Stephen. 2010. "Reading the Global: Comparative Education at the End of an Era." In *New Thinking in Comparative Education: honouring Robert Cowen*, edited by Marianne Larsen, 125–142. Rottterdam: Sense Publishers.

Carney, Stephen, Jeremy Rappleye, and Iveta Silova. 2012. "Between Faith and Science: World Culture Theory and Comparative Education." *Comparative Education Review* 56 (3): 366–393.

Cowen, Robert. 2003. "Agendas of Attention: A Response to Ninnes and Burnett." *Comparative Education* 39 (3): 299–302.

Cowen, Robert. 2006. "Acting Comparatively Upon the Educational World: Puzzles and Possibilities." *Oxford Review of Education* 32 (5): 561–573.

Crossley, Michael, Patricia Broadfoot, and Michele Schweisfurth. 2007. *Changing Education Contexts, Issues and Identities: 40 years of Comparative Education*. London: Routledge.

Epstein, Erwin H., and K. Carroll. 2005. "Abusing Ancestors: Historical Functionalism, and the Postmodern Deviation in Comparative Education." *Comparative Education Review* 49 (1): 62–88.

Heyneman, S. 2009, September. "The Future of Comparative and International Education." *CIES Newsletter* 151: 1–5. (paper version). http://cies.us/newsletter/sept%2009/Heyneman.html

Higginson, James Henry. 1999. "The Development of a Discipline: Some Reflections on the Development of Comparative Education as Seen Through the Pages of the Journal *Compare*." *Compare: a journal of comparative education* 29 (3): 341–351.

Klees, Stephen. 2010. "The Future of Comparative and International Education Revisited." CIES Perspectives, No 152, January 2010. http://www.cies.us/newsletter/jan10/index_jan10.html

Larsen, Marianne. 2009. "Comparative Education, Postmodernity and Historical Research: Honouring Ancestors." In *International Handbook of Comparative Education*, edited by Robert Cowen, and Andreas Kazamias, 1045–1059.

Levin, Henry M. 2009. "My Comparative Education, 1970–1975." *Comparative Education Review* 53 (3): 315–328.

Manzon, Maria. 2011. *Comparative Education: The Construction of a Field*. Hong Kong: Comparative Education Research Centre and Dordrecht: Springer.

Mason, Mark. 2008. What is comparative education, and what values might best inform its research? Presidential address given at the annual conference of the Comparative Education Society of Hong Kong.

Meyer, Hans-Dieter and Aaron Benavot. 2013. *PISA, Power, and Policy: The Emergence of Global Educational Governance*. Oxford: Symposium Books.

Nicholls, Jason. 2006. "From Antithesis to Synthesis: Reinterpreting the Brian Holmes/Edmund King Dialectic." *Research in Comparative and International Education* 1 (4).

Phillips, D., and M. Schweisfurth. 2006. *Comparative and International Education: An Introduction to Theory, Method and Practice*. London: Continuum.

Phillips, D., and M. Schweisfurth. 2009. *Comparative and International Education: An Introduction to Theory, Method and Practice*. London: Continuum.
Phillips, D., and M. Schweisfurth. 2014. *Comparative and International Education: An Introduction to Theory, Method and Practice*. 2nd ed. London: Bloomsbury.
Post, David. 2012. "Rank Scholarship." *Comparative Education Review* 56 (1): 1–17.
Rappleye, Jeremy. 2014. Preface to the 2nd edition. *Comparative and International Education: an introduction to theory, method and practice*. 2nd ed. London: Bloomsbury
Rust, Val D. 1991. "Postmodernism and Its Comparative Education Implications." *Comparative Education Review* 35 (4): 610–626.
Rust, Val D., Aminata Soumaré, Octavio Pescador, and Megumi Shibuya. 1999. "Research Strategies in Comparative Education." *Comparative Education Review* 43 (1): 86–109.
Takayama, K. 2011. "A Comparativist's Predicaments of Writing About 'Other' Education: A Self-Reflective, Critical Review of Studies of Japanese Education." *Comparative Education* 47 (4): 449–470.
Teelken, Christine, and Rosemary Deem. 2013. "All are Equal, but some are more Equal than others: Managerialism and Gender Equality in Higher Education in Comparative Perspective." *Comparative Education,* 49 (4): 520–535.

Thinking about gender in comparative education

Elaine Unterhalter

Institute of Education, University of London, London

> Comparative and international education has been both a particularly generative area for the exploration of themes in relation to gender and education, but has also tended to impose limits regarding how gender and education are understood. In reflecting critically on the history of my own work in this field, and some of the early scholarship of the 1970s and 1980s, this article poses questions about how and why particular theorisations of gender and education are selected and used. It also considers how and why particular integrations are made between gender frameworks, what this suggests about comparison, and what pointers this may help to provide for thinking about gender in the contemporary period. The analysis delineates the current epoch as one marked by a shift to a multi-polar world in which forms of political economy are realigning. Shifts associated with changing approaches to the public, the private and the personal entail gender identities and relations reconfiguring and a dispersed set of meanings. One outcome is that it can become difficult to connect ideas about gender in a simple way with an integrated social justice agenda. This has become apparent in education, which is crucial to policies of social protection, enhancing social justice, but is also linked with increasing monetisation of information and of the relationships of learning and teaching. The invocation of gender in both spaces, and the identification of its differences, requires particular acuity. In trying to formulate an approach that speaks to this process and developing a normative compass in contemporary times, the article tries to reflect critically on comparison as an intellectual move and a political position.

Comparative education has provided an ambiguous disciplinary space to look at issues about gender. On the one hand, some of the key works that have explored gender and education and tried to build theory in relation to global, international and trans-locational processes have been associated with the work of scholars in comparative and international education (e.g. Aikman 1999; Fennell and Arnot 2007; Moletsane 2005; Smyth and Rao 2005; Stromquist 1989, 1992, 1995; Vavrus 2003). On the other hand, because of the salience of comparison in *educational spaces*, to work in this field, some of the work of theorising gender as a relational and comparative term and what this might mean in education settings may not have ranged widely enough. Thus the comparative potential of gender as an analytical or normative idea or a practice, and its articulation with education as a particular kind of relational, intellectual and contextual engagement, appears to have been somewhat constrained. In this article I explore this ambiguous relationship. I do so partly reflecting critically on some of my own work in this area over 30 years, partly by reviewing some of the early compilations on gender, comparative and international education from the 1970s, and partly by considering steps to formulate an approach to gender and comparative education that speaks to particular disorienting features of the present moment.

The discussion proceeds as follows. I first outline some of my own attempts to map different meanings of gender in education, and some of the ways in which, in the process, I engaged and evaded some key issues regarding comparative education. I then trace some of the history of discussions of gender in comparative education, showing how, up until relatively recently, work on this issue has generally been linked with carving out a space to add gender into existing approaches with regard to comparison, rather than opening up more wide-ranging inquiry about meanings of gender, engagements with education or the dynamics of comparison. I suggest how features of the academic and policy climate may have contributed to these processes and some of the associated problems. In the final part of the article, in attempting to think about gender and education in contemporary times, I suggest the importance of further opening the space for more nuanced engagement with a more multi-dimensional and relational meaning of gender that might be appropriate for the current epistemic moment in comparative education.

Meeting myself: some critical questions

A key question this article is concerned with is why scholars in comparative and international education working on gender have noted some features of comparative dynamics and ignored others. I will try to present this problem through a critical reflection on my own work in this area. In 2005 I wrote an article, 'Fragmented frameworks', which tried to set up a taxonomy of work on gender and education drawing on different approaches to meanings of gender, education and development (Unterhalter 2005a). In a later refinement I distinguished between different ways of defining gender, and I used three metaphors to signal three different approaches to thinking about gender, linking these loosely with particular policy and practice regarding education, equality and global obligation (Unterhalter 2007a, 2009a, 2012). The distinction I made was between gender as a noun, gender as an adjective and gender as a verb. Gender as a noun signalled approaches to describing or analysing education systems, units or policies in terms of how many girls and boys, men and women were positioned in particular settings, for example with regard to enrolment, progression, attainment or employment. Gender as an adjective was a feature of work which looked at how gendered relations of power, distribution of resources, forms of struggle or representation took place in education settings, for example how curricula came to be gendered, the social divisions this drew on and the processes of exclusion and inclusion this produced and reproduced. Gender as a verb was to be found in those works that acknowledged that gender identities, performances or actions of all those engaged with education were not stable and changed, mixed and blurred in different contexts taking many discursive forms. For example, teachers might articulate official views in support of gender equality, but find these harder to enact in classrooms, if they were not reflexively engaged with identifying and trying to change prevailing stereotypes about gender identities or did not understand aspects of their own gendered autobiographies.

Comparison was explicit and implicit in this taxonomy. I portrayed the different approaches to gender as associated with different assumptions regarding the space of education. Thus, gender as a noun was most commonly associated with a view of the space of education as the school, the system of management, organisation or employment. Gender as an adjective considered the space of education as reproducing and contesting history, politics, ideas and power, while the notion of gender as a verb considered the space of education as active, peopled and changing in its movement between times, spaces and discursive forms. This analysis engaged some of the concerns of successive waves of work in comparative education, even if some of its more critical considerations of how these processes were articulated were not explored (Cowen and Kazamias 2009; Philips and Schwiesfurth 2007; Rappleye 2012).

The taxonomy of 'fragmented frameworks' presents the categories as clearly delineated, suggesting sharp divisions between theorisations and perceptions of education. However, in practice these distinctions often overlapped. This has been the case in my own work. For two decades before I wrote 'Fragmented frameworks' most of my research had drawn on analyses of gender as an adjective. This is evident, for example, in studies of domestic workers (Gaitskell et al. 1984) and political activism in South Africa (Gaitskell and Unterhalter 1989; Kimble and Unterhalter 1983), gender and apartheid education (Unterhalter 1991a), theorising citizenship taking account of issues of gender and education (Unterhalter 1999a), and women's movements for education in India (Unterhalter and Dutt 2001). However, in some studies of the distribution of schooling in South Africa, I had looked at gender as a noun (Unterhalter 1991b) and this was a theme I have taken up repeatedly in returning to the problem of how one might measure gender equality in education (see e.g. Unterhalter 2004, 2014 forthcoming; Unterhalter and Dorward 2013; Unterhalter and Oomen 2006). In a number of studies concerned with the analysis of autobiographical accounts of schooling by differently located South Africans, I had worked with the notion of gender as a verb (Parkes and Unterhalter 2009; Unterhalter 1999b, 2000, 2002, 2007b). This was one of the strands I used in a collaboration with friends in a six year study of two South African secondary schools (Morrell et al. 2009).

I do not think I have been unique amongst scholars working on gender, education and international development in using a wide palette of theorisations (see e.g. Bajaj and Pathmarajah 2011; Dejaeghere and Vavrus 2011; Maslak 2007). In reflecting on why I worked with particular theorisations at particular moments, the clearest explanation I can formulate rests on features of particular epistemic moments. Thus, growing up with the very visible effects of racial segregation and a repressive state in South Africa, and active both in student politics and later the exiled ANC in trying to change this, the epistemic resources I drew on in trying to develop an approach to gender came largely from critical engagements with Marxist theory, and the particular debates about this circulating within circles of academics and activists in Southern Africa, Western Europe and North America [for some explorations of these circles see Friedman (2014 forthcoming), Keniston (2013) and Moss (2014 forthcoming)]. However, in the early 1990s some major historical changes led to me adding layers to these foundational ideas. The first was the prospect that there would be a democratic government in South Africa and that the history of the distribution of education and what needed to change, where, had to be mapped. This was a key part of some of the work I did for the Research on Education in South Africa (RESA) project (1985–1995) that entailed working with the idea of gender as a noun. This experience of political settlement in South Africa and the part played by global solidarity movements and the UN system in helping to bring this about have had a powerful effect on my participation in work with global education movements and UN organisations, as I did on the Beyond Access project (2003–2010). Here too I recognised some of the importance of pragmatic politics. Part of this work entailed trying to improve approaches to the analysis and evaluation of gender in education, through expanding fields with regard to what was measured, going somewhat beyond a simple notation based on gender as a noun (Unterhalter 2005b; Unterhalter, Challender, and Rajagopalan 2005). From the mid-1990s I have worked in the UK higher education system, seeing many changes in institutional culture, and meeting students and colleagues from enormously diverse backgrounds. The epistemic opportunities associated with this institutional location have invited consideration of flux, change, inter-disciplinarity and the role of higher education, as these have characterised so many decisions and collaborations and been an important component of my work on gender, education and the capability approach (Unterhalter 2003, 2007b; Unterhalter and Brighouse 2014 forthcoming). In this environment, so enmeshed with diversity, it has been easy, indeed natural, to work with some of the potentiality of gender as a verb and I have explored this in some work on teaching in higher education (Unterhalter 2006, 2007c, 2009b, 2010). But some of the other challenges this location has presented relate to those of integrating frameworks or assessing new times, which I return to later in the discussion.

This brief autobiographical sketch highlights two issues. Firstly, the importance of understanding why I, or any other scholar, draw on certain theorisations at particular times, silencing others. Secondly, how a particular kind of approach to comparison is implicitly or explicitly implied by drawing out the distinctions in any taxonomy, and how an awareness of this can help in opening up a new heuristic space. In the next section, I address the first issue by looking at the history of some of the first writings on gender in comparative education. I then turn to consider the second by looking at some approaches to gender and comparative education, particularly in the light of assessing the contemporary epistemic moment.

Adding in gender to comparative education

The history of the scholarship on gender in comparative education can be read partly as a series of moves to address silences. Because of the evident need to fill the space of gender relations in studies of the comparative in education (however this was understood), it was gender that came to be added to a wider faming, rather than the wider framing being reconsidered in the light of a discussion of gender. Thus work in the field added gender to comparative investigations of units, such as schools or national education systems, to consideration of policies, for example on forms of curriculum, or to processes, such as migrations of education ideas from the global to the local. Gender in a number of familiar guises came to be added to comparison, but the process did not generate debates about the meaning of gender in education or the meaning of education or comparison. Rather it introduced gender as a refining category into the existing frameworks of comparative education.

The first step that was taken in the emergence of this field of inquiry appears to have been attention given to women and gender as a legal, rather than a social category. In 2005, in an overview of engagements with aspects of equality in comparative and international education, Nelly Stromquist (2005, 97–99) identified a special issue of the *Harvard Education Review* in 1979 as one of the earliest journal issues to deal with gender and education. This was followed by special issues of *Comparative Education Review* in 1980, which looked at issues of women and girls' education in the third world. *Comparative Education* in 1987 contained articles dealing with a wide range of countries, not just the third world, but delimited its concerns by using the term 'sex differences in education' (Sutherland 1987).

All three early instances of interventions in comparative education by writers on education and women, girls or gender, did not problematise *either* categories of gender or the process of comparing in education. The 1979 issue of *Harvard Education Review* comprised interviews with five women who had been involved with the attempt to use the legislative system in the US to prohibit gender inequality in any education institution (Harvard Education Review 1979). This was thus a key instance of comparison, in this case between different sites of legal engagement with the US education system, drawing on a particular, but narrow, meaning of gender, concerned with overcoming discrimination and inequity. This is not the first academic work that had looked at gender, women's rights and education,[1] but it may be one of the earliest that deployed a comparative framing.

The 1980 special issue of *Comparative Education Review* contained an introduction by Carolyn Elliott and Gail Kelly (1980) in which they provided an overview on why and how women's education had grown in 'third world nations', noting that the significance of this had not heretofore been studied systematically. Their remit with regard to the comparative education field, they considered, was to provide historically and culturally located analysis of women's education in Africa, Asia and Latin America that would allow for the differences to become apparent with work in this area in Europe, North America and Australia, particularly with regard to education and themes relating to family, work and culture. Thus their intention was not to problematise gender, the unit or process of comparison, or education, but rather to contextualise. Other articles in the issue noted gender as a purely descriptive category denoting numbers of women and men participating in different levels of education (Bowman and Anderson 1980), reaching particular levels of attainment (Finn, Reis, and Dulberg 1980), or experiencing different labour market outcomes (Ram 1980). The case studies in the issue considered obstacles to girls' enrolment in school (McSweeney and Freedman 1980), a number of studies of policy initiatives to involve more girls in school (Jones 1980; Wang 1980), discussions of women's education levels and work (Schiefelbein and Farrell 1980; Wainerman 1980), and an investigation into the portrayal of women and men in Indian textbooks (Kalia 1980). The one study that looked at girls' experiences of school, Biraimah's (1980) study in Togo, focussed on the significance of Western models of schooling and girls' responses to teachers as role models, rather than aspects of gender identity embedded within wider social relations. Although this was clearly a landmark issue for comparative education, in that the articles identified that there might be pedagogical and process factors that meant girls were treated differently to boys, in no way did it draw on any very complex theorisation of gender. Its stance with regard to comparative education pointed out the importance of context and history, but was not able to go into this to offer a wider theorisation of gender processes within and beyond schools. In terms of the taxonomy I developed, the whole issue is framed in terms of thinking about gender as a noun and describing the different conditions of women and men within existing education units (schools, textbook or attainment systems).

In 1987 *Comparative Education* published its first special issue on gender and education edited by Margaret Sutherland with the theme of sex differences in education. Patricia Broadfoot's (1987) introduction brought out that what was of interest was that 'sex differences' were embedded in the diverse cultural, religious, economic and social variables that meant that feminist demands for equality in education had to be located within these specificities. The very diverse articles in the special issue exemplified this approach. None dealt with gender as a social relationship or category of analysis. All located their concern with sex differences either within an analysis of the particular education units they delineate, for example different phases of education, subject areas or types of school (Moore 1987; Sutherland 1987) or policies in different countries (Byrne 1987; Kelly 1987), or considered how wider social forces, such as religion, socialism, policy history or labour market opportunities might explain sex differences in school (Al Hariri 1987; Eliou 1987; Kelly 1987; Szechy 1987). Here too what was evident was a discussion of gender as a noun that did not trouble the expected units of comparative inquiry. Sutherland's (1987, 8–9) account of gender and comparative education looked for explanations of the gender disadvantage of women in behaviourist or pragmatic responses to existing forms of social organisation, and termed attempts at change idealistic. Alone in this issue a study by Lynn Davies (1987), regarding the analysis of data on teachers and management in five African countries, posed questions about what kinds of relationships were being researched when gender was discussed, and what the reasons for this might be.

Comparative education in the 1980s was not unique in taking the perspective that gender was to be understood as a noun and education as a unit, such as a school. This was a commonplace in work on development economics, which at the time was exerting a major influence on the companion area of education and international development. The landmark publication that identified the significance of girls' education for international development is generally taken to be the edited collection put together by scholars linked to the World Bank (King and Hill 1993), although the importance of the education of women and girls for economic development had been noted by economists in the 1970s and 1980s, who drew attention to women's education being a key factor in relation to work both inside and outside the home (Boserup 1970; Stewart 1985). The importance of women's level of education was a given in many of the studies concerned with limiting population growth from the 1950s (Rindfuss, Bumpass, and St John 1980; Schultz 1993). The assumptions within all these studies linked to early articulations of development economics was that gender denoted stable categories either pertaining to men and women, or to economic relationships in the household and the work place. The foundational works in development economics which looked at gender as a political and social relationship, intertwining this with economic processes, started to be published in the 1980s (e.g. Beneira and Sen 1982), but this work, together with influential studies published in the 1990s, did not deal with education (Elson 1995; Kabeer 1994; Pearson 1994).

Writers on education and international development contested a number of the assumptions in the King and Hill analysis. There were challenges to the framing of the issues (Heward and Bunwaree 1999; Ilon 1992; Unterhalter 1996), some of the data used (Behrman and Rosenzweig 1994; Kingdon 1998) and the simplicity of the conclusions drawn (e.g. Jeffrey and Jeffrey 1998; Stromquist 1995). A special issue of IJED in 2000 looked at the way gender, now starting to be discussed in terms of constructed social relationships, was a key feature of donors' development discourse (Swainson 2000), the cultural relationships that contributed to girls being kept out of school (Colclough, Rose, and Tembon 2000) or girls being treated in particular ways in classrooms (Stephens 2000). However, as ideas about gender started to engage with different frameworks, notably gender as an adjective, the exploration of the education space became less historically located, and its relationship with some of the ideas that were key to comparative education appeared to recede. Thus, for example, the article by Peter Kutnick (2000) in the IJED special issue of 2000 looked at the differential attainment of boys and girls in the Caribbean, where the trend was different to that in many other counties where girls underperformed in comparison to boys. Kutnick drew on surveys with a large sample of children and teachers and observations in class of how girls and boys were addressed. But, although the article discusses data from Trinidad, Barbados and St Vincent, islands with very different economies, political histories and cultural mix, the article makes no reference to this. Instead its analysis focuses on children and discusses family background and teacher engagement as salient features of school attainment. This style of writing, where empirical data came to exercise strong explanatory power, edging out engagements with history or the gender dynamics of the society, set a trend for much work from 2000. In 2013, a rigorous review of literature on interventions regarding girls' education and gender equality, commissioned by DFID, concluded that a considerable part of the literature comprised studies where contextual critique was not given adequate consideration (Unterhalter, North et al. 2014). Alongside these data driven studies, a critical engagement with policy emerged as a feature of the education and international development literature on gender (Aikman and Unterhalter 2005; Fennell and Arnot 2007). Many contributors to this literature on policy were simultaneously engaged in undertaking research for policy makers and critically reviewing that policy.

My preliminary reading of the work on gender in comparative and international education from the publication of King and Hill (1993) to the present is that the main intellectual work has comprised identifying gendered social relations as a key aspect of the many modalities of education, but that the potential of reviewing gender comparatively has only been taken up by a handful of writers. Although in other disciplines, including women's studies, political philosophy, economics and cultural studies to name but a few, the boundaries and foundational ideas regarding how gender was understood were being investigated with great energy, these discussions seem to have had less resonance in comparative and international education than one would have expected. This silence is all the more puzzling because a key feature of all of these works on defining gender in other disciplines is that they surface particular kinds of problems of *comparison*. For example, comparison underpins the key problem in feminist economics and political philosophy as to whether and in what ways the private sphere was similar or different to the public sphere with regard to views about gender equality (Okin 1989; Philips 1999). Nnaemeka's (2004) nuanced consideration of feminism in Africa and the USA starts from ideas about different ontologies and their significance for politics. Comparison is also a key driver in feminist debates about justice. Thus, comparison animates the question posed by Nancy Fraser (1997) as to how and why redistributive ideas of justice, which stress the importance of not taking account of gender, in for example hiring practices for work, differ from recognitional ideas of justice, which do take account of gender, in order to acknowledge the salience of particular kinds of experience. Comparison also drives the distinctions that Floya Anthias (2002) makes between how to read the tensions between support for feminism and multiculturalism taking account of relative positional locations of different dominant and subordinate collectivities and how groups are positioned within these. Comparison is thus a key intellectual and political move in feminist theorising, and its limited use in comparative and international education over some decades is a puzzling silence.

The reasons for this silence await detailed treatment. The specialist journal *Gender and Education* was launched in 1989 but the searches undertaken for a rigorous literature review (Unterhalter, North et al, 2014) indicated that the journal had published very little material that dealt with comparative or international education and generally had not engaged in debates in this area. Over more than 20 years there appears to have been a disconnection between a rich comparative literature about gender and a somewhat static policy-oriented literature concerned with gender and education in international and comparative contexts. The reasons for this may lie with where and by whom gender and women's studies were taught, and how few opportunities there were for dialogue with those working on comparative and international education.

That moment of closure now appears to be ending. It is notable that the limits on the writing on gender in comparative and international education evident in earlier decades are no longer apparent. Research that is particularly analytically rich about the space of education and the multi-layering of ideas regarding gender is now being published. This works with the problematic of comparison, rather than limiting, refusing or ignoring it. For example, Jenny Parkes (2007) draws out the complexity of gender identities and educational public and private spaces in children's talk about violence in South Africa, while Elaine Salo (2003) looks at shifting identities of young people living in the townships of the Cape Flats. Joan Dejaeghere and Nancy Wiger (2013) work with Nancy Fraser's ideas about gender justice commenting on how this helps illuminate teachers' engagements with the concept of gender in Bangladesh. Karen Monkman (2011) considers how comparing different approaches to empowerment helps build a more nuanced approach to analysing gender, education and empowerment, and Erin Murphy-Graham (2012) draws on empirical data from Honduras to further deepen our insight into the theorisation of empowerment. It thus appears that this is a particular generative moment in which the potentials for theorising gender and problematising comparisons in education are being worked on *together*. Some reasons for this may be enhanced opportunities for networking and collaboration associated with particular conferences, and shared projects. Sometimes this generative theorising happens alongside more conventional assignments. Thus, policy attention on gender as a noun, and girls' schooling as a catchall answer to many development problems, as articulated in some large programmes such as DFID's *Girls' education challenge*, and USAID's programme on ending child marriage, has generated considerable amounts of donor assistance for research on these issues. Involvement in donor funded projects, linked with some of these concerns, have offered me opportunities to think more widely about theorising gender, education and comparison (Dejaeghere, Parkes, and Unterhater 2013; Unterhalter, Heslop and Mamedu 2013) and I think others have also been able to use the possibility to simultaneously access research funds and think critically about findings.

This fruitful scholarship leads me to consider that the contemporary problems regarding discussions of gender and comparative and international education appear less with regard to limits on perspective regarding gender, educational space and the potential of comparison; rather more associated with an older historical problem. That is, what comparison as a political and normative move may be able to tell us regarding the frameworks we currently draw on for thinking about gender and international education given some unsettling features of the present.

Comparison and the disorienting present

It is always difficult to make sense of contemporary times, but the current moment is particularly disorienting. The UN Secretary General Ban Ki Moon, in addressing the

General Assembly in 2013, highlighted, on the one hand, the hopeful prospect that the world might wipe out poverty, yet, at the same time, confronted challenges for which there was less optimism associated with the pressures on the planet, the large numbers of young people without jobs, the humanitarian and security disaster in Syria, the unresolved conflicts in many areas of the Middle East and North Africa, and the challenge of working with institutions designed for a previous era trying to tackle the challenges of the present (Moon 2013). Many academic commentators have noted significant political, economic, environmental and social changes accompanied by fragmented organisation at global, national and local levels, that has both positive and negative effects (Dietz, Havnevik, and Kaag 2011; Eyben 2013; Unterhalter and Dorward 2013).

In these conditions education is crucial to policies of social protection, enhancing social justice and processes of democratisation and enabling voice for the previously excluded. It is also a site associated with increasing monetisation of information and of the relationships of learning and teaching. For many large and small companies education is a commodity bought, sold, speculated about and planned with an eye to profit, rather than social justice. The relationship of these private associations with forms of state provision is complicated, as the enormous literature on public–private partnerships attests. Gender is a crucial component of both processes. It is highly salient to enhancing justice at local, national and global levels that is attuned enough to the complexity of diversity, but it is also implicated in the commodification of education and changes in social spending and wage relations. The expansion of low cost private schools exemplifies some of these relationships. These are often promoted as a clear response by poor parents to the failures of delivery in the public sector and their employment of women teachers can be an important employment opportunity. However, research in India indicates that parents appear to choose private schools for sons, while daughters remain in the inadequate public schools, thus cementing gender inequalities. In addition, the very low pay of women teachers in private schools does not help undo many local gender inequalities (Manjrekar 2013; Woodhead, Frost, and James 2013).

A controversial newspaper article by Nancy Fraser (*Guardian*, 14 October 2013) claimed that feminism had become the handmaiden of capitalism, and was implicated in neo-liberal reforms to drive down wages, undermine solidaristic organisation and promote individualism. Responses to the article suggested there was not a single version of feminism, that this was a very partial reading of experiences in the UK, the USA and elsewhere in the world. Fraser gave no consideration to the critiques feminist activists have made regarding violence against women or mobilising for changes in laws on property or health or international co-operation. The article did not mention education, but it is evident that the importance of girls' education has sometimes been a rationale for large private sector development initiatives (e.g. Nike project) whose social justice implications remain to be evaluated (Moeller 2013). Girls' education, as a key trope promising choice and freedom, for example through promotional films like the *Girl Effect*, has been associated with particular kinds of political economy. Getting girls into school is promoted as a silver bullet for development problems, which occlude discussions of what is taught, to whom, the socio-economic relations of schooling, work and livelihoods, the messy and difficult relationships associated with learning and teaching about sexuality and violence, and the politics of who presents what to whom (Koffman and Gill 2013; Ramdas 2012).

This leads me to worry that the taxonomy I developed regarding gender as a noun, an adjective and a verb, does not adequately fit the new language of diverse forms of education provision and the plasticity of gender when the personal is political in more sites and in more ways than feminist activists of the 1960s and 1970s anticipated. While in earlier periods, as I have reflected in the history of my own work, it was possible to suture together two quite different approaches, for example a concern with gender as a noun and an adjective, this does not seem an entirely appropriate move at present, even though it brings to the fore a comparative dynamic with regard to analysis. I consider there are features of the flux of the current moment that need us to add to the frameworks through which we can compare gender. Features of the current moment are that the public and the private in education often meld and the politics of this can become obscured. Individuals are thus addressed through a range of discursive forms that comprise both assumptions of ethical relationship and profit maximisation, sometimes in the same tropes. The state, global civil society and multilateral organisations are sometimes protective in the direction of social justice and sometimes neglectful of these relationships. Under these conditions it seems to me we need to capture conceptually the meanings and politics of gender dispersing into numerous sites. In earlier work (Unterhalter 2005a, 2012) I suggested an integrative move in relation to the taxonomy I developed, where empowerment or social justice bought together the three meanings of gender I had separated out. I am no longer so confident of this and consider that, side-by-side with this social justice reading of the present, we also need to be able to theorise the double entendres associated with women or gender equitable forms of relationship 'leaning in' to support exploitation or endorse conditions of vulnerability. I suggest this form of gender may be read as a kind of gerund, that is a verb that works as a noun. In understanding this process we need to document education agents (learners, teachers, managers, policy negotiators, parents) 'doing gender' and the historical location of the process of education gendering, turning the action sometimes into a commodity, sometimes into a form of social projection and engagement with justice, sometimes into a different way of reading or acting in the world.

Conclusion

Gender unsettles the existing containers of comparative education. As a set of relationships that operate at levels that are material, social, emotional, representational and ethical, metaphors of parsing work only in trying to distinguish some of these, but can never fully capture the textured interconnections and the histories of where relationships have come from and are going to. However, what I have tried to show in this article is that comparative moves, both of distinction, suture or dialectic, while inevitably bounded by particular epistemic moments and formed by communities of education practice, are nonetheless particularly rich in what they help us to see regarding the multiple forms of gender relations and the multi-dimensionality of this dynamic in education.

Acknowledgements

I am grateful to students participating in the module *Gender, Education and Development* at the Institute of Education, University of London in the Autumn term 2013 for very helpful comments in response to my early attempts to formulate some of the ideas in this paper. Sincere thanks to Bob Cowen, Michele Schweisfurth and Jenny Parkes for most insightful help and critical engagement with the text of the paper.

Note

1. Some much earlier academic (as opposed to practitioner or political and advocacy) works include: Boserup (1970) which discussed women's education and work in Africa; Woodhall (1973), which argued for a reconsideration of human capital theory to take account of gender; and Thorne and Henley's (1975) work on gender and language. A 1974 sociological study of schools in Victoria, reported only in 1986, gave considerable attention to gender (Porter 1986).

References

Aikman, S. 1999. "Schooling and Development: Eroding Amazon Women's Knowledge and Diversity." In *Gender, Education and Development: Beyond Access to Empowerment*, edited by C. Heward and S. Bunwaree, 65–81. London: Zed.

Aikman, S., and E. Unterhalter. 2005. *Beyond Access: Developing Gender Equality in Education*. Oxford: Oxfam Publishing.

Al-Hariri, R. 1987. "Islam's Point of View on Women's Education in Saudi Arabia." *Comparative Education* 23 (1): 51–57.

Anthias, F. 2002. "Beyond Feminism and Multiculturalism: Locating Difference and the Politics of Location." *Women's Studies International Forum* 25 (3): 275–286.

Bajaj, M., and M. Pathmarajah. 2011. "Engendering Agency: The Differentiated Impact of Educational Initiatives in Zambia and India." *Feminist Formations* 23 (3): 48–67.

Behrman, J. R., and M. R. Rosenzweig. 1994. "Caveat Emptor: Cross-country Data on Education and the Labor Force." *Journal of Development Economics* 44 (1): 147–171.

Beneria, L., and G. Sen. 1982. "Class and Gender Inequalities and Women's Role in Economic Development: Theoretical and Practical Implications." *Feminist Studies* 8 (1): 157–176.

Biraimah, K. 1980. "The Impact of Western Schools on Girls' Expectations: A Togolese Case." *Comparative Education Review* 24 (2): 196–208.

Boserup, E. 1970. *Women's Rolein Economic Development*. New York: St Martin's Press.

Bowman, M., and C. Anderson. 1980. "The Participation of Women in Education in the Third World." *Comparative Education Review* 24 (2): 13–32.

Broadfoot, P. 1987. "Intorduction and Acknowledgements'." *Comparative Education* 23 (1): 3.

Byrne, E. 1987. "Gender in Education: Educational Policy in Australia and Europe, 1975-1985." *Comparative Education* 23 (1): 11–22.

Colclough, C., P. Rose, and M. Tembon. 2000. "Gender Inequalities in Primary Schooling: The Roles of Poverty and Adverse Cultural." *International Journal of Educational Development* 20 (1): 5–27.

Cowen, R., and A. Kazamias, eds. 2009. *International Handbook of Comparative Education*. Dordrecht: Springer.

Davies, L. 1987. "Research Dilemmas Concerning Gender and the Management of Education in Third World Countries." *Comparative Education* 23 (1): 85–94.

DeJaeghere, J., J. Parkes, and E. Unterhalter. 2013. "Gender Justice and Education: Linking Theory, Policy and Practice." *International Journal of Educational Development* 33 (6): 539–545.

DeJaeghere, J., and F. Vavrus. 2011. "Educational Formations: Gendered Experiences of Schooling in Local Contexts." *Feminist Formations* 23 (3): vii–xvi.

DeJaeghere, J., and N. P. Wiger. 2013. "Gender Discourses in an NGO Education Project: Openings for Transformation Toward Gender Equality in Bangladesh." *International Journal of Educational Development* 33 (6): 557–565.

Dietz, T., K. Havnevik, and M. Kaag, eds. 2011. *African Engagements: Africa Negotiating an Emerging Multipolar World*. Leiden: Brill.

Eliou, M. 1987. "Equality of the Sexes in Education: And Now What?" *Comparative Education* 23 (1): 59–67.

Elliott, C. M., and G. P. Kelly. 1980. "Introduction: Perspectives on the Education of Women in Third World Nations." *Comparative Education Review* 24 (2): S1–S12.

Elson, D. 1995. *Male Bias in the Development Process*. 2nd ed. Manchester: Manchester University Press.

Eyben, R. 2013. "Building Relationships in Development Cooperation: Traditional Donors and Rising Powers." IDS Policy Briefing, 36 Brighton: Institute of development Stuides.

Fennell, S., and M. Arnot, eds. 2007. *Gender Education and Equality in a Global Context*. London: Routledge.

Finn, J., J. Reis, and L. Dulberg. 1980. "Sex Differences in Educational Attainment: The Process." *Comparative Education Review* 24 (2): 33–52.

Fraser, N. 1997. *Justice Interruptu*. London: Routledge.

Friedman, S. 2014. *Class, Race and Power: Harold Wolpe and the Radical Critique of Apartheid Auckland*. Park: Jacana.

Gaitskell, D., J. Kimble, M. Maconachie, and E. Unterhalter. 1984. "Class, Race and Gender: Domestic Workers in South Africa." *Review of African Political Economy* No. 27/8: 86–108.

Gaitskell, D., and E. Unterhalter. 1989. "Mothers of the Nation: A Comparative Analysis of Nation, Race and Motherhood in Afrikaner Nationalism and the African National Congress." In *Woman-Nation-State*, edited by N. Yuval-Davis, and F. Anthias, 58–78. London: Macmillam Press.

Harvard Educational Review. 1979. "An Interview on Title IX with Shirley Chisholm, Holly Knox, Leslie R. Wolfe, Cynthia, G. Bown and Mary Kaaren Jolly." *Harvard Educational Review* 49 (4): 504–526.

Heward, C., and S. Bunwaree, eds. 1999. *Gender, Education and Development: Beyond Access to Empowerment*. London: Palgrave Macmillan.

Ilon, L. 1992. "Fitting Girls' Schooling into Existing Economic Paradigms: Confronting the Complexities." *International Journal of Educational Development* 12 (2): 147–159.

Jeffery, P., and R. Jeffery. 1998. "Girls' Schooling and Population Policy." In *Feminist visions of Development: Gender Analysis and Policy*, edited by S. Jackson and R. Pearson. London: Routledge.

Jones, M. 1980. "Education of Girls in Tunisia: Policy Implications of the Drive for Universal Enrollment." *Comparative Education Review* 24 (2): 106–123.

Kabeer, N. 1994. *Reversed Realities: Gender Hierarchies in Development Thought*. London: Verso.

Kalia, N. 1980. "Images of Men and Women in Indian Textbooks." *Comparative Education Review* 24 (2): 209–223.

Kelly, Gail. 1987. "Setting State Policy on Women's Education in the Third World: Perspectives from Comparative Research." *Comparative Education* 23 (1): 95–102.

Keniston, B. 2013. *Choosing to be Free. The Life Story of Rick Turner*. Auckland Park: Jacana.

Kimble, J., and E. Unterhalter. 1983. "'We Opened the Door For You, You Must Go Forward': ANC Women's Struggles, 1912–1982." *Feminist Review* 12: 11–36.

King, E., and A. Hill, eds. 1993. *Women's Education in Developing Countries: Barriers, Benefits and Policies*. Baltimore: Johns Hopkins University Press.

Kingdon, G. 1998. "Does the Labour Market Explain Lower Female Schooling in India?" *The Journal of Development Studies* 35 (1): 39–65.

Koffman, O., and R. Gill. 2013. "'The Revolution will be Led by a 12-year-old Girl': Girl Power and Global Biopolitics." *Feminist Review* 105 (1): 83–102.

Kutnick, P. 2000. "Girls, Boys and School Achievement:—A Caribbean Perspective." *International Journal of Educational Development* 20 (1): 65–84.

Manjrekar, N. 2013. "Women School Teachers in New Times: Some Preliminary Reflections." *Indian Journal of Gender Studies* 20 (2): 335–356.

Maslak, M., ed. 2007. *The Structure and Agency of Women's Education*. Albany: State University of New York Press.

McSweeney, B., and M. Freedman. 1980. "Lack of Time as an Obstacle to Women's Education: The Case of Upper Volta." *Comparative Education Review* 24 (2): 124–139.

Moeller, K. 2013. "Proving "The Girl Effect": Corporate Knowledge Production and Educational Intervention." *International Journal of Educational Development* 33 (6): 612–621.

Moletsane, R. 2005. "Looking Back, Looking Forward: Analysing Gender Equality in South African Education 10 Years after Beijing." *Agenda* 19 (64) (2005): 80–88.

Monkman, K. 2011. "Introduction. Framing Gender, Education and Empowerment." *Research in Comparative and International Education* 6 (1): 1–13.

Moon, B. 2013. UN Secretary General Address to the General Assembly, 24 September New York: United Nations on line at http://www.un.org/sg/statements/index.asp?nid=7119 (accessed December 2013).

Moore, K. 1987. "Women's Access and Opportunity in Higher Education: Towards the 21st Centry'." *Comparative Education* 23 (1): 23–34.

Morrell, R., D. Epstein, E. Unterhalter, D. Bhana, and R. Moletsane. 2009. *Towards Equality? Gender in South African Schools During the HIV and AIDS Epidemic*. Durban: University of Kwazulu Natal Press.

Moss, G. 2014 forthcoming. *South African Radicalism and Politics in the 1970s*. Auckland Park: Jacana.

Murphy-Graham, E. 2012. *Opening Minds, Improving Lives: Education and Women's Empowerment in Honduras*. Vanderbilt University Press.

Nnaemeka, O. 2004. "Nego-feminism: Theorizing, Practicing, and Pruning Africa's Way." *Signs* 29 (2): 357–385.

Okin, S. M. 1989. *Justice, Gender and the Family*. New York: Basic Books.

Parkes, J. 2007. "Tensions and Troubles in Young People's Talk about Safety and Danger in a Violent Neighbourhood." *Journal of Youth Studies* 10 (1): 117–137.

Parkes, J., and E. Unterhalter. 2009. "Violence and the Struggle for Coherence in South African Transformation." In *Memory, Narrative and Forgiveness: Perspectives on the Unfinished Journeys of the Past*, edited by P. Gobodo- Madikizela and C. Van der Merwe, 380–400. Cambridge: Scholars Publishing.

Pearson, R. 1994. "Gender Relations, Capitalism and Third World Industrialization." In *Capitalism and Development,* edited by L. Sklair, 339–358. London: Routledge.

Phillips, A. 1999. *Which Equalities Matter?* Cambidge: Polity Press.

Philips, D., and M. Schweisfurth. 2007. *Comparative and International Education*. London: Continuum.

Porter, P. 1986. *Gender and Education: Sociology of the School*. Victoria: Deakin University Press.

Ram, R. 1980. "Sex Differences in the Labor Market Outcomes of Education." *Comparative Education Review* 24 (2): 53–77.

Ramdas, K. 2012. "What's Sex got to do with It?" *Stanford Social Innovation Review* 39.

Rappleye, J. 2012. "Comparative Education: The Construction of a Field." *Comparative Education* 48 (3): 403–406.

Rindfuss, R., L. Bumpass, and C. St. John. 1980. "Education and Fertility: Implications for the Roles Women Occupy." *American Sociological Review* 45: 431–447.

Salo, E. 2003. "Negotiating Gender and Personhood in the New South Africa Adolescent Women and Gangsters in Manenberg Township on the Cape Flats." *European journal of cultural studies* 6 (3): 345–365.

Schiefelbein, E., and J. Farrell. 1980. "Women, Schooling, and Work in Chile: Evidence from a Longitudinal Study." *Comparative Education Review* 24 (2): 160–179.

Schultz, T. P. 1993. "Returns to Women's Education." In *Women's Education in Developing Countries: Barriers, Benefits and Policies*, edited by E. King, and A. Hill, 51–93. Baltimore: Johns Hopkins University Press.

Smyth, I. A., and N. Rao, eds. 2005. *Partnerships for Girls' Education*. Oxford: Oxfam.

Stephens, D. 2000. "Girls and Basic Educationin Ghana: A Cultural Enquiry." *International Journal of Educational Development* 20 (1): 29–47.

Stewart, F. 1985. *Planning to Meet Basic Needs*. London: Macmillan.

Stromquist, N. P. 1989. "Determinants of Educational Participation and Achievement of Women in the Third World: A Review of the Evidence and a Theoretical Critique." *Review of Educational Research* 59 (2): 143–183.

Stromquist, N. P. 1992. *Women and Education in Latin America: Knowledge, Power, and Change*. Boulder, Co.: Lynne Rienner.

Stromquist, Nelly P. 1995. "Romancing the State: Gender and Power in Education." *Comparative Education Review* 39 (4): 423–454.

Stromquist, N. 2005. "Comparative and International Education: A Journey Toward Equality and Equity." *Harvard Educational Review* 75 (1): 89–111.

Sutherland, M. B. 1987. "Sex Differences in Education: An Overview." *Comparative Education* 23 (1): 5–9.

Swainson, N. 2000. "Knowledge and Power: The Design and Implementation of Gender Policies in Education in Malawi, Tanzania and Zimbabwe." *International Journal of Educational Development* 20 (1): 49–64.

Szechy, E. 1987. "The Problem of Female Education in Hungary." *Comparative Education* 23 (1): 69–74.

Thorne, Barrie, and N. Henley. 1975. "Language and Sex: Difference and Dominance."

Unterhalter, E. 1991a. "Changing Aspects of Reformism in Bantu Education, 1953–1989." In *Apartheid Education and Popular Struggles*, edited by E. Unterhalter, et al. eds, 35–72. Johannesburg: Ravan.

Unterhalter, E. 1991b. "Can Education Overcome Women's Subordinate Position in the Occupation Structure?" In *Education in a Future South Africa. Policy issues for Transformation*, edited by E. Unterhalter, H. Wolpe, and T. Botha, 65–84. London: Macmillan.

Unterhalter, E. 1996. "States, Households and the Market in World Bank Discourses, 1985-1995: A Feminist Critique." *Discourse: Studies in the Cultural Politics of Education* 17 (3): 389–340.

Unterhalter, E. 1999a. "Citizenship, Difference and Education: Reflections on the South African Transition." In *Women, Citizenship and Difference*, edited by N. Yuval-Davis and P. Werbner, 100–117. London: Zed.

Unterhalter, E. 1999b. "The Schooling of South African Girls: Statistics, Stories, and Strategies." In *Gender, Education and Development*, edited by S. Bunwaree and C. Heward, 49–64. London: Zed.

Unterhalter, E. 2000. "Remembering and Forgetting: Constructions of Education Gender Reform in Autobiography and Policy Texts of the South African Transition." *History of Education* 29 (5): 457–472.

Unterhalter, E. 2002. "Gender, Race and Different Lives: South African Women Teachers' Autobiographies and the Analysis of Education Change." In *The History of Education under Apartheid 1948-1994: The Doors of Learning and Culture shall be Opened*, edited by P. Kallaway, 243–255. New York: Peter Lang.

Unterhalter, E. 2003. "The Capabilities Approach and Gendered Education. An Examination of South African Complexities." *Theory and Research in Education* 1 (1): 7–22.

Unterhalter, E. 2004. "Gender Equality and Education in South Africa: Measurements, Scores and Strategies'." In *Gender Equality in South African Education 1994-2004. Perspectives from Research, Governments and Unions*, edited by L. Chisholm and J. September, 77–91. Cape Town: Human Sciences Research Council.

Unterhalter, E. 2005a. "Fragmented frameworks: Researching women, gender, education and development." In S. Aikman and E.Unterhalter, 'Introduction' in S. Aikman and E. Unterhalter eds. *Beyond Access: Developing Gender Equality in Education* Oxford: Oxfam Publishing, 15–35.

Unterhalter, E. 2005b. "Mobilization, Meanings and Measures." *Development* 48 (1): 110–114.

Unterhalter, E. 2006. "New Times and New Vocabularies: Theorising and Evaluating Gender Equality in Commonwealth Higher Education." *Women's Studies International Forum* 29 (6): 620–628.

Unterhalter, E. 2007a. *Gender, Schooling and Global Social Justice*. Abingdon: Routledge Taylor Francis.

Unterhalter, E. 2007b. "Remaking the Nation: Changing Masculinities and Education in South Africa." In *Education in Africa*, edited by D. Johnson and W. Beinart, 93–106. Oxford: Symposium Books.

Unterhalter, E. 2007c. "Gender Equality, Education and the Capability Approach." In *Sen's Capability Approach and Social Justice in Education*, edited by Melanie Walker and Elaine Unterhalter, 87–108. London/New York: Palgrave.
Unterhalter, E. 2009a. "Gender and Poverty Reduction: The Challenge of Intersection." *Agenda* 81: 14–24.
Unterhalter, E. 2009b. "Translations and Transversal Dialogues: An Examination of Mobilities Associated with Gender, Education and Global Poverty Reduction." *Comparative Education* 45 (3): 329–345.
Unterhalter, E. 2010. "Considering Equality, Equity and Higher Education Pedagogies in the Context of Globalization." In *Global Inequalities and Higher Education. Whose Interests are we Serving?*, edited by E. Unterhalter and V. Carpentier, 35–54. Basingstoke: Palgrave.
Unterhalter, E. 2012. "Mutable Meanings: Gender Equality in Education and International Rights Frameworks'." *Equal Rights Review* 8: 67–84.
Unterhalter, E. 2014, forthcoming. "Measuring education or the MDGs: Reflections on targets, indicators and a post 2015 framework." *Journal of Human Development and Capabilities*.
Unterhalter, E., and H. Brighouse. 2014, forthcoming. "Primary Goods, Capabilities and the Millennium Development Target for Gender Equality in Education." In *Capabilities, Gender, Equality: Towards Fundamental Entitlements*, edited by M. Nussbaum, and F. Comin. Cambridge: Cambridge University Press.
Unterhalter, E., C. Challender, and R. Rajagopalan. 2005. "Measuring gender equality in education." In S. Aikman and E.Unterhalter, 'Introduction' in S. Aikman and E. Unterhalter eds. *Beyond Access: Developing Gender Equality in Education* Oxford: Oxfam Publishing, 60–82.
Unterhalter, E., and A. Dorward. 2013. "New MDGs, Development Concepts, Principles, and Challenges in a Post 2015 World." *Social Indicators Research* 113: 609–625.
Unterhalter, E., and S. Dutt. 2001. "Gender, Education and Women's Power: Indian State and Civil Society Intersections in DPEP (District Primary Education Programme) and Mahila Samakhya." *Compare* 31 (1): 57–73.
Unterhalter, E., J. Heslop, and A. Mamedu. 2013. "Girls Claiming Education Rights: Reflections on Distribution, Empowerment and Gender Justice in Northern Tanzania and Northern Nigeria." *International Journal of Educational Development* 33 (6): 566–575.
Unterhalter, E., A. North, M. Arnot, C. Lloyd, R. Moletsane, E. Murphy-Graham, J. Parkes, M. Saito. 2014 forthcoming. *Interventions to Enhance Girls' Education and Gender Equality: A Rigorous Review of Literature*. London: Department for International Development.
Unterhalter, E., and M. Oomen. 2006. "GEEI: Measuring Progress on Girls' Education in Commonwealth Countries in Africa." In *International Handbook on the Inequality of Education*, edited by James Jacobs and Donald B. Holsinger, 538–557. Dordrecht: Springer.
Unterhalter, E., C. Yates, H. Makinda, and A. North. 2012. "Blaming the Poor: Constructions of Marginality and Poverty in the Kenyan Education Sector." *Compare* 42 (2): 213–233.
Vavrus, F. 2003. *Desire and Decline*. New York: Peter Lang.
Wang, B. 1980. "Sex and Ethnic Differences in Educational Investment in Malaysia: The Effect of Reward Structures." *Comparative Education Review* 24 (2): 140–159.
Wainerman, C. 1980. "The Impact of Education on the Female Labor Force in Argentina and Paraguay." *Comparative Education Review* 24 (2): 180–195.
Woodhall, M. 1973. "Investment in Women: A Reappraisal of the Concept of Human Capital." *International Review of Education* 19 (1): 9–29.
Woodhead, M., M. Frost, and Zoe James. 2013. "Does Growth in Private Schooling Contributeto Education for All? Evidence from a Longitudinal Two Cohort Study in Andhra Pradesh, India." *International Journal of Educational Development* 33 (1): 65–73.

Index

Note: Page numbers in **bold** type refer to figures
Page numbers followed by 'n' refer to notes

Abraham Moss Centre (Manchester) 50
academic mobility 58, 62–3, 108
actors 18, 109n; non-governmental 18
adult education 45–57; liberal 49–51
adult education institutes (AEI) 46
Adult Learning: It's never too late to learn (EC) 54
adult learning and education (ALE) 55
Africa 109n, 116–18, 122n
African National Congress (ANC) 114
Alexander, R. 33, 38
Alheit, P. 54
Alienworld 58–9, 62, 68
altruism 103
Anderson, C.A. 6
andragogy 47–8
Androgogy not Pedagogy (Knowles) 47
Anglo-Americans 27, 33, 37–9
Annual Global Monitoring Reports (GMRs) 19
Anthias, F. 118
anthropology 85, 98n
Archaeology of Knowledge, The (Foucault) 69n
Arinori, M. 90
Arnold, M. 7, 74–5, 79, 90
Asia 11n, 116; North 11n; South East 16
Auld, E.: and Morris, P. 18
Australia 50, 116
Austria 29
autonomy 35–8

Balzac, H. de 62
Ban Ki-moon 119
Bangladesh 119
Barbados 118
Barber, M. 28
Barking (UK) 30
Barnard, H. 7
Bauman, Z. 66–8
Beijing (China) 55n
Belgium 29

belief systems 105–6
Belzer, A.: and St Clair, R. 21
Benavot, A.: and Meyer, H.D. 20, 109n
Bereday, G. 6, 63, 74–5, 82n
Berlin, I. 78
Bernard, C. 87
Beyond Access Project (2003–10) 114
big data 15–26
Biraimah, K. 116
Birth of the Clinic, The (Foucault) 61
Bloch, M. 79, 88
Boserup, E. 122n
Boud, D. 54
Bourdieu, P. 68, 77
Braudel, F. 96
Bray, M. 109n
Bretton Woods Agreement 45
British academic and professional society (BAICE) 4
British Broadcasting Corporation (BBC) 31, 55
Broadfoot, P. 109n, 116
Bronfenbrenner, U. 28, 33–5
Brookfield, S. 54
Brookings Institution 20
Burghes, D. 30

Campbell, D.D. 52
capital: human 51–2; human capital theory 122n
capitalism 120
Caribbean 118
Carney, S. 108
Carroll, K.: and Epstein, E. 75
Centre for Research in International and Comparative Education (CRICE) 21
China 11n, 28, 34, 55n; Beijing 55n; Hong Kong 16–17; Shanghai 31
Christian theology 49
Chung, J.: and Crossley, M. 32
citizenship 53, 66
Civilizing Process, The (Mannheim) 66

INDEX

Clarke, P.: and Fuller, B. 32
class: middle 52; upper 52; working 64
Cold War period 8, 28
colonialism 8, 61; neo- 61
comparative analysis: historical emphases in 76–7, **76**
comparative education 75–7, 112–26
Comparative Education: The Construction of a Field (Manzon) 5
Comparative Education Society in Europe (CESE) 21
comparative/international studies in education 84–101
comparatography 73–83
comparisons/comparative education 58–72
Confucian countries 34
consanguinity 104–5
contemporary world 8, 102, 112
contextualist theory 33
continuing professional education (CPE) 51–2
Council for National Academic Awards (CNAA) 51, 55n
Cousin, V. 7, 75, 79, 90
Cowen, R. 3–14, 60, 107
Crisis and Hope in American Education (Ulich) 65
Crook, D.: and McCulloch, G. 79
Crossley, M. 6, 15–26; and Chung, J. 32
Cukier, K.: and Mayer-Schönberger, V. 20
cultural imperialism 8
culture of schooling 32–6
Cyprus 29

Dagenham (UK) 30
Dale, R. 3; and Robertson, J. 6
data: big 15–26
Davies, L. 117
de-contextualisation 60
de-territorialisation 60
Dejaeghere, J.: and Wiger, N. 119
Delors Report (1996) 54
democratisation 120
Denmark 29
Department for International Development (DFID) 118–19
Derrida, J. 68
Dewey, J. 54
dichotomy 91
differences: sex 117
doctoral research 48, 51
Dominice, P. 54
dualism 106
Dunlop, J.: et al. 46
Durkheim, E. 10, 58, 85, 95

Eckstein, M.: and Noah, H. 76
Economic and Social Research Council (ESRC) 21

economy: political 21, 97, 112
Edinburgh (UK) 62
Education for All (EFA) 19
educational research modalities: international transfer 15–26
eighteenth century 59, 62, 69n, 85–6
Einstein, A. 88
Elderhostel Institute Network 50
Elias, N. 66–7
Elliott, C.: and Kelly, G. 116
Elliott, J.G. 27–44, 79–80; et al. 33–4, 37–9; and Tudge, J. 35
Empires 8
empowerment 38, 119–21
Encyclopédie 85
engagement levels 36–8
England 4, 7, 21, 27–33, 39, 66, 75, 78–80; international education 4
English language 4
enlightenment 78; French 7; Scottish 7; Swedish 7
epistemic positioning 58–72
epistemology 3
Epstein, E. 3; and Carroll, K. 75
equality 106, 113; gender 113–14, 118
Esprit des Lois (Montesquieu) 85
ethical globalisation 10
ethnographic observations 102–11
Europe 3, 7, 11n, 15–16, 29, 47, 53, 59, 62, 114–16
European Commission (EC) 20, 53–5; *Adult Learning: It's never too late to learn* (2006) 54; Memorandum on Lifelong Learning (2000) 53
European Union (EU) 10, 11n, 48, 52–4
existentialism 49

Farrell, S.: and Reynolds, D. 29–32, 36
Faure, E. 54
feminism 118–20
Finland 16, 19, 27–8, 31–2
Foucault, M. 61, 69n
France 7, 16, 29, 46, 62, 74; (French) Enlightenment 7; Paris 66; University of the Third Age (U3A) 46–7, 50; University of Toulouse 50
Franklin, B. 62
Fraser, N. 118–20
Freire, P.: and Horton, M. 49
Fuller, B.: and Clarke, P. 32

gender: in comparative education 112–26; equality 113–14, 118; identities 112–13, 116, 119; inequality 116, 120
Gender and Education (journal) 118
Germany 29–30, 50, 65, 78–81; Holocaust 68; Nazi Party 64–6
global league tables 15–26

INDEX

Global, The 105–6
globalisation 1, 3, 8, 45, 60, 96, 108; ethical 10; modern 45
Goldstein, H. 21
governmental organisations 94
Grant, N. 75
Great Britain 48
Grek, S.: et al. 17

Halls, W.D. 74
Hans, N. 6, 9, 63, 74
Harbison, F.: et al. 46
Harvard Education Review 115–16
Harvard University (USA) 64–5
Hegel, G.W.F. 77
hegemony 16, 20–3
Henley, N.: and Thorne, B. 122n
Herbert, J.: and Stigler, J.W. 30–1
Herder, J.G. 59
Heyneman, S.P. 39; and Lee, B. 30
high-achieving countries 30–2; factors associated 30–2
Hildreth, A.: et al. 33–4
Hill, A.: and King, E. 117–18
Hintze, O. 79
Hirsch, H. 50
Hirst, P.: and Peters, R. 5, 46
Holmes, B. 6, 74
Holocaust 68
Homeworld 58–9, 62, 68
Homo Academicus (Bourdieu) 68
Honduras 119
Hong Kong (China) 16–17
Horton, M. 49; and Freire, P. 49
How the world's best performing systems come out on top (McKinsey Report 2007) 38
Hufton, N.: et al. 33–4, 37
human capital 51–2
human capital theory 122n
Human Career, The (Ulich) 64
Hume, D. 62
Husserl, E. 61

identities: gender 112–13, 116, 119
ideology 10, 68, 89
Illushin, L.: et al. 33–4, 37
imperialism 8; cultural 8; New 22
Importance of Teaching, The (Schools White Paper for England 2010) 17–19
imported pedagogies 32–8
India 114, 120
industrialised nations 36–7, 45
industrialised societies: modern 35
industrialism 46
inequality: gender 116, 120
information societies 3, 46
International Assessment of Educational Process (IAEP) 28–9

International Assessments of Mathematics, Second (IAEPM2) 28
International Assessments of Science, Second (IAEPS2) 28
International Association for the Evaluation of Educational Achievement (IEA) 15–16, 28–9, 31
international education 4, 112–13; England 4
International Handbook of Comparative Education 6
International Journal of Educational Development (IJED) 117–18
International Journal of Lifelong Education, The 48
International Labour Organisation (ILO) 48
international studies in education 84–101
international transfer: educational research modalities 1, 15–26
Iraq 9
Israel 69n

Japan 27–30, 78; Tokyo 74
Jarvis, P. 45–57
Jaspers, K. 66
Jefferson, Thomas 65
Judt, T. 8
Jullien de Paris, M-A. 7, 16, 59, 62

Kaloyannaki, P. 6
Kandel, I. 7, 74
Kant, I. 51
Kelly, G.: and Elliott, C. 116
Kenya 22; Primary School Management Project (PRISM) 22
Keogh, R.: and Walker, D. 54
Keppel, F. 64
Kerr, C.: et al. 46
Kim, T. 58–72
King, E. 6, 45, 74; and Hill, A. 117–18
Kirkwood, G.: and Kirkwood, C. 49
Knowles, M. 47–8, 55n
Kolb, D. 54
Kowalczyk, J.: and Sobe, N.W. 9
Kutnick, P. 118

Lacan, J. 61
large-scale international comparative surveys 16–19
Laslett, P. 50
Latin 5
Latin America 49, 116
Lauwerys, J. 6, 63
Lawn, M. 3, 20; et al. 17
league tables: global 15–26
learning: lifelong 45–57
Learning in the Fourth Age (L4A) 54
Learning Metrics Task Force 20
Learning to Be (Faure) 49

INDEX

Lee, B.: and Heyneman, S.P. 30
legitimacy 8
Lengrand, P. 49
Lesotho 36
levels of academic motivation/engagement 36–8
Levi-Strauss, C. 10
Levin, H.M. 109n
Lewy, G. 79
Li, J. 34
liberal adult education 49–51
Libya 9
lifelong learning/beyond 45–57
Lingard, B.: et al. 17
Liverpool (UK) 50
Local, The 105–6
London (UK) 62, 66
Luhmann, N. 92, 97
Luhmannian differentiation theory 92

McCulloch, G.: and Crook, D. 79; and Richardson, W. 82n
macrosystem 33–5
Manchester (UK): Abraham Moss Centre 50
Manen, M. van 63
Mann, H. 7, 75, 79, 90
Mannheim, K. 66
Manzon, M. 5, 60, 108–9n
Marxism 49
Marxist theory 114
Master's degree 48, 51–2
Mayer-Schönberger, V.: and Cukier, K. 20
Methods Wars (1960s) 4
Meyer, H.D.: and Benavot, A. 20, 109n
Meyer, J.W. 97
microsystem 33
middle class 52
Midwinter, F. 50
migration 89
Mill, J.S. 5, 87
Mills, C.W. 10, 58, 63
mobility 58–72; academic 58, 62–3, 108
modern globalisation 45
modern industrialised societies 35
Modern Practice of Adult Education, The (Knowles) 47
modern world 59
modernism 6; post 3, 109n
modernity 68, 97
Modernity and the Holocaust (Bauman) 68
Monkman, K. 119
Monroe, P. 93
Montesquieu 85
Morris, H. 50
Morris, P. 19
Moscow (Russia) 74
motivation levels 36–8
multiculturalism 118

Murphy-Graham, E. 119
Myers, C.: et al. 46

nation states 16, 59, 90, 94–7, 104–6
National Vocational Qualifications (NVQ) 52
nationalism 9, 58–9, 68
nations: industrialised 36–7, 45
Nazi Party (Germany) 64–6; Holocaust 68
neo-colonialism 61
neo-institutional theory 97
neo-liberalism 1, 3
neologisms 73
Netherlands 27–9
New imperialism 22
Ng, P.T. 31
Nguyen, M.: et al. 39
nineteenth century 5–7, 59, 69n, 75, 85–90, 95
Nisbet, R. 9
Nnaemeka, O. 118
Noah, H.: and Eckstein, M. 76
non-governmental actors 18
non-governmental organisation (NGO) 50, 94
North Asia 11n
Nottinghamshire (UK) 50; Sutton Centre 50
Nóvoa, A. 3; and Yariv-Mashal, T. 8, 17, 78

Open University (OU) 46, 55, 55n
Order of Things, The (Foucault) 61, 69n
Organisation for Economic Co-operation and Development (OECD) 15–17, 20, 27, 48, 60, 94; Programme for International Student Assessment (PISA) 15–20, 31, 38–9, 60, 104
organisations: governmental 94; non-governmental (NGO) 50, 94; supra-national 32
orthodoxy 84–101
Other 1, 58, 61
Ozga, J. 3, 17–18; et al. 17

Pacific Rim 29–30, 37, 96
Panorama (BBC) 31
Paris (France) 66
Parkes, J. 119
pedagogic practice/culture of schooling 32–6
pedagogy 27–44; imported 32–8
periodisation 8
Persian Gulf 105; Zoroastrians 105
Pescador, O.: et al. 109n
Peters, R.: and Hirst, P. 5, 46
Peterson, A.D.C. 1–2
Phillips, D. 73–83; and Schweisfurth, M.M. 76, 109n
philosophy 51, 54, 65, 70n, 73
physiology 87
Pilot, A.: et al. 39
Pink, D.H. 69
Poland 66, 74
political economy 21, 97, 112

INDEX

political sovereignty 95
Popper, K. 69, 78, 87
post-colonialism 3
post-Enlightenment 7
post-modernism 3, 69n, 109n
post-socialism 3
poverty 49, 120
power: social 5, 61
Primary School Management Project (Kenya) (PRISM) 22
Prince George's County Educators' Association (PGCEA) 48
process-person-context-time model 33
Programme for International Student Assessment (PISA) (OECD) 15–20, 31, 38–9, 60, 104
psychoanalysis 61
psychology 34

randomised controlled trials (RCTs) 18, 21
Reagan, Ronald: US administration (1980s) 36
Reber, A. 54
relativism 10
research: doctoral 48, 51; modalities 15–26
Research on Education in South Africa project (RESA 1985–95) 114
responsible body (RB) 46–7, 55
retirement education 50–1
Review of International Surveys Involving England Between (1964–90) 29
Reynolds, D. 37; and Farrell, S. 29–32, 36
Richardson, W.: and McCulloch, G. 82n
Ricoeur, P. 63
Ringer, F. 88
Rinne, R.: et al. 17
Robertson, J.: and Dale, R. 6
Robertson, S. 3
Rousseau, J-J. 59
Russell, B. 78
Russia 11n, 33; Moscow 74, *see also* Soviet Union
Rust, V.D.: et al. 109n

sacred texts 107–8
Sadler, M. 6, 18, 32, 39, 74–5
St Clair, R.: and Belzer, A. 21
St Vincent Islands 118
Salo, E. 119
Sarmiento, D.F. 90
Satre, J.P. 61
Savicevic, D. 47
Schneider, F. 93
schooling: culture of 32–6
Schriewer, J. 84–101
Schultz, T. 51
Schweisfurth, M.M. 2, 36, 77, 102–11; and Phillips, D. 76, 109n
Scottish Enlightenment 7

Segerholm, C.: et al. 17
sex differences 117
sexuality 120
Shanghai (China) 31
Sheldrake, R. 62
Shibuya, M.: et al. 109n
Shin, J. 31
silences 1–2, 3–14
Simmel, G. 67–8
Simola, H.: et al. 17
Singapore 16–17, 28, 31
siren songs 3–14
sixteenth century 67
Skocpol, T. 8
Smith, A. 62, 70n
Sobe, N.W.: and Kowalczyk, J. 9
social power 5, 61
social science 1, 7–10, 16–21, 46, 55, 59, 78, 84–9, 95
social stratification 106–7
social-scientific comparisons (epistemo-logic) 85–9
socialisation 36
socialism 117
societies: traditional 36–8
socio-centrism 89–90
socio-logic 89–94
Sociological Imagination (Mills) 63
sociology 9, 58, 66–8, 74, 85–7, 91
songs: siren 3–14
Sorenson, C.W. 31
Soumaré, A.: et al. 109n
South Africa 29, 114, 119
South East Asia 16
South Korea 27–8, 31
sovereignty: political 95
Soviet Union 34, 38; Sputnik (1957) 28
Spain 50, 79
Sputnik (Soviet Union) (1957) 28
Steinberg, L. 37
Steiner-Khamsi, G. 3, 10, 60
Stephens, M.: and Thomas, T. 55n
Stewart, D. 70n
Stigler, J.W.: and Herbert, J. 30–1
stonefish 10n
stones 3–14
Stowe, C. 7
stratification: social 106–7
Stromquist, N. 115
supra-national organisations 32
surveys: large-scale international comparative 16–19
Sutherland, M. 116–17
Sutton Centre (Nottinghamshire) 50
Sweden 29
Swedish Enlightenment 7
Switzerland 29–30
Syria 9, 120

INDEX

Taiwan 28–31
Tanzania 22
taxonomy 113–16, 120–1
Tenbruck, F.H. 84–5, 89, 95–6
Tennessee (USA) 49
Terlouw, C.: et al. 39
texts: sacred 107–8
theology: Christian 49
Theory of Moral Sentiments, The (Smith) 62
Third International Maths and Science Study (TIMSS) 29
Third World 3–4, 11n, 49, 116
Thomas, T.: and Stephens, M. 55n
Thorne, B.: and Henley, N. 122n
Tillich, P. 65
Time and Narrative and Narrative Identity (Ricoeur) 63
To Sell is Human (Pink) 69
Tokyo (Japan) 74
Topography of the Alien (Waldenfels) 68
Torrance, H. 21
traditional societies 36–8
trans-national comparativist 67–8
trans-societal structures/world systems (globo-logic) 94–8
transfer: international 1, 15–26
tribes (tribal): boundaries 104–5; elders 105–6, 109n; kinship 103–5; membership 102–6, 109n
Trinidad 118
Tröhler, D. 9
Tudge, J.: and Elliott, J.G. 35
Tunisia 69n
twentieth century 18–20, 59, 85, 90, 94–6

Ulich, R. 63–7
undergraduate education 48, 51
United Kingdom (UK) 15–22, 27–32, 36, 39, 46–9, 109n, 115, 120; Barking 30; Dagenham 30; Department for International Development (DFID) 19; Economic and Social Research Council (ESRC) 21; Edinburgh 62; Liverpool 50; London 62, 66; Manchester 50; Nottinghamshire 50; University of London 15; University of Nottingham 47, 55n; University of Surrey 46–8, 55n
United Nations Educational Scientific and Cultural Organization (UNESCO) 16, 19, 49
United Nations (UN) 114, 119
United States Agency for International Development (USAID) 119

United States of America (USA) 7, 10, 15, 21, 28–34, 36–9, 45, 48, 52, 64, 75, 116–20; civil rights movement 49; Founding Father 62; Harvard University 64–5; Jefferson 65; Reagan administration (1980s) 36; Tennessee 49
universalism 94
Universalists, The 106
University of London (UK) 4
University of Malaya (Malaysia) 21
University of Nottingham (UK) 47, 55n
University of Surrey (UK) 46–8, 55n
University of the Third Age (France) (U3A) 46–7, 50
University of Toulouse (France) 50
Unterhalter, E. 10, 112–26
upper class 52
Uprichard, E. 20
Urry, J. 62

vocational education 51–2
Vulliamy, G. 21–2

Waal, E. de 10
Waldenfels, B. 68
Walker, D.: and Keogh, R. 54
Wallerstein, I. 97
Waterkamp, D. 64–5
Watson, K. 73
Wealth of Nations, The (Smith) 62
Weber, A. 66
Weltanschauung (world view) 58–9, 63
West 37, 38–9
Wiger, N.: and Dejaeghere, J. 119
Willis, W.: et al. 37
Wissenschaften (scientific knowledge) 58–9, 63
Woodhall, M. 122n
working class 64
World Bank 16, 19–20, 117
World Education Forum (WEF) 17
world society 96–7
world systems 94–8
world systems theory 81, 97–8
World Wars: I (1914–18) 66; II (1939–45) 50, 87

Yariv-Mashal, T.: and Nóvoa, A. 8, 17, 78
Yeaxlee, B. 49, 55n

Zhao, Y. 34
Zoroastrians 105